GOD INTERRUPTS HISTORY

GOD INTERRUPTS HISTORY

Theology in a Time of Upheaval

LIEVEN BOEVE

NEW YORK • LONDON

2007

The Continuum International Publishing Group Inc
80 Maiden Lane, New York, NY 10038

The Continuum International Publishing Group Ltd
The Tower Building, 11 York Road, London SE1 7NX

www.continuumbooks.com

Printed in the United States of America

Library of Congress Cataloging-in-Publication Data

Boeve, L. (Lieven)
[God onderbreekt de geschiedenis. English]
God interrupts history : theology in a time of upheaval / Lieven Boeve.
p. cm.
Includes bibliographical references and index.
ISBN-13: 978-0-8264-2812-7 (hardcover : alk. paper)
ISBN-10: 0-8264-2812-6 (hardcover : alk. paper)
ISBN-13: 978-0-8264-2813-4 (pbk. : alk. paper)
ISBN-10: 0-8264-2813-4 (pbk. : alk. paper)
1. Theology – Methodology. 2. Christianity and culture – Europe. 3. History – Religious aspects – Catholic Church. I. Title.

BR118.B5313 2007
230.01 – dc22

2007006457

Contents

Part III
God Interrupts History
Narratives on God, Incarnation, and Time

Preface

How are we to practice theology in the contemporary Western European context? In the past five years, the search for an answer to this question led me more or less as a matter of course to the present book. On a variety of occasions, it became clear to me that the method employed by modern theology to conceptualize the Christian faith in relation to its surrounding context had come under pressure. On account of evident shifts in the context, a methodological reassessment appeared to be necessary. The results of my research in this regard are offered here in the present volume, a cultural-theological book with strong methodological accents. The proposition that "God interrupts history" not only deals with theological content but at the same time with the methodology one employs to explore it.

The completion of this study obliges me to express my sincere gratitude to my colleagues, assistants, and friends who make up the Research Unit Systematic Theology, the Research Group Theology in a Postmodern Context, and the GOA Orthodoxy Group (K.U. Leuven). For many years, they have created an appropriate and critically challenging environment facilitating theological reflection of the type found in these pages. I am also grateful to the Research Foundation of Flanders (FWO) and the Research Fund (BOF) of the K.U. Leuven for their financial support. A final word of gratitude is extended to Brian Doyle, who was responsible for the English translation of this study.

Introduction

My previous monograph, entitled *Interrupting Tradition: An Essay on Christian Faith in a Postmodern Context,* engaged in a cultural theological study of the way in which the Christian faith ought to relate to a dramatically shifting context: from modern to postmodern, from preponderantly Christian to increasingly multi-religious. In dialogue with the critical consciousness of the so-called postmodern context, I sought to establish conceptual patterns that might serve the Christian narrative in its endeavor to assume contextual plausibility and theological legitimacy. I ultimately arrived at the hypothesis that the Christian narrative can only be guaranteed a future as an "open narrative," conscious of its unique particularity but at the same time open to otherness. Indeed, I suggested, it is perhaps in the encounter with the other and otherness that God reveals Godself today.[1]

The present study is a continuation of this research trajectory. Its goal is to elaborate a number of methodological backgrounds for the development of a contextual theology, which we have styled a "theology of interruption." After several provisional studies, it has become clear to me in recent years that such a theology functions according to a specific method. While the method in question is in line with the modern theological method of the post-conciliar authorities, it also departs therefrom. The present volume thus represents a thorough reworking of these provisional studies, bringing them together into a single cohesive project, in the conviction that what started as intuition now requires more systematic elaboration and explanation.[2]

1. Cf. L. Boeve, *Interrupting Tradition: An Essay on Christian Faith in a Postmodern Context,* Louvain Theological and Pastoral Monographs 30 (Leuven: Peeters / Grand Rapids: Eerdmans, 2003).

2. Bibliographical details concerning the articles in question can be found toward the end of this book.

1. Point of Departure: Recontextualization and the Question of Method

The processes designated by sociologists as modernization, secularization, and individualization have changed the features of Western European society considerably in a relatively short period of time.[3] Virtually without question, its Christian conceptual horizon lost the self-evident character it once enjoyed in providing meaning to the lives and everyday social existence of ordinary men and women. Younger generations are no longer to be identified as a matter of course as Christian by birth, and if they are Christian, it is usually a matter of personal choice — a choice that their environment can potentially call into question. At the same time, on both the local and global levels, Christians find themselves in the midst of an enormous variety of other religions and alternative fundamental life options. Immigration, the new media, the so-called religious revival, and the emergence of new religious movements bring Christians uninvited into contact with a plurality of approaches to life and society, and the practices that give concrete shape thereto. Secularization may have ruptured the all-embracing character of the Christian conceptual horizon, but it has clearly not been able to rid the world of religion altogether.

Postmodernity has taught us, moreover, that we are not the masters of the world surrounding us, of our society, and not even of our own identity. Our fundamental life options and religious narratives are being confronted repeatedly with difference and otherness. They would appear to be nothing more than specific ways of dealing with life, society, and reality as a whole. When our narratives are absolutized to constitute the single all-embracing narrative, they are brought face to face with their limits and often cause victims. We have become conscious that our narratives have historically evolved, are contextually embedded, and are the result of a multitude of accidental circumstances. It is for this reason that we are much more sensitive nowadays toward the other located at the boundary of our narrative, and to the plurality of narratives itself.

This situation represents a challenge to Christians to reflect anew on the relationship between their faith and the current context in which they live. In line with generations of Christians before them, they are

3. We will return to these specific terms and the relationship between them in the first chapter.

being called upon to consider how they ought to give plausible and legitimate expression to their Christian faith in the same context. The Christian faith can only survive by *recontextualization,* since the credibility thereof is always contextual.[4] In principle, every stage of the Christian tradition is inseparably bound to a specific historical context, which has made an essential contribution to its profile. The Christian faith is not detached from the context or culture in which its adherents live, rather it is interwoven with the said context and culture. When the context or culture changes, then Christian faith evolves with it. Recontextualization is thus also an ongoing task that can never reach completion. Indeed, Christians participate together with their contemporaries in the prevailing context, sharing as they do in the sensitivities, attitudes, ideas, and ambiguities that characterize it. The same holds true for theology. It is theology's task to reflect, in relation to the changing context, on the internal comprehensibility and the external credibility of the Christian faith.

The present study takes the process of recontextualization seriously and endeavors to determine the best manner of implementing it in the present day. Our line of approach is *methodological* in character. How should we conceptualize the relationship between theology and context with a view to achieving the best results? How does the Christian narrative relate to the context and what precisely is the impact of the latter on the former? What, for example, does today's religious revival signify for Christian faith? How should we understand the frequent appearance of religious symbols in the media detached from their original — traditional — setting? How do we reflect theologically on the fact that the standard rituals associated with important transitional moments in people's lives have managed to survive the devastating erosion experienced by long-established religious practice? Which theological method is the most appropriate in this regard? What should it be able to achieve? Of what should it be wary? In what way should such a method relate to other theological perspectives?

---

4. For the development of tradition in terms of recontextualization see *Interrupting Tradition,* chapter 1. See also chapter 2 in the present volume. The concept of recontextualization functions both descriptively and normatively. As a *descriptive* category, it assists us to analyze the ways in which tradition has been challenged by contextual change and novelty — varying from stubborn condemnation and suppression of this novelty to its uncritical embracing and adaptation. As a *normative* category, recontextualization calls for a theological program in which insight into the intrinsic link between faith and context inspires theologians to take contextual challenges seriously, in order to come to a contemporary theological discourse that can claim both theological validity and contextual plausibility.

2. Dialogue Partners

In describing his relationship with the theology of his teacher and friend Karl Rahner, Johann Baptist Metz argued that the theology of every new generation of theologians should be understood as a *Korrektivtheologie* with respect to its forerunner. Metz was certainly among the first to recommend Rahner's transcendental-idealistic theological project, but at the same time, he distanced himself from it in order to develop his own political theology. Metz wrote that it is praxis which determines the theological agenda: new experiences make it simply impossible to reproduce the theology of the past. Indeed, the continuity of the theological project is to be found in the fact that new theology "understands itself as a corrective with respect to existing theological projects and systems, and — in a critical-corrective relationship with the latter — saves and passes on the content and intention thereof."[5]

The line of thought that we will develop in the following pages can be described in a similar fashion. Our immediate dialogue partner in the present volume is in fact the modern theology with which countless post-conciliar students of theology were raised. Important examples such as Rahner and Metz, together with Hans Küng, David Tracy, and Edward Schillebeeckx, have inspired an entire generation. Each in their own way, they endeavored to engage in theology in dialogue with modernity, and were able to identify points at which the Christian narrative could be grafted onto modernity's potential for freedom and liberation. For many of them, it was a question of a "mutual and critical correlation" of the salvific message of the Christian faith with the achievements as well as the shadow side of the modern context. Where human dignity was put into practice, God was inescapably present; where the degradation of human suffering clashed with modern critical consciousness, God was also part of the scene. Correlation theology thus sought to establish a bridge between culture and faith. The project of modernity was one that Christians together with other "people of good will" could support and to which they could contribute as Christians. In short, such theological endeavor took the presupposition that it was possible to identify *continuity* between modernity and Christian faith as its point of departure.

---

5. Cf. J.-B. Metz, *Glaube in Geschichte und Gesellschaft: Studien zu einer praktischen Fundamentaltheologie* (Mainz: Grünewald, 1977), p. 12.

The modern context, however, has passed into history. And if we bear in mind that precisely the modern theologians focused particular attention on the intrinsic relationship between Christian faith and context, then it goes without saying that also their theological approaches should be questioned today, and where necessary corrected. Today also, theology is and remains *Korrektivtheologie*. Indeed, in a situation one might describe as postmodern, strategies of correlation would no longer appear to function at their best. Patterns of reflection have emerged that are critical of the facile acceptance of continuity and consensus, patterns that draw attention to the boundaries, particularities, and contingencies of every form of meaning giving, rooted in a profound mistrust of totalizing conceptual frameworks. Such reflection finds its counterpart at the societal level in processes of detraditionalization, individualization, and pluralization that have found their way into everyday life and have increasingly become a force to be reckoned with. The overlap between human existence and Christianity as a provider of meaning has become smaller. Fewer and fewer people are interested in the Christian message. Others prefer to see it as a sort of wisdom teaching, the inspiration behind which is perhaps also to be found outside the Christian narrative. Consensus would appear to have vanished; the religious situation has become one of plurality. At the same time, the present-day religious revival does not appear to be leading people in their droves back to the fold. Of course, all this has far-reaching consequences for the practice of theology if we bear in mind that the latter presented itself in modern terms as reflection rooted in continuity and consensus. Indeed, is it not fair to say that such a modern approach suffers from an incapacity to explain the specific and particular narrative character of the Christian faith in relation to the context? Or is it precisely the other way round: has the correlation between faith and context not lost sight of this particularity, because the presupposition of continuity is so determinative of its method? Or should we be thinking rather of a — remediable — "correlation flaw"?

In light of this evidently stalled correlation, others have argued that only anti-modern or postmodern conceptual patterns rooted in difference or *discontinuity* can be of value in redefining the relationship between the Christian faith and concrete context. It is thus claimed that this is the lesson to be learned from the bankruptcy of modern theology, namely, that it was too quick to seek reconciliation with the modern world. A fine example of this perspective can be found in Joseph Ratzinger's analysis of the relationship between Christian faith and present-day European culture elaborated in his recently published *Values in a Time of Upheaval,* written shortly before he was elected as Pope Benedict XVI.[6] As a matter of fact, Ratzinger maintains that Europe is undergoing a crisis with respect to the values that shaped the continent and that it is caught up in a dynamic that is further depleting the said values.[7] Europe is threatened in its very existence by a culture—without precedent—in which God has disappeared from public awareness, either by way of denial or doubt with respect to God's existence, or as a result of the privatization of the religious and the irrelevance of God for the public domain. Worse still: "There is an obvious parallel here to the Roman Empire in the days of its decline: it continued to function as a huge historical framework, but its own existential vigor was dead, and it was already living thanks only to those who in fact wanted to destroy it."[8] Only a culture founded on the firm ground of Christian faith provides for the energy to reverse this decline. "Today, at this precise hour in history, Europe and the world need the presence of God [. . .] As Christians, we are responsible for maintaining the presence of God in our world, for it is only this presence that has the power to keep man from destroying himself."[9] It is not dialogue with the world that one should expect to find on the theological agenda, but rather the *conversion* of a world characterized by the absence of faith and declining values. The current context, certainly the European context, has alienated itself to such a degree from the Christian faith that an emphasis on the Christian alternative as a rupture with the world is the only approach that can claim legitimacy.

3. Between Bridge and Rupture

Having arrived at this point, it is important for the arrangement of our theological project that we make a distinction between two different

6. Cf. J. Ratzinger (Benedict XVI), *Values in a Time of Upheaval* (New York: Crossroad, 2006). See also J. Ratzinger, "Europe in the Crisis of Cultures," in *Communio: International Catholic Review* 32 (2005): 345–56. For a comprehensive presentation of Joseph Ratzinger's position with respect to dialogue with the contemporary world, see our "Europe in Crisis: A Question of Belief or Unbelief? Perspectives from the Vatican," *Modern Theology* 23 (2007): 205–27.

7. Cf. Ratzinger, *Values in a Time of Upheaval*, p. 145: "[T]he dissolution of the primal certainties of man about God, about himself and about the universe—the dissolution of the consciousness of those moral values that are never subject to our own judgment—all this is still our problem. In a new form, it could lead to the self-destruction of European consciousness."

8. Ibid., p. 140.

9. Ibid., p. 165.

methodological options as a remedy for the problems facing the modern theological endeavor (together with a third that simply continues with the correlation approach). On the one hand, there are approaches that reject the theological *necessity* of dialogue with the context because Christian faith in essence is not affected by it. On the other hand, there are theological approaches that maintain the necessity of such dialogue but want to reconsider the *nature* thereof because of the altered situation. Contrary to the first position, the second presupposes the basic theological premise that it actually makes a difference for the Christian faith to be involved with the context, and indeed that there is an *intrinsic link* between the significance of revelation, faith, church, and tradition, and the context in which they are given form. Faith and church are not in opposition to the world, they participate in constituting the world and, furthermore, they are in part constituted by the world. Given the fact that God reveals Godself in history and that it is precisely in history that God can be known by us, history ultimately becomes co-constitutive of the truth of faith.

Our theological project subscribes to this second option. Our conviction is that there is a lesson to be learned from the way in which modern and anti-modern theologians deal with the changing context and determine the relationship of the Christian faith to that context. It will have been apparent thus far that the discussion between modern and anti-modern theology tends to be focused on the question whether the said relationship should be conceptualized in terms of continuity or discontinuity. The relationship between the modern world and Christian faith is either one of continuity and dialogue, or discontinuity and mutual exclusion. In each instance, Christian faith and (post)modernity appear in a one-to-one relationship: either the mutually critical relationship of two partners working toward the same goal or the opposition of two cultures with the essence of the human person and the world as the wager.

In the present study, we will question whether either of these one-to-one patterns represents the most useful way of examining the present-day situation. Both take a secularizing paradigm as their point of departure, which they each evaluate in a different way. While it is true that Europe is no longer understood in its totality from the perspective of the Christian conceptual horizon, the "process of secularization" did not simply lead to a primarily secular society with which Christianity is thus obliged to interact. Europe, rather, is undergoing a process of detraditionalization, whereby no single given tradition (including both religious traditions and secular atheism) is capable of continuing unquestioned. In addition, and to an increasing degree, European society is also to be characterized as pluralized at the level of both culture and individual fundamental life options, brought about in part by detraditionalization and in part by the processes of increased mental and physical mobility. For this reason, it is not the presupposed discontinuity or continuity between the Christian and the secular that determines today's spectrum of fundamental life options but rather the multiplicity of conceptions of humanity and the world, the plurality of religions and other convictions, of which the Christian faith and radical Enlightenment thinking (in their own variety) have evolved into but two positions among the many. It is on the basis of such an analysis that the Christian faith — as part of the pluralized context — is invited to reconsider its place and the role it should play in the further evolution of the European project. Such an exercise will have consequences for our self-understanding, for the evaluation of the situation in Europe, and for the way in which Christians actively participate in European society.

4. The Study in Outline

It is this exercise to which we commit ourselves in the present study. This book is divided into three parts, each with three chapters. The first part focuses on the present-day need to re-evaluate theological method. In parts two and three, we will examine three mainly methodological issues and three mainly thematic issues. "Mainly" in both instances, because content and method are always the closest partners.

In part 1, we offer an analysis of the methodological issue at stake. To this end, the first chapter presents a study of the current so-called post-secular and post-Christian context, which we analyze in terms of detraditionalization and pluralization. We argue that it would be better for theology today to consider the context from the perspective of a paradigm of pluralization than from that of a paradigm of secularization. In the second chapter, we explore the consequences of our analysis for the establishment of a contemporary theological method. We examine the problems related to modern correlation theology and its presupposition of continuity and offer critique of strategies that exclusively champion discontinuity. The result is a more extended development of the methodological contours of the way in which "recontextualization" structures the relationship between Christian faith and context. In this regard, we will make use of the category of "interruption," a category that succeeds in keeping continuity and discontinuity together. We will elucidate the pertinence of this category on both contextual and theological grounds. The product of our research is thus a theology of interruption, which implies a radical hermeneutic of both tradition and context. In the short third chapter, we present an additional theological consideration. Given the altered nature of the relationship between Christian faith and the current context — in terms of both systematic and practical theology — it seems opportune to make a distinction between the way in which the Christian faith relates to the context from both an *ad intra* and an *ad extra* perspective.

In the second and third parts of the book, we apply our hermeneutical-theological method in specific case-studies. Part 2 offers a study of the place of religious experience in acquiring faith, the relationship between life rituals and sacraments, and the relationship between faith and science. We explore the way in which the renewed cultural interest in religious experience, the survival of classic life rituals and the emergence of new rituals, and the debate surrounding creationism and "Intelligent Design" oblige theology to renew its orientation. In each instance, a "contextual interruption" of the Christian faith and of theological reflection leads to a "theology of interruption," which in turn profiles Christian faith and theology in context and tradition.

In the three chapters of part 3, we explore religious phenomena that exhibit cultural importance in a surprising and often novel way. What are the challenges of such a cultural interest in religion for theological reflection? The revival of religion and so-called "something-ism" direct us to a reflection on negative theology. The confrontation with religious plurality, and the questions it raises with respect to religious truth claims, lead to an exploration of the constitutive meaning of the belief that God became a human person in Jesus Christ. Present day apocalyptic sensitivities, to conclude, guide us to a rediscovery of the apocalyptic tension that ought to be a determinative feature of the Christian faith. As with the other chapters of this book, the process of recontextualization also results at this juncture in a theology of interruption.

The reader will not be surprised to find that we conclude the present study with a brief commentary on the hypothesis proposed by Johann Baptist Metz more than thirty years ago, namely, that the shortest definition of religion is . . . interruption.

Part I

THEOLOGY IN A POST-SECULAR CONTEXT

About Recontextualization and Interruption

In line with every past generation, Christians and their theologians are being challenged today to explore the relationship between their Christian faith and the surrounding world in which they take part. Indeed, it is because of this relationship that changes in the context have the capacity to place Christian intuitions, ideas, practices, and behavioral strategies under pressure.

In the first chapter, we offer an analysis of the present-day context. We discuss the religious situation in Europe and examine the claim that the latter should be identified as post-secular and post-Christian. We also draw attention to the so-called religious revival that would appear to be putting an end to secularization's hegemony, and to the increasing awareness of religious plurality. In the second chapter, we demonstrate that these contextual shifts imply a transition for theological method, from correlation to recontextualization. It will become apparent, moreover, that "interruption" is an appropriate contextual-theological term to give expression to the relationship between Christian faith and its concrete context in a critical and dynamic way. The third chapter differentiates between the perspective *ad intra* and the perspective *ad extra* evident in this relationship between the Christian narrative and the context.

Chapter One

The European Religious Situation

A "Post-Secular" and "Post-Christian" Context

Reflecting on the relationship between Christian faith and the current situation calls in the first instance for a detailed analysis of the religious situation in Europe. Under the influence of the apparent religious revival that is said to be at work on the old continent, this situation is not infrequently described as *post-secular.* Modernity did not banish religion from culture and society, it simply changed its appearance. For that reason, we begin by offering some methodological reflections on this concept. With the help of a number of observations from sociology of religion, we then provide a description of the present-day context as (the result of) an ongoing process of "detraditionalization" and "pluralization." It will become apparent that our situation can be analyzed not only as post-secular but also as *post-Christian.* By way of transition to the following chapter, we finally provide a brief investigation of the challenges such recent evolutions imply for theology.

1. A Post-Secular Europe?

Defining the current European religious situation as "post-secular" in one way or another relates this situation to the secularization process. Conventional sociology of religion endeavors to explain the gradually diminishing impact of the Christian tradition, institution, and faith practices on the individual and social level via the theory of secularization.[1]

1. For the Low Countries, but also for Europe as a whole, the work of the Louvain sociologist K. Dobbelaere in close collaboration with B. Wilson, has been of particular importance. See, for example, his *Het "volk-Gods" de mist in? Over de Kerk in België,* Nikè-reeks: didachè (Leuven: Acco, 1988), pp. 20–23. Dobbelaere himself introduces "the laicization thesis" in this regard (pp. 42–44). See also R. Laermans, ed., *Godsdienst en Kerk in een geseculariseerde samenleving: Een keuze uit het werk van Karel Dobbelaere* (Leuven: University Press, 1998). For a contemporary defense of the secularization paradigm see, for example, S. Bruce, *God Is Dead: Secularization in the West,* Religion in the Modern World (Malden, MA/Oxford/Berlin: Blackwell, 2002).

Based on the presuppositions of the so-called zero-sum theory, it is argued that modernization consists of a process that excludes religion from modern society and culture. In short, the sum of modernization and religion is always zero: the more religion, the less modernization; and especially the reverse: the more modernization, the less religion. The secularization thesis interprets modernization as a process whereby religion is slowly but surely expelled from modern society and culture. Once the secularization process is completed, a secular Europe will be realized, a Europe in which religion no longer plays a role in the construction and legitimation of individual and social identities. It would now appear, however, that this thesis has ultimately been falsified by the facts, and that many have come to recognize this reality. Religion has not been banished; rather, it has again received a prominent place on the agenda, in Europe as well as in the world as a whole.

In this regard, the use of the category "post-secular" can imply at least two meanings. From a *chronological* perspective, it might be understood as an attempt to describe how the evolution from a pre-modern overall Christian context to a modern secular society in the present is continued in the evolution from a secular to a post-modern, post-secular society. The term "post-secular," however, can also hint at a *methodological* issue with regard to the secularization thesis itself, and thus the way in which the religious transformations in Europe have been analyzed and explained. In other words, using the term "post-secular" has to do with the discussion of whether the term refers to an historical description of the process from pre-modern to post-modern, which changed religion in Europe (the *facts*), or pertains rather to the way in which we analyze these changes, i.e., the history of our ways to describe this process (our *view* of the facts).[2]

Of course, such a methodological usage of the term is not without impact on the way in which the current religious situation in Europe is interpreted, its history re-described, and the future of religion in Europe envisaged (both on the individual and social level). Thinking in terms of a post-secular methodological perspective on religion in the European context then should help us, as we will later demonstrate, to situate and understand the various phenomena and views that are mentioned with reference to the current European religious situation: new religious movements (both inside and outside the classical religions)[3];the

2. This is only valid, of course, for the people for whom such a distinction is still relevant.

3. See the voluminous bibliography of R. Nanniga, *Cults and New Religious Movements: A Bibliography: www.skepsis.nl/cultsbib2.html* (accessed May 1, 2007).

vague religiosity of many of our contemporaries, referred to ironically by some as "something-ism";[4] the strong religious imagination apparent in some new religious movements; the reference to, or appearance of, classical religious symbols, narratives, and rituals in contemporary (popular) culture;[5] the widespread search for spirituality (instead of "ethics,"[6]) including the replacement of the term "religion" with "spirituality";[7] the remarkable survival of the traditional rites of passage (some speak, for example, of a kind of *à-la-carte* Catholicism);[8] the tendency to religious indifference and relativism, and to practical agnosticism and atheism instead of theoretical agnosticism and atheism; the reverse tendency to fundamentalisms and neo-conservatisms, both in classical religions as well as in classical atheism, etc. It should also assist us in situating and understanding contemporary intellectual approaches to religion, both theological and philosophical.

Based on such a changed methodological perspective, we might reflect on the way in which religion in contemporary Europe contributes, or has the potential to contribute, to the identity construction and legitimation patterns of individuals and societies. We might think of regenerating old ways or constructing new ways to do so; we might reflect on the conditions necessary for establishing religious identity in view of religious plurality, interreligious communication, and so on. It goes without saying, however, that especially for theological reflection an adequate analysis of the current religious situation as "post-secular" exhibits important consequences for the way in which Christian thinkers perceive their faith and its relation to the contemporary context, in terms of both individual believers and believing communities, the churches.

---

4. See chapter 7 for a theological discussion of this religious phenomenon. In the Netherlands, the phenomenon has tended to be called "something-ism" (Dutch: "ietsisme"). Cf. S. W. Couwenberg, "Onttovering van het geloof en het 'ietsisme' als eigentijdse uiting van religieus verlangen," *Streven* (January 2004): 10–20.

5. The success of Dan Brown's *Da Vinci Code* and everything that goes with it provides an excellent illustration of this point.

6. The evident shift in relevant literature is significant in this regard. Authors who once published on "business ethics" are now writing about the spirituality of the (corporate) leader. Cf., for example, J. Verstraeten and J. Van Gerwen, *Business en ethiek: spelregels voor het ethisch ondernemen* (Tielt: Lannoo, 1990); J. Verstraeten, *Leiderschap met hart en ziel: spiritualiteit als weg naar oorspronkelijkheid* (Tielt: Lannoo, 2003).

7. See, for example, L. Voyé, "Een nieuw 'religieus' verlangen?" in *God: Hoe voelt dat?* ed. L. Boeve (Leuven: Davidsfonds, 2003), 33–69.

8. See K. Dobbelaere and L. Voyé, "Religie en kerkbetrokkenheid: ambivalentie en vervreemding," in *Verloren zekerheid: De Belgen en hun waarden, overtuigingen en houdingen*, ed. K. Dobbelaere et al. (Tielt: Lannoo, 2000), 117–52.

2. The Detraditionalization of Europe

In the meantime, the secularization thesis has come increasingly under fire. The process of modernization has evidently not led to the disappearance of religion or the human inclination to religiosity. Nevertheless, established, institutional religions — the Christian churches in particular — do not seem to be thriving in the European context.

"Desecularization" and the Religious Shifts in Europe

The secularization thesis, including the "zero-sum theory," has been placed under serious doubt today by authors such as Peter Berger and Harvey Cox, two of its former proponents.[9] Religion ultimately survived modernization. For Cox, secularization was the myth of the twentieth century, prophesying "the final disappearance of religion, ignorance and superstition."[10] In the meantime, however, the opposite would appear to be the case: the world is experiencing a process of *desecularization,* giving rise to "counter-secularization" movements.[11] In hyper-modern Japan, for example, religion is alive and well. Elsewhere, the growth of the Pentecostal movement and the resurgence of Islam cannot be ignored.

It would seem, however, that Europe is an exception to this "desecularization thesis,"[12] even if Berger is correct when he claims that the situation is highly ambiguous. There can indeed be no doubt that a significant number of Europeans have left and are still leaving the Christian churches, first in the Northern Protestant countries of Western Europe and, in more recent years, also in the Catholic South. Berger refers here to the emergence of a "massively secular Euro-culture." Nevertheless, together with European sociologists of religion, he wonders whether "secularization" is an appropriate term to analyze and define the European situation: "a body of data indicates strong survivals of religion, most of it generally Christian in nature, despite the widespread alienation

9. Cf. P. Berger, *The Sacred Canopy: Elements of a Sociological Theory of Religion* (Garden City, NY: Doubleday, 1967); *The Heretical Imperative: Contemporary Possibilities of Religious Affirmation* (Garden City, NY: Anchor, 1979); H. Cox, *The Secular City: Secularization and Urbanization in Theological Perspective* (New York: Macmillan, 1965).

10. H. Cox, "The Myth of the Twentieth Century: The Rise and Fall of 'Secularization,'" in *The Twentieth Century: A Theological Overview,* ed. G. Baum (Maryknoll, NY: Orbis, 1999), 135–43, p. 135.

11. Cf. P. Berger, "The Desecularization of the World: A Global Overview," in *The Desecularization of the World: Resurgent Religion and World Politics,* ed. P. Berger (Grand Rapids: Eerdmans, 1999), 1–18, pp. 2–4.

12. Cf. Berger, "The Desecularization of the World," pp. 10–11; Cox, "The Myth of the Twentieth Century," pp. 136–39.

from the organized churches. A shift in the institutional location of religion, then, rather than secularization, would be a more accurate description of the European situation."[13] Cox arrives at an analogous question, also with an explicit reference to Christianity: "Could Christianity in Europe be moving away from an institutionally positioned model and toward a culturally diffuse pattern, more like the religions in many Asian countries, and therefore more difficult to measure by such standard means as church attendance and baptism statistics?"[14] Modernization in Europe has caused a *transformation of religion,* not its disappearance.

Yves Lambert, Director of Research at the "Groupe de Sociologie des Religions et de la Laicité," also doubts whether Europe is the exception to the "desecularization thesis," and likewise claims a religious mutation in Europe.[15] In an article published in 2004, he argues that, whereas the 1981 and 1990 results of the European Values Study surveys[16] could be interpreted as supportive of the secularization thesis, thus underlining the "European exception,"[17] the 1999 survey reveals three significant new tendencies, especially among the young, which nonetheless place the thesis under reconsideration. The process of "un-churching" is still continuing, with progressively lower church attendance rates, less confidence in the church, etc. It is also clear that a number of young people have already grown up without ever belonging to a religion. Among young Christians, however, a religious renewal is observable, while for the whole of the younger generation (eighteen- to twenty-nine-year-olds) there is an evident increase in "believing without belonging."[18]

---

13. Berger, "The Desecularization of the World," p. 10.

14. Cox, "The Myth of the Twentieth Century," p. 139.

15. Y. Lambert, "A Turning Point in Religious Evolution in Europe," *Journal of Contemporary Religion* 19 (2004): 29–45.

16. The European Values study started in the 1970s under the impetus of Jan Kerkhofs (K.U. Leuven) and Ruud de Moor (University of Tilburg). Surveys have already been organized on three occasions in several European countries (in 1981, 1990, and 1999/2000). Lambert's study makes a comparison of the results of the three surveys with respect to the nine countries in which they were available: Ireland, Italy, Spain, Belgium, France, West Germany, the Netherlands, Great Britain, and Denmark.

17. For the "European exception," see Grace Davie, "Europe: The Exception That Proves the Rule?" in *The Desecularization of the World,* ed. P. Berger, 65–83, and Berger, "The Desecularization," pp. 9–11. Berger makes reference to a second exception: "There exists an international subculture composed of people with Western-type higher education, especially in the humanities and social sciences, that is indeed secularized. This subculture is the principal 'carrier' of progressive, Enlightened beliefs and values. While its members are relatively thin on the ground, they are very influential . . . " (p. 10).

18. This expression stems from G. Davie, *Religion in Britain since 1945: Believing without Belonging* (Oxford: Blackwell, 1994).

On the basis of the first two surveys (1981, 1990), one might affirm that age, generally speaking, is an important factor with regard to a person's claim to being religious in terms of opinion, belief, and behavior: "the younger the person, the more likely they are to be irreligious."[19] Based on the 1999 survey, Lambert maintains that there is evidence enough to reconsider this affirmation seriously. He offers three points in support of his argument:

First, "in all countries, young people who declare themselves as Christian, appear more religious in 1999 than in 1990 and 1981 [...], regardless of whether the indicators are of personal religiosity (being a religious person, getting comfort and strength from religion, beliefs especially in a personal God and life after death) or of institutional religiosity (attachment to ceremonies, appreciation of the spiritual and moral contributions of churches)."[20] This growing religiosity, however, does not result in a more active Christian engagement, such as participation in local faith communities or doing voluntary work. Moreover, regular church attendance is also on the decline among young Christians. The religiosity of young Protestants, however, is "noticeably inferior."

Second, the phenomenon of "believing without belonging" is becoming a permanent feature in the more secular countries of Europe. Lambert defines it here as the development of an "autonomous, diffused, 'off-piste' religiosity [which] is illustrated mainly through variables which are less typically Christian":[21] importance of meditation and contemplation; belief in a higher power, spirit, or force, rather than a personal God; belief in life after death (including reincarnation); an interest in different religious traditions rather than one particular tradition. In general, this group claims to be in search of spirituality (rather than "religion").

Third, the young people who have never belonged to any religion seem to be a new category if the data are anything to go by. The vast majority (62 percent) of those who state that they presently do not belong to a religion have never belonged to one.

Lambert thus concludes that there has indeed been a religious mutation in Europe, which would make Europe a little bit less of an exception (but only slightly less so). When asked for his interpretation, Lambert ventures "a kind of return in the swing of the pendulum following the phase of the great religious breakdown, the permissive thrust, and the

19. J. Stoelzel, *Les valeurs du temps present: une enquête européenne* (Paris: PUF, 1983), 231–32, as quoted in Lambert, "Turning Point," p. 35.
20. Lambert, "Turning Point," pp. 37–38.
21. Ibid., p. 38.

ideological radicalization of the 1960s and 1970s."[22] The younger generation would seem to attach new importance to more traditional values such as faithfulness, social order, and so on. The exceptions here are the ethical items that affect private self-determination, such as the use of soft drugs, abortion and euthanasia, homosexuality, suicide, and so on. There are indications of a selective re-activation of traditions and a new openness to religion.

Some of Lambert's remarks are important in this regard, as they seem to point to what is at the basis of resurgent religiosity in Europe. (1) As regards the stronger belief in life after death, Lambert suggests that this may have been influenced by the "over-valuation of self-realization which might have made death even more unacceptable." (2) Second, openness to religion holds true "to the extent to which its role is from now on non-authoritarian. [. . .] It can find new credibility as a source of meaning, ethics, sociability, identity, faith, or as an autonomous quest." (3) "On the other hand, religion is *relativized,* passed through the filter of individual subjectivity, confronted by indifference or the autonomous spiritual quest." He continues, "This is what I call 'pluralistic secularization,' which tends in Western Europe to slightly de-secularize the most laicized of countries (France, for example) and, on the other hand, to further secularize the most confessional ones (Sweden for example)."[23] He concludes, "In Europe, God is neither as dead nor as alive as some now maintain."[24]

In short, Europe has undergone an important transformation at the religious level, moving from a predominantly institutional Christian society to a society in which religiosity and spirituality tend to be a feature of a person's autonomous, subjective establishment of meaning.

"Believing without Belonging": Post-Secular and Post-Christian?

At this point, I would like to draw our attention to the language used to deal with the religious situation in Europe, especially as regards the categories of "religion" and "believing without belonging."

First, the use of the category "religion" is often ambiguous. On the one hand, "religion" seems to refer to classical, traditional religion (most often Christianity) and institutional religion (Christian churches), while on the other, it also refers to a kind of general religious attitude, perhaps better referred to as "religiosity," often more general than, or even to be

22. Ibid., p. 42.
23. Ibid., p. 43.
24. Ibid., p. 44.

distinguished from, Christian religion. As concerns the latter, one may ask whether "*believing* without belonging" is too strong a definition for this kind of religiosity.

No doubt a sort of "Christian believing without belonging" is a real phenomenon — albeit more in the past than in the present. It concerns Christians who have distanced themselves from the churches, most often dissatisfied with their conservative ethics, inflexible doctrinal positions, hierarchical community structures, and outdated liturgical language. As far as Belgium is concerned, for example, many of these un-churched people (all officially Catholic through infant baptism) tend to refer to themselves as "Christians" and explicitly no longer as "Catholics." In the Belgian sub-report of the 1999 EVS survey, K. Dobbelaere and L. Voyé comment on this un-churched Christian believing, stating that it only lasts for one generation because religion in one way or another requires the support of plausibility structures. The figures demonstrate that the following generation is less Christian: "un-churched Christians" are a dying breed,[25] because a deep-seated detachment from the church seems to initially presuppose an equally deep-seated attachment thereto.

As a general category, however, one can legitimately ask whether "believing without belonging" really has to do with "believing" (in terms of "Christian believing"), especially in the long run.[26] Does it make any sense to interpret (or recuperate) the resurging, more general, multifaceted religiosity in Christian terms, as a sort of left-over Christianity without institutional or traditional embeddedness (as Cox would appear to suggest)? For Lambert also, the expression "believing without belonging" refers in the first instance to the individual — *off-piste* — quest for spirituality, as an autonomous answer to questions of ultimate meaning and religious wonder. After all, the most important empirical indicators

25. Cf. Dobbelaere and Voyé, "Religie en kerkbetrokkenheid," p. 128: "Extremely few people un-churched by accident of birth become churched later in life, while a large number of those one would consider churched by accident of birth later drift to the margins of the church if they do not abandon it altogether." Dobbelaere and Voyé ask themselves whether this shift should be blamed on increasing irreligiosity or dissatisfaction with the church as an institution. While many lapsed churchgoers certainly lay the blame on the latter, the authors observe at the same time that "un-churched" religiosity has difficulty surviving from one generation to the next: later generations of un-churched are thus already less religious than the first." The authors conclude: "Religiosity, in other words, needs to be supported by plausibility structures and in Belgium only one such structure is clearly visible. If one clashes with the Catholic church, the only alternative is to join the un-churched. [...] In the long term, however, and certainly over several generations, this clearly gives rise to irreligiosity" (pp. 129–30).

26. Cf. S. Hellemans, "From 'Catholicism against Modernity' to the Problematic 'Modernity of Catholicism,'" in *Ethical Perspectives* 8 (2001): 117–27, p. 124. Hellemans prefers to use the expression "longing without belonging" instead of "believing without belonging."

of this religiosity are not explicitly Christian. It is for this reason that "post-Christian" is perhaps a more appropriate term to describe the group in question, certainly from the perspective of the Christian faith. The category "post-Christian" then refers to the fact that most members of this group are only partially initiated and enjoy nothing more than a fragmentary involvement with faith and faith communities, although they are for the most part baptized and may well have been educated in confessional schools. This becomes manifest, for instance, in their occasional and declining participation in Christian rites of passage and their poor, non-integrated knowledge of the Christian tradition — often in spite of many years of catechesis and religious education in schools.

From "Secularization" to "Detraditionalization" and "Individualization"

Based on these cultural-sociological considerations, it would seem that the question of whether we are living in a post-secular Europe can be answered in the affirmative, if we understand "secular" in terms of the secularization thesis. At the same time, however, we cannot deny the reality of secularization, understood as the process of "de-institutionalization" and "individualization/subjectivization" of religion resulting in the transformation of religion in Europe. This transformation has given rise to a multi-faceted religious panorama in which Christian faith and church practice have strongly diminished, to such a degree that post-secular Europe can equally be styled post-Christian Europe.

Bearing this in mind, it is perhaps better to employ the term "detraditionalization" when one refers to the processes classically associated with "secularization," since the latter continues to refer in one way or another to the secularization hypothesis and the secularization of European society proposed therein. At the same time, the term "detraditionalization" not only alludes to Europe's declining institutional Christian horizon but also hints at the more generally observed socio-cultural interruption of traditions (religious as well as class, gender, etc.), which are no longer able to pass themselves effortlessly on from one generation to the next. Identity formation is no longer a question of growing into pre-given ideological patterns, which condition one's perspectives on meaning and social existence. It is from this broader perspective that the hampering of the transmission process of Christian tradition is observed. Christianity is no longer a given and unquestioned horizon of individual and social identity.

The titles given to the three subsequent books containing the Belgian results of the European Values Study are particularly telling. In 1984, the research group in charge of this study published "The Silent Turn," showing that Belgium was turning away from a more traditional Roman Catholic profile.[27] In 1992, the same group published "The Accelerated Turn," claiming that the process of change was evolving faster than ever.[28] The title of the third book, "Lost Certainty," indicates that the processes of detraditionalization are reaching their end. In little less than a few decades, Belgium has evolved from a society broadly perceived as Catholic into a detraditionalized society.[29]

It must be clear by now that detraditionalization is understood as a descriptive category, indicating the socio-cultural developments that influenced Europe in modern times. In this regard, detraditionalization is not only a feature of post-Christian reality, rather it affects all religious and ideological affiliations. All of them in one way or another have to deal with this changed socio-cultural reality.

Detraditionalization and *individualization* are two sides of the same process. On the structural level, every individual is charged with the task of constructing his or her personal identity. Traditions no longer automatically steer this construction process, but are only possibilities together with other choices from which an individual must choose. One single determined tradition is no longer unquestioned or taken to be of decisive importance. In other words, personal identity has become more and more (structurally) reflexive. Every choice has its alternatives in relation to which one must answer for one's options. At the same time, those who opt for classical or traditional identities are also making a choice. Under the influence of detraditionalization and individualization, the relationship to tradition has changed also in this regard and has

---

27. See J. Kerkhofs and R. Rezsohazy, ed., *De stille ommekeer: oude en nieuwe waarden in het België van de jaren tachtig* (Tielt: Lannoo, 1984).

28. See J. Kerkhofs, K. Dobbelaere, and L. Voyé, *De versnelde ommekeer: de waarden van Vlamingen, Walen en Brusselaars in de jaren negentig* (Tielt: Lannoo, 1992).

29. See K. Dobbelaere, M. Elchardus et al., *Verloren zekerheid. De Belgen en hun waarden, overtuigingen en houdingen* (Tielt: Lannoo, 2000). Some of the research group's results are offered here by way of illustration. When Belgians are asked to define themselves in terms of religious affiliation, 47.4 percent describe themselves as Catholic, 1.2 percent as Protestant and 15.3 percent as Christian without being Protestant or Catholic (p. 119). In 1967, 52 percent of the Flemish people (for Belgium 42.9 percent) attended Sunday services on a weekly basis; in 1998 this was reduced to 12.7 percent (Belgium 11.2 percent) (p. 126). In 1967, 96.1 percent of newborn children were baptized in Flanders; 73 percent in 1998. The Belgian figures for 1998 are still more than 8 percent lower (64.7 percent). Marrying in the church (and not in a civil marriage alone): for Flanders 91.8 percent in 1967, 51.2 percent in 1998; for Belgium 86.1 percent in 1967, 49.2 percent in 1998 (p. 123).

become more reflexive. People are aware to one degree or another that their choices could have been different. Of course, there are (cultural) instances and processes that endeavor to steer identity construction at the individual and social level, the media and the processes of economization being the most significant in this respect.[30] The latter is particularly omnipresent. Economization determines both the way in which culture manifests itself to us and the way in which we have access to it and can relate to it. This double function gives rise to an inclusive consumer culture that presents itself as the intermediary par excellence between us and our cultural context. In the first instance, the process of economization reduces our culture to a series of consumer goods. Commodification separates cultural objects from their original associations and narratives, and makes them available for exchange on the market, items to be acquired for a price that frequently does not square with their real value. At the same time, the consumer culture structurally influences the way in which we relate to culture. We are trained in the discipline of consumption and learn to see culture from a market or consumer perspective and to make use of it as such. The way we relate to religion and tradition is likewise no longer free of such influences.[31]

As is the case with detraditionalization, individualization is also a descriptive category intended to designate a cultural trend. It is thus to be distinguished from individualism, for example, which foregrounds the individual as a normative category in the process of identity construction. In the sociological sense, the process of individualization refers to the structural possibilities available to us in the formation of our personal identity and the increase in potential reflexivity that is brought about thereby. The question of whether the possibilities in question are or are not realized by every individual has nothing to do with the process as such or with its structural character.

It should be noted, however, that the distinction between individualization (the necessity of identity construction resulting from detraditionalization) and individualism (absolute self-determination) tends to be forgotten in many, primarily pessimistic, analyses of contemporary culture. The rejection of the latter, however, does not release Christianity from its responsibility to come to terms with the former.

30. For this paragraph, see my *Interrupting Tradition,* chapters 3 and 4.

31. See, for example, the important study by V. Miller, *Consuming Religion: Religious Belief and Practice in a Consumer Culture* (New York: Continuum, 2004), and European reactions thereto in *Bulletin ET* 17:1 (2006) (Special Issue: *Consuming Religion in Europe*).

Individualization indeed has an irreducible effect on the way Christians today understand their faith, but it need not automatically lead to individualism.

3. The Pluralization of Religion in Europe

Our focus on the interpretation of the European Values Study data, however, might make us forget another important feature: the pluralization of religion, which goes much further than Lambert's "pluralistic secularization."[32] The religious plurality of our day extends beyond the plurality resulting from "pluralistic secularization," no matter how widespread and important the latter phenomenon may be. Indeed, one of the notable shortcomings of the EVS is its under-representation of other (world) religions, including Islam.[33] Furthermore, information from the EVS survey on other religions focuses mainly on the way in which Christians and "post-Christians" perceive them.[34]

The religious reality, however, is far more complex. In a contribution entitled "Serving God in Brussels" (1995), K.U. Leuven anthropologist Johan Leman offers a portrait of the various forms of religious affiliation in metropolitan Brussels.[35] He first mentions the diversity of Christian churches and communities (autochthonous and other): Catholic, Protestant of different denominations, Anglican, Greek Orthodox, Syriac Orthodox, and the many Christian sects (e.g., Jehovah's Witnesses), which can often be distinguished further on a social and regional basis. As far as the autochthonous communities are concerned, Jews likewise

---

32. Cf. the subsection "Desecularization and the Religious Shifts in Europe" on page 16 above.

33. Lambert, "Turning Point," p. 30. "At least 15 million people in Western Europe adhere to the Muslim faith or have close cultural ties or affiliations with the Islamic world. In the course of a few decades, Islam has emerged as Europe's second religion after Christianity. Especially remarkable about this phenomenon is that it has occurred gradually, generally peacefully, and, in some measure, as a consequence of the economic needs of European countries. Despite notable difficulties [e.g., the events of September 11, 2001], Islam is slowly but inexorably becoming part of Europe's social, cultural, and even political landscape"; from S. T. Hunter, *Islam, Europe's Second Religion: The New Social, Cultural, and Political Landscape* (Westport, CT: Praeger/CSIS, 2002), back cover.

34. Those who consider themselves Christians, Lambert comments, demonstrate "a kind of positive relativism toward religion and at least an open-minded attitude" ("Turning Point," p. 41).

35. See J. Leman, "Religions, Modulators in Pluri-Ethnic Cities: An Anthropological Analysis of the Relative shift from Ethnic to Supra-Ethnic and Meta-Ethnic Faith Communities in Brussels," *Journal of Contemporary Religion* 14 (1999): 217–31. Leman's study has shown that religion is an important factor of integration, adaptation, and lack of adaptation among non-native residents (as well as more socially dominant groups) in major cities.

represent a recognizable group, and it is clear that a significant number of middle-class people are inclined toward different forms of oriental spirituality. Allochthonous communities tend for the most part to be of Buddhist and particularly Muslim descent, and differ according to regional origin. Their residence often leads to an accommodation of their religious views and practices toward the Belgian context, although a reaction against such accommodation is also manifest and has given rise to various forms of fundamentalism.

Religious *pluralization* does not limit itself to the aforementioned description, however. Together with detraditionalization, it is also evident in relation to the population of Europe as a whole. The result is broad spectrum of religious and other fundamental life options and an increasing awareness of this plurality. In addition to Christians (subdivided into various different denominations), there are atheists, agnostics, Muslims, Jews, Buddhists, lapsed Christians, post-Christians, the uninterested, adherents of new religious movements (such as New Age), people we might describe for want of a better word as syncretists, etc. In addition, each group can be further subdivided into a multiplicity of tendencies and lifestyles, some institutionally recognizable and some not.

Indeed, geographic as well as mental mobility have brought the plural world of religions and convictions onto our doorstep. Migration, tourism, and the communication, media have confronted those developing a "religiosity without belonging" as well as those committed to a classic religious tradition with religious diversity.[36]

At this juncture it is important again to make the distinction between pluralization as a descriptive category and (formal) pluralism and relativism as means of relating to pluralization. Similarly, when the Christian faith rejects the latter, it is compelled nonetheless on account of pluralization to determine its own position in the current context in a different manner than before. More than has hitherto been the case, the Christian's participation in a particular tradition demands a degree of reflexivity and a recognition of the specificity of the Christian fundamental life option in

36. For the former, religious plurality presents the manifold ways in which human beings can construct their religious identities. Often religious traditions are conceived of as reservoirs of narratives, rituals, practices, worldviews, etc., from which they can choose in order to construct their religious identity. The tangible confrontation with religious otherness leads many of them to a reflection on their own religious identity and truth claims that often seem to result in a theological-pluralist position on theological truth — which in the long run probably leads to more detraditionalization and once again often to post-Christian positions (cf. chapter 7). In chapter 8, however, I will argue that this is only one way in which plurality can be dealt with and, in the case of a Christian theological reflection, not the most promising and fruitful one.

relation to other fundamental life options, including atheists and agnostics, "something-ists" and the indifferent, Muslims, Buddhists, members of new religious movements, etc.

4. The Analysis of the Contemporary Religious Situation of Europe

It might be opportune, therefore, to employ pluralization in combination with detraditionalization, also as a tool to analyze the current context, aware at the same time of the fact that both processes influence one another. The following considerations would support this suggestion and necessitate a change of perspective with respect to the concrete religious situation.

In the first instance, consciousness of the reality of religious plurality clearly has an impact on the detraditionalization process going on in European societies. Three elements are worth mentioning in this regard. (1) It further relativizes the (until recently) unquestioned monopoly position of Christianity in answering questions of meaning and value. (2) Consciousness of religious plurality feeds the intuition of a general religiosity, constitutive for being a human person as such (the idea of the *homo religiosus,* human beings being incurably religious). Particular traditions are then understood as specific examples or manifestations of such general religiosity. (3) Religious plurality is both the outcome and the engine of detraditionalization and individualization. To construct their religious identities, individuals use (fragments from) old and new religious traditions that have been detached from their original traditional embeddedness. In this regard, one might speak of a religious market situation in which established churches and religions, as well as new religious movements and trends, are caught up in the game of supply and demand. As such, the idea of "tradition" itself as a given reality, into which people are initiated in order to receive their identity rather than constructing it, becomes lost.

In combination with detraditionalization, the category of religious pluralization also refers to the fact that the outcome of modernization is not a secular society without religion, a kind of "Euro-secularism."[37] On the contrary, a dynamic multi-religious society, full of complexity and ambiguity, has taken over. Aside from classical world religions, many

37. In line with what Berger calls "a massively secular Euro-culture" ("The Desecularization of the World," p. 10).

new religious movements and fundamental life options are present in Europe, ranging from fundamentalist positions to *à-la-carte* consumerism of religious narratives, rituals, and practices.[38] As a consequence, this also implies that the rather classic analysis of the religious situation in European societies in terms of a *continuum* between "churched Christians" and "atheist humanists" is too simplistic when it comes to adequately analyzing the current state of affairs.[39]

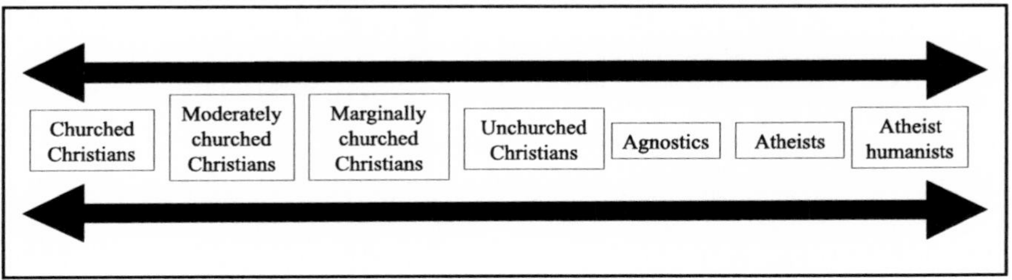

An analysis in terms of a *plural arena of interacting religious positions* would appear to be a more adequate analytical procedure than the continuum illustrated in the figure above. The diversity of individual religious convictions, including vague religiosity, nihilism, and religious indifference, represent distinct positions in this plural field, to be distinguished in their own right, next to the variety of classical religious traditions. In this way, the established parameters of the secularization hypothesis (more or less churched Christian to more or less unchurched/atheist) are left behind and justice is done to the dynamic complexity of the plural religious arena and to the relative independence of the various positions on this arena. Christianity has not been replaced by a secular culture, but by a plurality of life options and religions — among which the secularist (atheist) position, in all its variants, is only one — that have moved in to occupy the vacuum left behind as a result of its diminishing impact.

---

38. An analysis that firmly supports this can be found in C. Partridge, *The Re-Enchantment of the West*, vol. 1: *Alternative Spiritualities, Sacralization, Popular Culture and Occulture* (London/New York: T&T Clark, 2004).

39. Aside from this, one may remark that a considerable degree of sociological research in the media and academic world still conceives of its instruments within such continuum-thinking together with many systematic and pastoral-theological strategies. Questionnaires inquire whether a person believes (in God) according to the classic continuum, without any form of "confessional" specification of the person's faith, without providing the opportunity to indicate the faith tradition that steers his or her belief and the extent to which this tradition may or may not have been integrated.

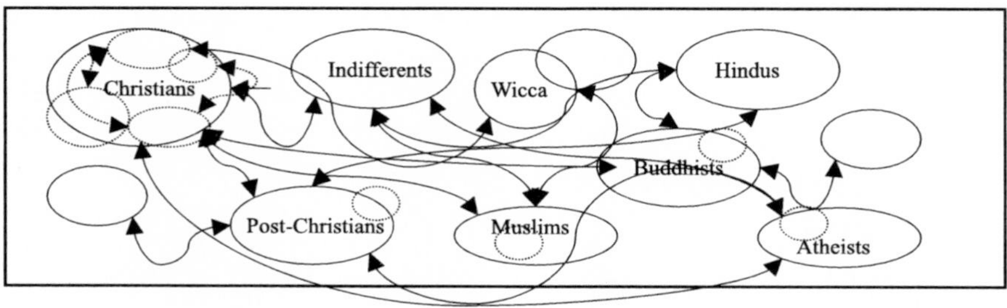

The space occupied by religion and other fundamental life options is filled with a variety of different groups, all of which often can be further specified into a multiplicity of different positions: Christians, atheists, agnostics, post-Christians, the indifferent, Muslims, Jews, the adherents of New Age, individualists, etc. Identity construction and reflection on one's fundamental life option takes place within this space, and every choice we make in this regard establishes itself as a position within the same space. The concrete arena of fundamental life options then is one of active diversity and dynamic interaction, based on contact with other positions. Such interaction has the potential to result in conflict and confrontation, but it can also lead to mutual exchange and initiate learning processes of every sort. A contemporary reflection on religion, therefore, urges that we take a fully accepted plurality of positions as our point of departure. At the same time, this implies in turn that there can be no neutral position, no detached observer's perspective, since each position (including the one claiming to be able to speak about the others) is always already one among many. Furthermore, it implies our recognition of the fact that fundamental life options — from the social-structural perspective — are a matter of choice, and a choice we are ultimately required to justify.

5. Conclusions and Theological Questions

One can indeed legitimately qualify the current European religious situation as *post-secular*. Secularization in this regard did not lead to a secular culture, but to a transformation of religion in Europe on the basis of which the classical Christian tradition lost its overall and pregiven unquestioned position. The impact of the Christian tradition on meaning and social life has diminished because of the process of detraditionalization. Together with the growing presence and consciousness of religious plurality, this has led to a Europe that might be considered *post-Christian* with equal legitimacy.

The detraditionalization and pluralization of religion in Europe, however, bear important consequences for the institutional religions of Europe, and Christianity in the first instance. These two processes not only inverted the privileged status of Christianity in Europe, they also have an effect on contemporary Christian believers and communities, those (still) belonging to the churches, albeit often in varying degrees. Detraditionalization also changes the way in which Christians themselves relate to the Christian tradition. Since the necessity to be Christian no longer exists on the cultural level, contemporary Christians — structurally speaking — must more than before "choose" to be a Christian, whether or not they live out their faith, from their own spiritualities, as a vocation or "being chosen." As with all identity formation, Christian identity has also become potentially *reflexive,* and the option to be a Christian has been individualized. The pluralization of religion only reinforces this reflexive potential. For many, these structural changes lead to a serious relativization of their bonds with the Christian tradition (especially its claim to anteriority), leading them to adopt marginally Christian and even post-Christian positions. In this respect, the Christian tradition is in danger of becoming little more than a reserve supply of narratives and rituals, side by side with other narratives and rituals, which can be used as a resource in the construction of personal religious identity and in the individual search for spirituality. Others feel extremely uncomfortable with this reflexivity, and turn to more traditionalist and fundamentalist positions, stringently reinforcing the bond between social and individual identity and the tradition transmitted from the past.

When confronted with these two opposing reactions to the same processes, an obvious question arises: are there ways to *both* productively engage this structural reflexivity in a theological reflection on what it is to be a Christian today, *and* simultaneously maintain the dynamic integrity of the Christian tradition? Can such reflexivity become a driving force stimulating a reflection on Christian tradition whereby the latter is neither reduced to a storehouse nor set in stone? Or does this structural reflexivity indeed automatically lead toward "religiosity without belonging" and relativism, and their counterpart in traditionalism and fundamentalism?

What type of theological reflection do we need for this purpose? Which theological method is most appropriate? Both challenges, detraditionalization and pluralization, have led theologians for some time now to reflect on the relationship between the Christian faith and tradition on the one hand, and the context in which it finds itself on the other.

Chapter Two

A New Method

Recontextualization Leads to Interruption

Christian faith and tradition are always anchored in a context and given expression therein. No single attempt to explain the core (or essence) of faith and tradition can escape this fact. Furthermore, the intrinsic bond between faith, tradition, and context is precisely Christianity's strength, a strength that can be described theologically as the incarnational driving force of the Christian faith. We have referred elsewhere to this process in both descriptive and normative terms as "recontextualization."[1] In the present chapter, we will discuss the way in which our manner of recontextualization has shifted on account of the changes in the context we analyzed in the preceding chapter. We will demonstrate that this has significant consequences for the way we speak about tradition and its relationship with the context in theological and pastoral terms. Indeed, the modern correlation paradigm served until recently as the established manner to account for the intrinsic relationship between theology and context. This correlation method (in several variants) shaped the work of many post-Conciliar theologians (such as Hans Küng, Edward Schillebeeckx, and David Tracy). We will argue in the following pages that this theological method is in need of thorough revision, bearing in mind that the processes of detraditionalization and pluralization force us to think differently concerning faith and the Christian tradition than in the past.

In the present chapter, we will explore the project of modern correlation theology and endeavor to determine why it no longer functions as a method today. On this basis, we will develop the method of recontextualization as an alternative. We will conclude by explaining how the notion of "interruption" allows us to conceptualize the relationship between faith, tradition, and theology, on the one hand, and context, on the other, in a plausible and theologically legitimate manner. It will be shown

1. Cf. the introduction to the present study, footnote 4.

that "interruption" is the motor of a concrete theological hermeneutics of faith, tradition, and context.

1. The Modern Correlation Method No Longer Functions

Modern correlation theology is experiencing difficult times. Anti-modern theologians who sharply criticized this theology shortly after Vatican II[2] are now crying victory. New theological movements such as "Radical Orthodoxy," with John Milbank[3] at the helm, argue that theology's "sell-out" to secular modernity has made it impossible to associate God with the world and ultimately led to postmodern nihilism.[4] Both tendencies point to the need to hark back to pre-modern conceptual patterns in order to reflect on the cause of the Christian faith in today's literally post-modern context. Appeal is frequently made to Augustine and the distinction he makes between the "city of God" and the "city of man." In relation to the contemporary context, such theologians then primarily stress discontinuity. For them, modern theology has been too eager to appeal to the continuity between faith and context, going too far in adapting Christian faith to (post)modernity, so much so that it has little if anything to say to the present context.

The Project of Modern Correlation Theology

In theology "correlation" has been understood in a number of different ways. In its most general sense, the concept gives expression to the intuition that faith, faith tradition, and reflection on faith do not take place in isolation. On the contrary, they are closely related to life, culture, society, history — the context in which they are embedded. In line with this

2. See, for example, J. Ratzinger, "Communio — Ein Programm," *Internationale Katholische Zeitschrift Communio* 20 (1992) 454–63, on the occasion of the 20th anniversary of *Communio:* post-Conciliar theologians have opted for what they consider interesting at the cost of what is true by presenting old liberal insights as new Catholic theology (p. 455). The theology of *Communio,* on the contrary, must allow God's word to give answer to the questions people raise and should therefore "not remain within the circle of professionals, theologians or church makers, who hurry from one academic sitting to the next and thereby reinforce their disappointment with respect to the church both for themselves and for others" (p. 461 — translation mine).

3. Cf., for example, J. Milbank, " 'Postmodern Critical Augustinianism': A Short Summa in Forty-Two Responses to Unasked Questions," *Modern Theology* 7 (1991): 225–37; J. Milbank, C. Pickstock and G. Ward, eds., *Radical Orthodoxy: A New Theology* (London: Routledge, 1999).

4. See, in addition, section 3, pages 37–41 of the present chapter.

general definition, it is possible to identify "correlation" in many theologies down through the centuries. The question of correlation becomes a pertinent issue in the modern period, however, when the context is progressively established and recognized as autonomous on account of secularization. At that moment, the need arose to provide an explanation of how correlation would function in a theological method. This was clearly the goal of the German-American theologian Paul Tillich, who himself coined the term "correlation." The correlation method became the driving force behind his systematic theology, which aimed explicitly at translating the core of the Christian faith into a modern context.[5]

Broadly speaking, the project of the modern correlation method endeavors to establish a correlation between Christian tradition and the modern, secular context. Christian faith and theology strive to build a bridge between the two. In this sense, it would be correct to say that the majority of modern theologies are to be considered correlation theologies, although many of those involved would be inclined to question and even correct the term itself.[6] It is also in this sense that we employ the term "correlation" in the present study: as a resolutely *modern* way of conceiving the relationship between tradition and context.

A brief explanation seems appropriate at this juncture. In modernity's striving for rationality and emancipation, human persons got rid of the all-encompassing religious horizon, which had completely determined their individual and social existence. They discovered themselves as subjects both capable of and responsible for their achievement of maturity as subjects. Although this claimed autonomy of the subject was at first rejected by the church and theology, afterwards they embraced it. Rationality, human freedom, and social liberation were considered privileged *loci theologici* from which to recontextualize the Christian faith in a God who is salvifically involved with human beings and their histories. Where human beings strove after human dignity, God could

---

5. Cf. P. Tillich, *Systematic Theology* (Chicago: University of Chicago Press, 1951–64), 3 vols.

6. See, for example, F. Schüssler Fiorenza, *Systematic Theology: Tasks and Methods*, in *Systematic Theology: Roman Catholic Perspectives*, ed. F. Schüssler Fiorenza and J. P. Galvin (Minneapolis: Fortress Press, 1991), 1:3–87, pp. 55–61; D. Tracy, "The Uneasy Alliance Reconceived: Catholic Theological Method, Modernity, and Postmodernity," *Theological Studies* 50 (1989): 548–70, passim. In dialogue with Tillich, among others, Schillebeeckx was to argue that the notion "interrelation" provided a better indication of the way his late-modern theology functioned. Interrelation, in addition to experiences of harmony ("things fall into place"), would be better placed to conceptualize experiences of conflict ("things do not fall into place") in the interchange between tradition and context (see E. Schillebeeckx, *Theologisch geloofsverstaan anno 1983* [Baarn: Nelissen, 1983], pp. 9–10). Cf. below, chapter 4.

not be absent. Secular culture was no longer considered to be alienated from Christianity, rather it was the place in which God was actively present in the struggle for an authentic subjectivity and social justice. Modern theologies thus presumed the principle that there is continuity between modernity — with its focus on rationality and emancipation — and Christian faith as their point of departure. What was at stake, therefore, was the correlation of the salvific message of Christian faith with the modern context: "faith and (modern) living were in line with each other." Correlation theologies thus endeavored to establish consensus between culture and faith: Christians were at least as modern as the average modern human being. The modern project was an endeavor in which Christians could participate, together with all other "people of good will" — and they could do so on theological grounds.

The following elements are important for the continuation of our diagnosis:

1. The presuppositions behind modern correlation theologies concern the premise that theology is concerned with a dialogue between two partners: Christian tradition and the modern secular context. The concept of "co-relation" testifies to this and most of the discussions regarding this term concern the nature of the two partners and of the relationship or hermeneutics in which they are involved.

2. On the basis of this dialogue, the theologies in question often engage in a criticism and reconstruction of Christian tradition for which the epistemological standards of the context are regulative (although in most cases, these standards are criticized where they become exclusive of religion altogether — in the terms used at the time, secularist instead of secular). The definition of rationality, including its claims to universality, transparency, and communicability, remains profoundly modern. In as far as secular reason reaches truth, Christian faith cannot but comply with it. Faith thus adds to, or qualifies, what human beings know by secular reason alone. Furthermore, in the act of faith, the will supplements reason. Given these standards of rationality, in addition to various attempts at demythologization, the discourse of ethics has often been conceived as the primary bridge between the modern context and Christian faith, testifying to the latter's lasting validity, plausibility, and rationality. Explained from the perspective of theological methodology, Christian particularity (expressed in narratives and doctrines, rituals, and practices) is not an obstacle to universal truth; rather it is within this very particularity that universal truth is communicated and revealed in its fullest realization.

3. Immediately resulting from our second point, this claim to universality reveals the presupposition of a fundamental continuity, a potential consensus between modern culture and Christianity when related to each other in a mutually critical manner — i.e., there should be no discrepancy between being a sincere modern human being and being an authentic Christian.

It is very important to note, however, that this theoretical presupposition was accompanied by an existing factual overlap between context and Christian faith. There remained a common cultural horizon, very much influenced by Christian tradition. Up until the beginning of the 1980s, a significant proportion of the population of a large number of Western European countries continued to take their Christian identity for granted as something automatically given at birth.

The End of the Modern Correlation Theology Project

This form of theologizing no longer appears to function today. As a result of the processes of detraditionalization, correlation strategies and their implicit, modern presuppositions, tend to be the subject of serious question.

1. For theologians who analyze the contemporary situation in terms of plurality, there is no longer an easily identifiable secular culture to which Christian faith is related and in which Christians live their faith. Theology is no longer engaged in a dialogue between two partners but immersed in a dynamic, irreducible, and often conflicting plurality of religions, worldviews, and lifeviews. Many Christians today, especially in Western Europe, are becoming increasingly aware that the Christian faith (with its own plurality) is only one position among others on the field of religions and convictions.

2. At the same time, modern epistemological standards (universality, transparency, and communicability) have been criticized by many postmodern authors. Since the 1980s, postmodern sensibilities have questioned some basic presuppositions of modern secular culture, drawing more attention to heterogeneity, difference, and radical historicity. Inspired by the lessons of twentieth-century history, such authors have become suspicious of totalizing "grand narratives" and have drawn attention to the limits, contextuality, particularity, and contingency of any construction of meaning. They have developed conceptual patterns that have their roots in a sensibility toward radical plurality, otherness, and difference, and that foster the awareness of the ever-persisting

danger of misunderstanding plurality and difference in a totalizing or functionalizing manner.[7]

3. It is from such a perspective that contemporary philosophy and the human sciences tend to criticize any facile presupposition of consensus, continuity, and harmony. Indeed, such conceptual frameworks often imply mechanisms of inclusion or exclusion.

4. Moreover, the factual overlap between Christianity and culture has progressively disappeared. It was already apparent from the succession of results emerging from the European Values Study that the process of detraditionalization has reached its conclusion.[8]

At the level of systematic theology and in terms of pastoral effectiveness, the correlation method would appear to have become a counter-productive strategy. In concrete terms, its failure has given rise to a far-reaching dilution of the Christian tradition in an effort to reestablish continuity with the context by way of establishing consensus. More recently, for example, this has lead in several instances to the hasty theological recuperation of the contemporary search for spirituality and the renewed desire for religiosity (both of which are frequently post-Christian by nature). In so doing, one is tempted to forget the specificity of the Christian faith as it acquired shape in concrete narratives and communities. The apparent discontinuity between post-Christian religiosity and Christian faith is then painlessly erased.

2. From Continuity to Discontinuity?

When the modern partner in correlation theology is deconstructed, correlation theology is confronted with a problem. We already made reference above to the critique of anti-modern and postmodern theologies with respect to correlation theology. We also noted that thinking in terms of continuity is characteristic of a particular type of theologizing, one that has evolved from dialogue with modernity. The loss of plausibility

7. I treated this topic in my "Critical Consciousness in the Postmodern Condition: A New Opportunity for Theology?" *Philosophy and Theology* 10 (1997): 449–68, and in "When Secularization Turns into Detraditionalization and Pluralization: Faith in Search of Understanding" in *ET-Bulletin* 12 (2001): 258–70, as well as in "The Particularity of Religious Truth Claims: How to Deal with It in a So-called Postmodern Context," in *Truth: Interdisciplinary Dialogues for a Pluralist Age*, ed. K. De Troyer and C. Helmer, Studies in Philosophical Theology 22 (Leuven: Peeters Press, 2003), 181–95. A more detailed study is presently in the making with "Naming God in Open Narratives: Theology Challenged by Postmodern Thought" as its working title.

8. Cf. chapter 1.

encountered by modern presuppositions of rationality and emancipation — modernity's so-called master narratives — evidently has provided critics of this type of theologizing with new ammunition. It would indeed seem that anti-modern theologians have been proven right. The "absolutized autonomy" of subject and world turned out to be a fiction that led to the downfall of both. Theology ought, therefore, to take the discontinuity between Christian faith and the contemporary context as its point of departure. Some favor a genuine post-modern theology in the chronological sense of the term: a theology after modernity, a theology that leaves modernity behind, or at the very least its secular presuppositions. Such theologians read the postmodern crisis of modernity as the destruction of modernity, and thus reject modern secular thinking and its ensuing postmodern nihilism as without a future. By way of remedy, they present conceptual schemes that claim a more original relationship with God as the point of departure for all reflection on humanity and the world.

As we noted above, the "Radical Orthodoxy" movement, which has taken the Anglo-Saxon world by storm and acquired a place of importance therein, represents a persuasive illustration of such a manner of thinking. This movement welcomes the postmodern criticism of modernity only insofar as it enables it "to reclaim the world within a theological framework."[9] For such thinkers, the criticism in question is only valuable in as much as it makes apparent the devastation caused by secular modernity, with its resultant anxiety brought on by a lack of values and meaning. Yet the "self-conscious superficiality of today's secularism" offers the opportunity to establish a new, postmodern theological project. This group clearly no longer trusts the project of modern correlation theologies, which endeavor to establish an internal link with "universal accounts of immanent value." "Instead, in the face of the secular demise of truth, [this postmodern theology] seeks to reconfigure theological truth."[10] Hereto it proposes a return to a neo-Augustinian conceptual framework, in which the modern perplexing difficulties brought to the fore by postmodern nihilism are resolved. The central key in this regard is the Augustinian/Platonic category of "participation." The finite only

---

9. For an outline of the principles of the Radical Orthodoxy movement see the introduction ("Suspending the Material: The Turn of Radical Orthodoxy") of Milbank, Pickstock, and Ward, eds., *Radical Orthodoxy,* 1–20; see also J. Milbank, "The Program of Radical Orthodoxy," in *Radical Orthodoxy? — A Catholic Enquiry*, ed. L. P. Hemming (Aldershot: Ashgate, 2000), 33–45. See also "Christian Experience of God: Rupture with the Context?" on page 75 in chapter 4 of the present volume.

10. Milbank, Pickstock, and Ward, eds., *Radical Orthodoxy,* p. 15.

preserves its own integrity — in fact, even its worldliness — when it participates in its infinite eternal source, whereas in modern epistemology and postmodern nihilism the integrity of the finite ultimately dissolves.

The point of departure of such anti-modern and self-declared postmodern theologies, therefore, is the deconstruction of the (post-)secular partner of modern correlation theology and thereby the bankruptcy of the latter's theological project. The contemporary context is interpreted in terms of nihilism and the disintegration of meaning, and can only be saved by opening it up to a more original dependence on God. Correlation theology's principle of continuity between context and tradition is thus replaced by a principle of rigid discontinuity. Theological discourse is at odds with modern human discourse.

3. Consequences for Theological Method: From Correlation to Recontextualization

The anti-modern diagnosis accuses modern correlation theology of being too contextual. The modern context is said to have infected the Christian faith and thereby disempowered it. The remedy is to affirm a theological discourse that breaks with the dynamics of the modern and postmodern context and offers a radical counter narrative. From this point onwards, theology must account for discontinuity with the context. Far reaching recontextualization would thus also appear to be out of the question. In spite of the fact that we share elements of the analysis that modern correlation theology has encountered difficulties in the postmodern context, we firmly reject the negative results of the said analysis and the proposed remedy at the same time. As is the case with modern correlation theology, such forms of theologizing tend to analyze the contemporary context from a perspective of secularization rather than in terms of plurality (unless immediately understood as relativism, chaos, and the absence of perspective). In line with the primary hypothesis upon which the present study is based, however, modern correlation theology is *not* suffering from *too much* recontextualization but rather *too little*. A consistent recontextualization of the correlation method leads to a more profound methodological reflection on "recontextualization" as a theological method for today.

What does this imply for theology today? First of all, dialogue with the context should not be suspended. Counter to theologies that take discontinuity between Christian faith and contemporary context as their point of departure, we claim that there is an intrinsic link between the two.[11] History and context make an essential contribution to the development of tradition and the way in which Christian faith is given shape in space and time. However, while there can be no presupposition of discontinuity, we question at the same time, in contrast to the modern correlation theologies, the presupposition of continuity. The way in which tradition and context are related to one another should serve as the subject of an adequate theological methodology. And precisely engaging in a dialogue with the current context offers an escape from this dilemma.

Plurality, Difference, and Particularity as Opposed to Consensus, Harmony, and Continuity

From both the descriptive and normative perspectives, the current context teaches theology to be aware of plurality, difference, and particularity, and warns against the facile appeal to consensus, harmony, and continuity. Theology must therefore dare to question the very habits it has made its own in dialogue with the modern context (and at the same time with modern philosophy, the humanities and sciences).

1. Taking a substantial continuity between the Christian faith and modern culture and society as one's point of departure is no longer plausible. Such continuity likewise no longer functions in the pastoral domain. It becomes particularly difficult to determine the particularity or specificity of the Christian faith if one bases oneself on wide-ranging, human conceptual patterns, such as the results of the social sciences or philosophy, unless one has already more or less identified the former with the latter. There is no automatic link between the generally human and Christian particularity. It is not because human persons can be defined as ritual beings that the Christian sacraments — which do indeed ritualize human existence — are legitimate, significant or, for that matter, even true.[12] It is not because humanity would appear to be incurably religious and the majority holds a belief in "something more" that human beings are open to the salvific message of the God of Jesus Christ proposed by the Christian tradition.[13] Christian particularity is not only an enlargement or substantiation of general religiosity, characterizing the human species and accessible to all.

---

11. This intrinsic link is elaborated in theological terms in chapter 8 via the category of incarnation.

12. Cf. chapter 5.

13. Cf. chapter 7.

2. In addition, there are questions as to the identification of such universal human structures. In both the (social) sciences and in philosophy, such a methodological plurality holds sway that the results thereof are not always complementary. In instances in which social scientists and philosophers claim to be normative, (hidden) presuppositions and (hidden) agendas often play an important role. Plurality comprises conflict, heterogeneity, and incommensurability. If one takes such plurality as one's point of departure, the possibility of sidetracking into one or other meta-discourse is immediately blocked. Such a meta-discourse also constitutes part of the said plurality, even if it pretends to be able to take stock of the latter from an observer's perspective.

3. If one analyzes the many ways of living, thinking, and acting, the many religions and fundamental life options, in terms of radical plurality, then, the first and irreducible level of our reflection is our particularity itself. The starting point is thus the specific narrativity of a fundamental life option whether religious or not, the level of the concrete particular narrative. Human beings do not live from reflexive structures, but from narratives. Thinking in terms of underlying universal structures is an *a posteriori* procedure, and should not be considered the *a priori* establishment of the required preconditions or general validity criteria governing every fundamental life option.

For precisely these three reasons, it is of vital importance for theology that it does not postpone the theological dimension of its reflection too long, in the hope that it might come to the surface almost automatically in and through dialogue with the context. The awareness of the specific particularity of the Christian faith option places precisely the specificity of this option in the foreground, namely, the confession that God became involved with human history in and through Jesus Christ. No one is denying, of course, that Christians are human beings like every other. Being Christian, however, is an irreducible qualification of such being human (analogous to the way in which other fundamental options qualify the "being" of other human beings). In short: it is not in the first instance as human beings that Christians are Christian, but it is as Christians that they are human, irreducibly determined by their particular Christian narrativity — just as others are also human in the first instance on the basis of their own irreducible particular identities. It is thus necessary to develop conceptual patterns that recognize and account for the irreducible significance of the particular. It is also at this juncture that dialogue with the contemporary context has the potential to be productive.

From Correlation to Recontextualization

As a descriptive and normative concept for conceiving of the development of tradition and theology, the goal of the "method of recontextualization" is to radicalize modern correlation theory by "recontextualizing" it.[14] In addition to the notion of continuity, we must also ascribe a place to particularity, contextuality, narrativity, historicity, contingency, and otherness. Indeed, the point of departure of such a renewed recontextualization is to be found in the determination to take the radical historicity and contextuality of the Christian faith and of theology seriously.

The theological method we propose here certainly *cannot* be described as *anti-correlative.* In principle, one might even be at liberty to speak of a "postmodern correlation," in order to specify continuity with the concern of modern theology to engage in a methodologically anchored dialogue with the context. Common sense suggests, however, that we avoid the (modern theological) term "correlation," since it still exudes a spirit of continuity and a longing for harmony and synthesis between tradition and context. Moreover, "correlation" inevitably refers to a significant relationship of two terms, even if one characterizes the said relationship as "critical correlation." In our postmodern context, however, the particularity of the Christian narrative, as far as it qualifies the life of Christians today, is always situated in a plurality of narratives. This plurality represents the irreducible point of departure to conceive of the relationship of Christian faith with the context (*ad extra*). Simultaneously, it is the same confrontation with plurality that keeps the internal process of recontextualization in operation (*ad intra*).[15] It is for this reason that we opt for the term "recontextualization"—which can be understood as "post-correlative" in relation to modern correlation theology, precisely because of the need for recontextualization on the basis of an evolved context. What is at stake here should become more evident in the following chapters.

---

14. This has been further developed in two articles that represent a re-reading of the correlation methods of Hans Küng and Edward Schillebeeckx: "Kan traditie veranderen? Theologie in het postmoderne tijdsgewricht," in *Collationes* 26 (1996): 365–85, with reference to H. Küng, *Theologie im Aufbruch: Eine ökumenische Grundlegung* (Munich: Piper, 1987), building on H. Küng and D. Tracy, eds., *Paradigm Change in Theology: A Symposium for the Future* (Edinburgh: T&T Clark, 1989); and "Erfgenaam en erflater: Kerkelijke tradities binnen de Traditie," in *Traditie en initiatie: Perspectieven voor de toekomst*, ed. H. Lombaerts and L. Boeve, Nikèreeks 36 (Leuven: Acco 1996), 43–77, with reference to E. Schillebeeckx, *Mensen als verhaal van God* (Baarn: Nelissen), 1989.

15. We will explore this point further in chapter 3.

From a Secularization Paradigm to a Detraditionalization and Pluralization Paradigm

In line with the analysis undertaken in the first chapter, this shift can be described as a transition in terms of theological method from a paradigm of secularization to a paradigm of detraditionalization and pluralization. Indeed, today's culture can no longer be adequately identified with secularity, with which Christian faith is obliged to relate; correlation theologians then emphasize continuity between faith and world while anti-modern theologians emphasize the rupture between them. For those who analyze the present situation in terms of plurality, however, the determinative experience of Christians today tends increasingly to be that the Christian faith is one among the many positions in the arena of fundamental life options. Confrontation with other positions (Buddhist, Muslim, or atheist, for example) does not only challenge Christianity to engage in inquiry and dialogue, it simultaneously and immediately invites Christianity to (re)discover its own position and (re)emphasize its own distinctive features. This does not imply that the tradition as a whole and unrevised should be set in contrast to other positions. What it does imply is that the process of recontextualization begins in the very confrontation with plurality and otherness. Christian faith should not be understood as a "counter culture," but it can likewise no longer be described as a partner of an essentially secular culture. On the contrary, it is located in the midst of an internally pluralized arena in which it is obliged to determine its own position in relation to the other fundamental life options surrounding it. While this is surely a social and cultural task, it is also a (inter)subjective task, and to the extent that our own identities have become pluralized even an intra-subjective one.

4. Method between Continuity and Discontinuity: Interruption

Neither the presupposition of continuity nor that of discontinuity is appropriate for the construction of a methodological theological reflection on the relationship between theology (or tradition, or faith) and the context. It is for this reason that we must search for a fitting theological category that can support the methodological recontextualization in which we are engaged as regards the precise relationship between Christian faith and present-day culture. By way of response we propose the notion of "interruption." In what follows, we will not only endeavor to demonstrate that the category of interruption is capable of structuring the mediation between tradition and context in a *contextually* adequate manner, but we will also demonstrate that it is *theologically* legitimate. In other words, from the perspective of recontextualization, the contextual interruption of modern theology leads to a postmodern theology of interruption.

Interruption: Between Bridge and Rupture

Where anti-correlationist (anti-modern) theologies strongly relativize or deny the intrinsic involvement of Christian faith and theology with the context and thus stress the discontinuity between both, the category of interruption holds continuity and discontinuity together in an albeit tense relationship. Interruption is after all not to be identified with rupture, because what is interrupted does not cease to exist. On the other hand, it also implies that what is interrupted does not simply continue as though nothing had happened. Interruption signifies an intrusion that does not destroy the narrative but problematizes the advance thereof. It disturbs the anticipated sequence of sentences following one after the other, and disarms the security devices that protect against disruption. Interruption refers to that "moment," that "instance," which cannot occur without the narrative, and yet cannot be captured by the narrative. It involves the intrusion of an otherness that only momentarily but nonetheless intensely halts the narrative sequence. Interruptions cause the narrative to collide with its own borders. They do not annihilate the narrative; rather they draw attention to its narrative character and force an opening toward the other within the narrative.

Modern correlation methods work from an essential or factual continuity between Christian faith and the secular context. Secular critical positions with respect to this context almost never call the modern views on rationality and humanity into question, but rather only deal with problematic evolutions *within* the secular context, for example, evolutions that do not serve humanity. Theological positions in dialogue with such context frequently justify their critique of church and tradition by appealing to the aforementioned continuity: from the perspective of a modern theology of creation, theology and the church cannot ignore whatever is found to be genuinely rational and human in the surrounding culture and society. Modern "mutually critical correlation" does indeed presuppose that the search for and the realization of rationality, humanity, truth, and justice provides a bridge between the Christian faith and the secular context. Correctly understood, Christian faith and modernity are partners on the journey toward a more rational, more human world. Seen as such, the mutually critical correlation functions both as a driving force and a critical instance of a modern Christian faith. The postmodern critique of modernity's rationality and emancipatory ideologies on the one hand, and the related discovery of plurality and difference on the other, however, have thrown the presuppositions of this modern Christian project into disarray. In the terminology of "interruption," the theological project of modern correlation theology has been interrupted *from within the context* itself. Rationality and humanity, truth and justice, are no longer univocal terms. In every instance, rather, they are signified from within a particular narrative that qualifies their content from the outset. Although these concepts seem to connect several particular positions when understood in abstract terms, in practice they appear to be the points that differentiate these positions the most. Where secular rationality (also with respect to humanity and emancipation) appeared in the past to be able to engage in a meta-discourse in which truth claims could be regulated legitimately and without loss, the concrete context in which the Christian narrative now finds itself, offers, by contrast, a plurality of narratives, all of which are characterized by specific truth claims about rationality, humanity, and justice, without a universally shared set of rules.

Interruption as the Exponent of Contextual Critical Consciousness

It is on this point that the category of interruption can demonstrate its primary use as the exponent of what can be termed our contemporary *contextual* critical consciousness.

1. The confrontation with religious otherness alerts the Christian narrative specifically to the very particularity of its own truth claim and interrupts any pretence toward absoluteness. The postmodern contextual critical consciousness, gained from the confrontation with plurality and difference, informs the Christian narrative of its borders at this juncture and criticizes the tendency, inherent in every narrative (thus also in the Christian narrative), to withdraw into its own self-secured identity. The modern maneuver to link the Christian narrative, and thus its truth claim, in a qualified manner with a secular meta-discourse, has not only become unreliable but has also proved counter-productive. At the same time, post-secular forms of Christian neo-traditionalism and fundamentalism do not take into account the interruption of otherness caused by the confrontation with irreducible religious plurality. Due to the latter,

however, the Christian narrative is thrown back upon its own narrativity and particularity. It is critically challenged to formulate its truth claims on two fronts: first, with respect to this irreducible narrativity and particularity, and second, as regards the truth claims of others. This is obviously what is at stake in the case of inter-religious communication. Any attempt to denote religious plurality by way of a meta-discourse and to transcend the conflict of truth claims by way of a universal epistemological framework does not take the radicality of these truth claims seriously. Such an epistemological observer's position is and remains totalizing; the confrontation with the other, with difference, is ultimately done away with.[16] In concrete terms, this means that, apart from modern approaches, fundamentalist or traditionalist tendencies, both in the Christian narrative and outside it, are also exposed to criticism.

2. On the other hand, the rediscovery of its own particularity is also the manner in which the Christian narrative can be interruptive in the current context. Such interruption not only critically engages with other narratives that have closed themselves off or harden themselves in a fundamentalist way, it also warns us of the erosion of the particularity and alterity in many current discourses that seemingly take a sympathetic view toward religion and other fundamental life options but often imply a post-Christian functionalization of religiosity, and relativization of its particularity. Being Christian or participating in Christian practices and narratives in such an instance is conceived of as little more than a filling in of the necessary religious dimension of being human, of the *homo religiosus*. Belief then is often appreciated as a most effective therapy against loss of meaning and depression, the driving force behind social integration and solidarity. Christian rituals and celebrations are considered useful because they fulfil the human need for ritualization. Christian values can be productive in raising and educating children and young people because they offer the latter a general framework in which they can orient

16. This is why, from a structural point of view, classical inclusivist and pluralist solutions in fact run parallel to each other. They both demarcate a single framework — which is also, in principle, no less particular than any other — as a meta-discourse on the basis of which all other narratives are perceived; for inclusivism the framework is Christianity, for pluralism a more original religious structure to which particular religions relate. In spite of this criticism, it will become evident from our observations in chapter 8 that an important aspect of inclusivism is nevertheless worth preserving. Only as a participant in one's own Christian narrative, inclusive of its own truth claims, can one approach the particular truth claim of the other. At the same time, one should not do away with an intuition of pluralism, namely, that the multiplicity of religious truth claims puts the Christian truth claim under serious pressure and urges a theological reflection. However, it is the nature of the solution — the search for *one* meta-discourse into which differences are then subsumed — that is sharply criticized here.

themselves. The notion "God" is understood as a so-called "transcendental signifier," allowing us to refer to that which cannot be defined and always, in principle, escapes our language, while simultaneously making our language possible. A renewed appreciation of the specificity of one's own particularity, however, invites one to protest against such functionalizing reductions. Christian rituals, narratives, concepts, and communities can and indeed often do fulfil these functions. They should, however, not be reduced to such functions. Moreover, when religion is only sought for in order to realize these functions, it often stops generating the aforesaid positively perceived effects. The latter seem to be side-products which cannot be strived for independently. The same also applies *mutatis mutandis* to other religions and fundamental life options. When taking their own particularity seriously, they too cannot accept that they are not acknowledged and respected for their distinctive identity. In this regard, and rooted in the awareness of their own particularity, fundamental life options can criticize and counter (i.e., interrupt) the creeping inclination to uniformity that is progressively mastering our society. Through the processes of economic globalization,[17] plurality and otherness are recuperated in terms of market perspectives. The market renders diversity marketable, consumable, and exchangeable. As was the case with modernity's master narratives, this master narrative of postmodernity also produces its victims.

Toward a Theology of Interruption

In line with the contextual critical consciousness, the confrontation with the other interrupts the Christian narrative at the point at which it tends to close itself off. When it does so, however, there are always victims. Engaged in ongoing processes of recontextualization, today's theologies cannot avoid dealing with this interruption. Recontextualization, however, can never be legitimate on merely contextual grounds; at the same time it also requires a *theological* legitimization.

1. Only when interruption is also a theological category can the Christian narrative allow itself to be interrupted and become a narrative of interruption. As a theological category, interruption structures the way in which we reflect upon the relationship in which God is engaged with God's creation. Moreover, there are good grounds for developing

17. See the subsection " 'Secularization' to 'Detraditionalization' and 'Individualization' " on page 21 of the present volume.

such theological thinking patterns. After all, in the concreteness of particular histories, the God professed by Christians repeatedly breaks open the narratives of human beings and communities, including narratives about Godself. This serves in the first instance as a key that allows us to read and understand the God we encounter in the Old Testament. When Israel is kept enslaved in Egypt, God sends Moses to lead them away from their confinement in slavery and misery. When the Jewish people closes itself off from God, serves other gods, disrespects the poor and the strangers, and their kings become corrupt, then prophets in the name of God denounce such self-enclosement and call for reform. Each time, narratives are broken open by God or on behalf of God. The New Testament is likewise an account of the continuing interruption of closed narratives. Jesus forgives sins and heals the sick on behalf of God, opening new opportunities for those who were outcasts in the eyes of the religious and social authorities. On behalf of the same God, Jesus criticizes those who reduce religion to the mere observance of the Law, or to a scrupulous offering of the required sacrifices, or to political activism, etc. Jesus asks us to become like the children, like the poor, the outcast, and the persecuted (because they are blessed), like the widow who only has a single penny to sacrifice. He invites us to follow in the footsteps of the father embracing his younger, prodigal son (and not to partake in the incomprehension of the older son). He teaches us to recognize him in the poor, the sick, the hungry, the thirsty, the prisoner, the naked, in short in the vulnerable and wounded other: " 'Lord, when was it that we saw you hungry and gave you food, or thirsty and gave you something to drink?' [. . .] 'Truly I tell you, just as you did it to one of the least of these who are members of my family, you did it to me' " (Matt. 25:37b–40b).

On closer inspection, the entire metaphorical constitution of the Christian narrative appears to be permeated by the interruption, on God's behalf, of narratives, including one's own narrative, through confrontation with otherness.[18] This is also illustrated by important motifs such as vocation, exodus, desert, mountain, cross, resurrection, conversion, pilgrim, etc. The Christian narrative is never allowed to close itself. When it does, then the God of love breaks the narrative open. Interruption functions here as a *theological* category. Ultimately, the resurrection of the Jesus who died on the cross is the paradigm of interruption. God interrupts the closing of Jesus' narrative by the religious and political

18. See further chapter 7 of *Interrupting Tradition.*

authorities and radically opens it. It is precisely here that God makes clear that the narrative of the one who lives like Jesus, professed by his disciples as the Christ, cannot be closed in death, but that such a narrative has a future beyond death. Following Jesus means engaging the challenge of the other who interrupts our narratives.

In the New Testament the perspective on God as "interrupter" is thus radicalized. By professing Jesus of Nazareth as the Christ, Christians hold that God becomes manifest precisely in the all-too-human. They further profess that radical transcendence implies an unabridged radical immanence, that the One who surmounts history absolutely is nonetheless only encountered in the concrete contingent particularity of history. For Christians, professing Christ is then also the interruption *par excellence* of history. It is this God and this interruption to which the Christian narrative bears witness, a witness that never attempts to completely grasp or contain this God or this interruption. Moreover, whenever this narrative tends to close itself, it is itself interrupted — broken open — precisely by the same God who prevents the Christian narrative from closing itself and who, when this nonetheless occurs, becomes its first victim. Even when God is eliminated, however, interruption still occurs. Belief in the Resurrection is the sharpest expression of this. When narratives are forced shut, even unto death, God nevertheless still breaks them open.

2. It thus follows that a fully accepted particularity of the Christian discourse is not a refutation of its truth, but rather the very precondition thereof. It is only through the incarnation that God becomes fully revealed. This implies at the same time that each Christian narrative stands under God's judgement and can only bear witness to God in a *radical-hermeneutical* manner. The Christian truth claim is held precisely within this tension (which is actually the same tension present in the prohibition of idolatry and in the Chalcedonian dogma of the incarnation). For this reason, a Christian narrative may not close itself on theological grounds. From a theological-epistemological point of view, the encounter with the other is in fact the place in which God's interruption can be revealed and where the borders of one's own Christian narrative in naming this God can become visible. That is why present-day interreligious communication, for instance, is not only a contextual necessity but also a theological one. As a participant in interreligious dialogue, the Christian may learn both to take her or his own particular Christian narrative very seriously as the way toward God, and at the same time to qualify this narrative nonetheless in a radical-hermeneutical way because of this relationship

with the same God. The "peculiarity" of the Christian truth claim, therefore, is that Christians cannot claim the truth, and yet they are always already living in relation to it, in respect for the radical-hermeneutical tension of a narrative that both concerns God and is interrupted by God.

3. It is through the encounter with concrete others and otherness that the Christian narrative is challenged and interrupted. It is such interruption that has the potential to become the locus in which God is revealed to Christians today. Theologically speaking, interruption is *not a formal, empty category;* it is charged rather with the narrative tradition of the God of love revealed in concrete history, of the God who became human among humans. *Imitatio Christi* then summons Christians to a praxis of being both interrupted and interrupting — respecting the very otherness of the other while at the same time also becoming the other of the other, questioning, challenging the other, criticizing him or her where he or she tends to become hegemonic. The category of interruption thus appears to be an adequate means to conceive of God's salvific engagement with history. For Christians, the challenge introduced by otherness then becomes a *locus theologicus.* As a particular narrative, the Christian narrative is interrupted by the God it testifies to as the One who interrupts closed narratives, and by whom it is challenged to become itself interrupter of closed narratives. In and through this double praxis of interruption, the Christian community lives its Christian identity and contributes to the recontextualization of a narrative tradition, both retrieving and renewing it, for the sake of its contemporaries and future generations.

4. In addition to the epistemological-theological considerations outlined above, there are also *political-theological* considerations to be borne in mind. Wherever closed narratives are operative, one encounters the victims thereof. Whenever a narrative profiles itself as a meta-discourse, other narratives are either suppressed or excluded, invalidated or silenced. The God of the interrupted Christian narrative therefore requires us to place such a meta-discourse under critique and to break open the narrative(s) of those it has pushed aside. A radical theological hermeneutic of contingency thus implies an equally radical theological hermeneutic of suspicion. Where diversity and otherness are being stealthily reduced to the multiplicity of market goods or eradicated in the name of an inviolable hegemonic truth claim, Christians are obliged to interrupt on behalf of God the "Interrupter."[19]

---

19. See chapter 9 and the general conclusion.

5. Conclusion

It will have become clear by now that a postmodern recontextualization should not be understood as an anti-correlationist maneuver. The intrinsic involvement with context of all theology is, after all, the point of departure for the concept "recontextualization." What can (and should) be discussed, however, is the nature of this involvement and the way in which it influences contemporary theologizing. In the *ad extra* legitimization of the Christian narrative, a theology of interruption will therefore draw less attention to similarities and points of overlap between the Christian narrative and other narratives. Indeed, the greatest differences often reside in what we perceive to be common, precisely because of the irreducible particularity of the narrative within which one is living. The other is not in the first instance an ally or familiar partner, but rather one who challenges our narratives in his or her irreducible otherness. It is precisely the encounter or confrontation with the other as other that compels the Christian narrative — *ad intra* — toward self- and world-critique, toward recontextualization, at both the theological-epistemological and the political-theological levels.

Chapter Three

An Adjusted Dialogue with the Context

Distinguishing between an Inner and an Outer Perspective

The altered situation in which Christians find themselves today places their identity under question and influences the way in which they enter into dialogue with present-day culture and society while simultaneously constituting a part thereof. Such a tensive relationship between Christian faith and its surrounding culture, however, need not be a source of insurmountable problems. A contemporary recontextualization, making use of the contextual-theological category of interruption, has the potential to succeed in locating this tension in its correct perspective and to make it theologically productive. In line with the first two chapters, this new situation calls for appropriate and strategic analysis and reflection, both from a systematic- and a pastoral-theological perspective. Before we proceed to elaborate this procedure in the following chapters, therefore, it seems opportune at this juncture to make a methodological distinction between an external and an internal perspective with regard to the theologian's engagement, dialogue, or communication with the current context. On the one hand, *ad extra,* the growing awareness of plurality and otherness realizes the discovery of one's own Christian narrative particularity. On the other hand, the challenge of the new plural context and the confrontation with other particularities instigate an *ad intra* examination of the consequences thereof for the further development of this particular narrativity.[1] It is necessary to account for this methodological consideration, since theologians are already involved in

1. In modern theology, both dimensions were either undifferentiated or not considered essential. The *ad intra* dimension was ultimately the same as the *ad extra* dimension: Christianity allowed itself to be criticized and enriched by secular culture, and thus endeavored to gain (or maintain) acceptability and relevance within this secular culture. Expressed in modern categories, the particularity of Christianity was formulated in such a way that it was perfectly

every instance with the culture in which they live, and as such they also share in its constitution. It is also important to note here that the distinction we are making is not an absolute one; in practice, both dimensions continually intersect.

1. The Outer Perspective: The *Ad Extra* Dimension of the Communication between Christian Faith and the Context

In the first instance, we must account for Christianity's relationship with detraditionalized and pluralized culture and society in which it finds itself, both at the interpersonal level — with non-Christian or no longer Christian groups — and at the intra-personal level, insofar as our "fragmented selves" also consist of a variety of different worlds. We can term this the *ad extra* dimension. The problem here is that Christians today find communicating what they stand for more difficult in the public forum because the common presuppositions and language they once employed to this end are increasingly diminishing. From a more technical perspective, the question posed here is that of the *communicability* of the particularity of the Christian narrative. The Christian experience of reality can only be adequately communicated to those who have a minimal familiarity with the Christian narrative or are at least prepared to become acquainted with it. The problem here, therefore, is one of language.

Some examples might serve to illustrate this point. Without any concept or narrative concerning God, one can have no experience of God — and will have absolutely no idea what an experience of God might mean. Religious experience, therefore, cannot simply be identified with the experience of God, nor is such identification necessary for it to be termed religious experience as such (certainly if "religious" is understood etymologically, i.e., as deriving from *religare*).[2] Furthermore, the very elements that bind the three so-called prophetic religions — also referred to as "religions of the book" or "religions of revelation" — serve at the same time to distinguish them from one another. Islam, Christianity, and Judaism

---

plausible, and could even be considered a pre-eminent expression of the modern person, culture, and society.

2. This is precisely the reason why the pluralistic theologian John Hick no longer speaks of God when he names the transcendent referent of the religions but uses "the Real." For more background information and comments, see T. Merrigan, "Religious Knowledge in the Pluralist Theology of Religions," *Theological Studies* 58 (1997): 686–707, pp. 695–96.

differ considerably in their perception of the "prophet," Mohammed, Jesus, or Moses respectively; in the role their sacred scriptures (Qur'an, Bible, and Torah) play within the respective religious tradition; and the way in which the revelation of God in history is understood. Christianity's particular experience of faith, in itself constituted by a complex variety of experiences, locates contemporary Christians in the midst of a plurality of religious and other fundamental life discourses.

Paying greater attention to the irreducible particularity of the Christian narrative is one of the lessons learned from the encounter with the plurality of religions and fundamental life options. The Christian narrative forms its own (albeit dynamic[3]) symbolic space, its own hermeneutical horizon, i.e., its own hermeneutical circle. Becoming acquainted with Christianity is thus something like learning a language, a complex event that presupposes grammar, vocabulary, competence, and familiarity, as much as it does empathy.

Given the difficulties experienced, however, some might wonder whether communication about Christian faith can be structured (or even taken over) by referring to the structural analogies, and sometimes even family relationships, between the Christian faith and other religions and fundamental life options. After all, each supports some kind of spirituality (which often includes an experience of and relationship with something transcendent), each advocates an ethics, holds ideas on the meaning of personal and social life, expresses its convictions in narratives and rituals, etc. Indeed, some might be inclined to call this a general or universal human substratum upon which the various religions then build, furnishing this anthropological basis with their own respective cultural-religious interpretations.

While it is no doubt the case that evidence of parallel structures can contribute to our understanding of one or other specific religion and its particular raison d'être, it can never replace its narrative "thickness." At the structural level we are dealing with reflexive speech, a way of thinking that recognizes the *a posteriori* structures in our narratives. Human beings, however, do not live from reflexive structures but from the narratives themselves. Moreover, theories that set out to determine what is universally human are often just as contextual and particular as the object of their investigation. They are far more exponents of the surrounding culture than occupying an "objective" observer's position, having transcended the very culture and society in which they live. While

3. In this regard, see our reflections on the inner perspective.

every form of theoretical reflection entails distantiation, it also — and simultaneously — presupposes internal involvement.

2. The Inner Perspective: The *Ad Intra* Dimension of Our Communication with Culture and Society

In contradistinction to the *ad extra* dimension, we can also consider Christianity's relationship with the context from an internal perspective. As we already mentioned above, the Christian narrative tradition is thoroughly contextual and it recontextualizes itself from its involvement in contemporary life and current contextual experience. History is replete with shifts in culture and society that have driven the Christian tradition toward recontextualization. Time and again, this tradition was placed under such intense pressure that it ultimately led to a critically creative elaboration of the newness in the context, in some instances even while going through a thorough transformation. It is on this level that renewal of tradition takes place and is given form.

A recent example of this process can be observed in the renewal of the language of faith in which the relationship with God is no longer interpreted and conceptualized in exclusively patriarchal terms, in so doing giving expression to the contemporary Christian experience of God in Christian narrative communities.

And as was the case with the outer perspective, also for the inner perspective the confrontation with contextual newness can be considered a *language problem:* the old language is no longer able to evoke adequately the new experience of faith. Because of this, Christianity's own discourse (or, as stated above, its own symbolic space, hermeneutical horizon or circle) begins to shift in the process of recontextualization.

3. Problems with This Methodological Distinction

One of the problems associated with many current pastoral and theological analyses and strategies is that both methodologically distinct dimensions are conflated. In the first instance, this misunderstanding arises from the fact that the methodological distinction between inner and outer cannot always be made with equal clarity in practice. An encounter with someone of another religion or fundamental life option can result simultaneously in a heightened awareness of the limits of communicability *ad extra* (because of one's own narrative particularity), and instigate an *ad intra* recontextualization of the particular narrativity (which in its turn becomes the basis for communication *ad extra*). In the second instance, both cases are related, as we have stated, to a problem of language. We shortly elaborate on the confusion this often seems to generate.

1. Searching for a new language *ad intra* as a result of the altered experience of faith is often wrongly seen as the solution for problems on the *ad extra* level. The fact that the Christian faith can no longer make itself understood in the public forum is then attributed in the first instance to a deficiency of contemporary, contextually rooted faith language. It is through a new and contextually adapted language of faith that the current communication problem should be solved. This problem is especially felt today, for example, when it comes to communicating the unique place of Jesus Christ for the interpretation of the Christian relationship with God. The same difficulty occurs when attempting to clarify what "hope" means for Christians, or endeavoring to explain the credibility and relevance of Christian sacramental praxis.

The presupposition behind this position is that the Christian faith has alienated itself from culture — frequently on account of its traditionalistic and institutional rigidity — and must (and thus also can) make a return move back to culture. Underlying this, moreover, is the idea that this alienation is also the apparent reason for the massive exodus from the church in recent decades. A further presupposition is the idea that each person is at least open toward a Christian interpretation of life and society, if only this were to be presented well enough — a sort of unproblematic inclusivism.

Surely, there can be little doubt that a tradition which refuses to recontextualize itself ultimately sets up fundamental obstacles to dialogue with culture and even jeopardizes such dialogue. It would be a misconception, however, to think that recontextualization is capable of solving the entire communication problem, let alone that it has the capacity to convince non-Christians, ex-Christians (or even potential Christians) once again of the validity of the Christian narrative. The *ad extra* problem is not in the first place a matter of the renewal of faith language, but of the familiarity with it (initiation).

2. The reverse situation of turning to the *ad extra* dimension when faced with *ad intra* problems is also not uncommon. Issues that demand recontextualization, such as access to the priesthood, or family ethics (but also with respect to the examples given earlier: the uniqueness of

Christ, Christian hope, sacramental praxis) are not infrequently countered with references to the irreducible specificity of the language of the tradition. It is argued that only those who have truly mastered this language can really comprehend and accept that matters are as they are and thus not open to change. The necessary but often difficult recontextualization process is thereby prematurely short-circuited. Particularity is absolutized and played off against contextuality, more specifically against contextually new experiences of being Christian.

An additional example of employing an *ad extra* solution for an *ad intra* problem can be found in the reduction of Christianity's essence to the structurally and universally human (which we discussed above), which then functions as a kind of meta-discourse behind/beneath/above Christian narrativity. The Christian sacraments, for example, then draw their meaningfulness (and legitimation) exclusively from the fact that rituals and ritualization are a human necessity. Such a strategy is employed in equal measure by those who support the status quo and by those who desire change in relation to *ad intra* problems and issues.[4]

4. Where Is the Boundary between the Inner and the Outer Perspective?

Although the boundary between the *ad intra* perspective and the *ad extra* perspective was dissolved on two occasions in the preceding paragraphs, the designation of this boundary continues to be an extremely difficult task. It is for this reason that those who draw a very wide and rather vague boundary, something not completely unusual in a time of accelerated detraditionalization, are *de facto* conflating *ad intra* and *ad extra* perspectives. The ambiguity of much post-Christian religiosity is disregarded when it is too quickly recuperated as a promising instance of recontextualization (*ad intra*). In so doing Christian faith is subjected to an overextended dynamic of accommodation and assimilation. It is striking that people who think of culture and society in terms of secularization rather than pluralization frequently fall into this trap. The experience of human wholeness then comes to form the primary point of contact for current theologizing. While I do not wish to minimize the

4. With respect to the problem of ordination, for example, those who support the status quo tend to employ anthropological arguments to support the immutability of rituals and traditions, including ordained ministry, while those who seek change claim that the equality of women in society implies that they should have as equal access to the ordained ministry (at least in principle) as their male counterparts.

importance of the experience of human wholeness for theology, it nevertheless appears under a different light when viewed from the perspective of pluralization and individualization. Christianity is not obliged to accommodate — or indeed recuperate — everything that is recognized to be fully human. In a perspective of plurality and difference, the necessary dialogue with such experiences acquires a different structure. It is no less true, however, that those who draw a narrower and more defined boundary in the process lose access to valuable new impulses for recontextualization.

Part II

BETWEEN BRIDGE AND RUPTURE

Religious Experience, Rituals, and the Dialogue with Science

In the second part of the present volume we will present a number of exercises in which the methodological shift described in part one is explained in greater detail. Interruption is thus employed as a conceptual category and hermeneutical key in the service of a critical-productive recontextualization of theology, allowing us to steer an appropriate middle course between strategies of continuity and discontinuity.

To this end, we plan to enter into a twofold dialogue with the (late-modern) theological project of Edward Schillebeeckx. In chapter 4, which deals with the place of religious experience in theological epistemology, we will take the discussion between Schillebeeckx and Antoon Vergote on the role of experience in the Christian faith as our point of departure. Chapter 5, entitled "The Sacramental Interruption of Rites of Passage," can be read as a critical-constructive commentary of the article in which Schillebeeckx made his new sacramentological project public. In this response it will be shown in practice that method indeed shifts according to the context. While no effort will be made to bring the extensive theological work of this major Flemish-Dutch theologian into discredit — it remains the commanding result of an intense dialogue between theology and modernity — it is nevertheless important to be aware that the context has changed and that the task of every new generation is to engage in what Metz called *Korrektivtheologie*.[1] We are convinced,

1. Cf. Introduction (section 2) on page 4 of the present volume.

furthermore, that those whose goal it is to continue Schillebeeckx's theological project today must ultimately radicalize his methodology in the way we suggest.[2]

Chapter 6 is devoted to the discussion between faith and science, a discussion that has surfaced with regularity since the dawn of modernity. Creationism and Intelligent Design, positivism and neo-Darwinism compel theology to adopt a position that is capable of avoiding the pitfalls of harmony and conflict models.

Religious experience, rituals, and the relationship between religion and science are frequently occurring themes in our contemporary culture. Drawn to this renewal of interest, the theology of interruption may discover that it has much to say about it from its own theological inspiration, not so much as a counter-cultural voice but rather as a voice in the midst of culture. The context thus appears to encourage theology to renew itself from within and to re-establish a contextually plausible and theologically legitimate place for itself in a culture within which it most assuredly has a role to play, albeit a different role when compared with the past.

2. See the conclusion to chapter 5.

Chapter Four

Theology and the Interruption of Experience

It would be inaccurate to describe a reflection on the status of experience in Christian faith and theology as an unengaged academic exercise. Those who embark on such a venture today find themselves in the midst of a debate that has already been going on for years and that certainly since modernity — with its turn to the subject — has been one of pressing concern. Since that time, philosophers and theologians have appealed to experience to both legitimate and delegitimate religious truth claims, adopting a variety of positions in the process. The continuous discussion on the place of spiritual or mystical experience in reflection on the relationship between different religions is just one example of this. A further example is the impassioned dispute (especially in the last decades of the previous century) between the so-called "Chicago" and "Yale" schools on the relationship between faith experience and the development of tradition and thus, by extension, the legitimacy of the correlation method in modern theology as a whole.

The category of experience also crops up in contemporary religious philosophical and theological discussions that examine the way in which Christian belief relates, or needs to relate, itself to the so-called postmodern context. It is into this debate that we tread in an effort to reconceptualize the concept of religious experience as an "experience of interruption." We do so in discussion with modern theologies in which experience, often in a tense relationship with tradition, is portrayed as the primary instrument Christians can use to bring their faith up to date. On the other hand, we also enter into debate with (literally) postmodern theologies that portray religious experience as a rupture with the present culture of nihilism and loss of meaning and which jettison every intrinsic relationship between context and Christian belief.

Before going further, however, we must first determine what we understand by the term "experience." Most thinkers who try to answer this question start from the supposition that experience is a paradoxical and complex fact with multiple dimensions.[1] Many make a distinction between three standard meanings for experience that are also found in everyday language (and which can be distinguished at least in German and Dutch): experiment, momentary sensation or "experienced occurrence" (Dutch *belevenis,* German *Erlebnis*), and "being experienced" (Dutch *ondervinding,* German *Erfahrung*). But in its broadest sense, almost all dimensions of human understanding can be linked to this concept: sensory (and non-sensory) stimulus, perception, observation, sensation, participation, interpretation, *savoir-faire, savoir-vivre,* practical knowledge, insight — even tradition as a collective term for a knowledge that has proven valuable in the past and which can serve as a guide for living, thinking, and acting today. Experience as *experiment,* "testing," has positive scientific connotations and is embedded in a logic of experimental verification. With *sensation* or "experienced occurrence" (Dutch *belevenis,* German *Erlebnis*), attention is focused especially on an intense subjective experience with at least a strong affective component. Experience as "*being experienced*" points rather to a *savoir-penser,* a *savoir-faire,* or a *savoir-vivre* acquired in and from the past. To a large extent, this *savoir-vivre* gives shape to the identity of an individual or group; it enables one to deal in a qualified way with what occurs in everyday situations, thus allowing one to experience the here and now "in perspective." In experience as "sensation," the intensity of the subjectively lived "here-and-now" dimension often comes into tension (and sometimes even rupture) with the prevailing interpretative frameworks that determine everyday life. Experience as "being experienced," "savoir-vivre," on the other hand, does not so much require to be interpreted but rather is interpretation. This is not to deny the "experiential dimension" of daily life, but it nevertheless implies that interpretation is already taking place and even constitutes the precondition for this dimension. Interpretation is not to be understood as a conscious act of a reflexive subject who wants to grasp an as yet uninterpreted fact or occurrence and therefore as secondary. On the contrary, interpretation is already provided in what makes experience experience. As we shall see

1. See, for example, D. Mieth, "Annäherung an Erfahrung — Modelle religiöser Erfahrung im Christentum," in *Religiöse Erfahrung: Historische Modelle in christlicher Tradition,* ed. W. Haug and D. Mieth (Munich: Fink, 1992), 1–16; D. Mieth, "What Is Experience?" *Concilium. International Journal for Theology* 14 (1978): 113, 40–53. Further, M. Dumas, "Introduction à l'expérience en théologie: Pluralité, ambiguïté et nécessité," in *Théologie et culture: Hommages à Jean Richard,* ed. M. Dumas, F. Nault, and L. Pelletier (Québec: Presses de l'Université Laval, 2004), 123–42.

below, however, this implies that we have already taken a position in the debate, certainly if we want to investigate religious experience and its function within Christian faith and theology.

1. Lessons from a Modern Debate: Experience in Modern Correlation Theologies

"Modern correlation theology" is — as already mentioned in chapter 2 — a collective expression used for a diversity of theological approaches that, despite internal differences, generally proceed from the notion that two poles, tradition and context, need to be brought into relationship with each other. This modern theological project strove to reflect on Christian faith on the basis of dialogue with a context of modernization and secularization. With such Catholic representatives as Hans Küng, Edward Schillebeeckx, and David Tracy, it cannot be denied that this method of theologizing has been of extreme importance to the renewal of theology in the second half of the twentieth century. From a theological epistemological point of view, the category of experience occupies a very important place in this theological method.

The modern theological emphasis on experience did not, however, occur in a vacuum. It reflects a change in the way modern men and women set about the acquisition of knowledge. While few would be likely to conceive of religious experience in a positive-scientific way (experience as verifying hypotheses), a similar logic is nevertheless evident to a certain degree. The truth and plausibility of faith needs to be experienced — i.e., only the actual living of Christian faith can substantiate its truth claims. The increasing role of experience in faith and theology thus fits in with the modern rejection of a knowledge that is simply handed down from the past without the possibility of testing it in the present. Truth is not so much something that approaches us from times gone by but rather something that needs to be confirmed in the here and now. Playing with the two already mentioned standard meanings of the word, one might affirm paradoxically that truth is not a matter of having experience (as a *savoir-faire* learnt from the past) but of having *an* experience (the subjectively experienced here-and-now). The truth of the faith does not reside in tradition or in doctrines, but rather in a faith experience that precedes tradition and doctrine (and on the basis of which this tradition and doctrine can either be upheld or placed under critique). Even though many modern theologians will admit that there is no experience without an already given interpretative framework — all experience is already interpreted experience — experience continues nonetheless to hold pride of place.

This manner of theologizing, however, has not only had its supporters, it has also had its critics. Reference can be made in this regard — without going into detail — to the post-conciliar discussions between theologians of the respective *Concilium* and *Communio* groups,[2] as well as to the heated debate in the US between the so-called Chicago and Yale schools.[3] The Low Countries likewise experienced a similar discussion in the 1980s with religious experience as the burning issue. It involved a dispute between two internationally renowned thinkers, Edward Schillebeeckx and Antoon Vergote. We will examine this discussion here as a means of establishing a basis for further development. At the same time, we will endeavor to learn some lessons from its content for the continuation of our reflection.

Edward Schillebeeckx: Experience as a Bridge between Christian Tradition and Modern Context

For Edward Schillebeeckx, Flemish Dominican and emeritus professor at the Radboud University of Nijmegen,[4] "experience" is not only a

2. In 1973, a number of theologians, among them W. Kasper, K. Lehman, J. Ratzinger, and H. U. von Balthasar, established the journal *Communio* as a more conservative counterpart to the journal *Concilium*, set up after the Second Vatican Council (by H. Küng, K. Rahner, J.-B. Metz, E. Schillebeeckx, and also Ratzinger, among others) with the "spirit of the Council" as its inspiration. See in this regard the comment made by Ratzinger, co-founder of *Communio*, on the occasion of its 20th anniversary in J. Ratzinger, "Communio — Ein Programm," *Internationale Katholische Zeitschrift Communio* 20 (1992): 454–63: "post-conciliar theologians have opted for the novel at the price of the true by presenting old liberal insights as new Catholic theology" (p. 455). And further: "the theology of *Communio* should let God's Word be the answer to people's questions and thus cannot remain in the domain of the experts, theologians, or church makers, who hurry from one meeting to another, and thereby reinforce their dispiritedness about the church in themselves and others" (p. 461, our translation).

3. With David Tracy and George Lindbeck as respective protagonists. For an overview of this debate, cf. J. C. K. Goh, *Christian Tradition Today: A Postliberal Vision of Church and World*, Louvain Theological and Pastoral Monographs 28 (Leuven: Peeters/Grand Rapids: Eerdmans, 1999). See also "Christian Experience of God: Rupture with the Context?" on page 75 of the present volume.

4. For a more detailed study, see my "Experience According to Edward Schillebeeckx: The Driving Force of Faith and Theology," in *Divinizing Experience: Essays in the History of Religious Experience from Origen to Ricoeur*, ed. L. Boeve and L. P. Hemming, Studies in Philosophical Theology 23 (Leuven: Peeters Press, 2004), 199–225. For the present study we rely on Schillebeeckx's earlier methodological works, including his *Tussentijds verhaal over twee Jezusboeken* (Baarn: Nelissen, 1978); English trans., *Interim Report on the Books Jesus and Christ* (London: SCM/New York: Crossroad, 1980). Schillebeeckx maintained similar positions thereafter in "Erfahrung und Glaube," in *Christlicher Glaube in moderner Gesellschaft*, vol. 25, ed. Böckle (Freiburg/Basel/Vienna: Herder, 1980), 73–116. He reformulated a number of these ideas in his farewell lecture — *Theologisch geloofsverstaan 1983* — when he retired

key term for our understanding of what inspired the first Christians when they bore witness to Jesus as the risen Christ, but also a means of grasping what revelation is and how it occurs, as well as what is at stake in Christianity's two-thousand-year-long tradition up to the present. Furthermore, the category of experience for Schillebeeckx is of crucial importance for analyzing the current situation. Finally, via the "correlation" of both experiences — that of the tradition and that of the current situation — Schillebeeckx proposes a way for Christians today to live their faith in a contextually plausible and relevant way in the said situation.

1. First of all, experience is essential for those who wish to understand what *Christian faith* is all about. Schillebeeckx's three "Jesus books" leave little doubt in this regard. In *Jesus: An Experiment in Christology,* he attempts to describe Jesus' specific experience of God as an "abba" experience, fitting in with and giving expression to the intimate relationship between Jesus and his Father.[5] Furthermore, it was the Easter experience of the first disciples after Jesus' crucifixion that brought them together again and thus constituted the beginning of the Christian community. Ultimately, as Schillebeeckx tells us in his second "Jesus book," *Christ: The Christian Experience in the Modern World,*[6] it is the experience of grace, the experience of having found salvation from God in Jesus Christ, which is given multiple expression in the New Testament. In the third book, *Church: The Human Story of God,* Schillebeeckx repeats that experience is the driving force behind the Christian tradition — which is in fact a tradition of Christian experience — up to the present day.

Indeed, there can be no revelation without experience: revelation can only be discerned "in and through human experiences." In addition to a subjective dimension in the experience of revelation, Schillebeeckx also distinguishes an objective aspect, a cognitive claim — sometimes also called the interpretative direction of the revelatory experience — that unfolds itself together with the experience. Within the experience itself

---

from his position at Nijmegen. Almost all of these revised ideas were later included in the first part of *Mensen als verhaal van God* (Baarn: Nelissen, 1989); English trans., *Church: The Human Story of God* (New York: Crossroad/London: SCM, 1990). In our text, however, we rely mainly on *Interim Report.*

5. Cf. E. Schillebeeckx, *Jezus het verhaal van een levende* (Bloemendaal: Nelissen, 1974); English trans., *Jesus: An Experiment in Christology* (New York: Seabury Press/London: Collins, 1979), pp. 210–21 — "abba" = Daddy, Father.

6. Cf. E. Schillebeeckx, *Gerechtigheid en liefde: Genade en bevrijding* (Baarn: Nelissen, 1977); English trans., *Christ: The Christian Experience in the Modern World* (London: SCM, 1980).

intrinsic interpretative elements are present, which constitute the objective kernel of experience (the *interpretandum*), to be distinguished (but not separated) from other interpretative elements (the interpretaments) that originate from the situation in which the experience takes place. Schillebeeckx takes love as his example at this juncture: in their experience of love, lovers obviously know that their experience is about love.[7] The experience of love thus speaks for itself; it has a certain transparency of its own. This does not mean that interpretative elements (interpretaments) coming from elsewhere — from literature, for instance, or popular culture — do not matter. Interpretation does not come in addition to the objective aspect of experience, but rather as its self-expression it is deeply interwoven in the actual experience itself.[8] Applied to the experience of the (first) Christians, such first-order expressions as "Jesus is the Christ" and "He lives" refer to the common fundamental basic experience of "having experienced salvation in and through Jesus." It is this basic experience that is expressed in the New Testament writings, in various interpretative ways, in relation to the Old Testament and the then-contemporary context. Although this fundamental basic experience does not exactly coincide with the New Testament interpretations, the former nevertheless is not disconnected from the latter. In fact, it is even impossible to disconnect the one from the other because such basic experience is already contained from the outset within pre-existing interpretative frameworks — frameworks that are also influenced by underlying theories and models. There is no such thing as "un-mediated experience."

Christian faith is essentially about this basic experience, certainly if we ask ourselves what Christian faith can still mean for us today, and this is Schillebeeckx's primary concern: a stubborn adherence to certain traditional interpretaments may result in restricting access to this basic experience (the *interpretandum*). Just as the New Testament bears witness to this basic experience in various ways depending on the situation, so too does the "living tradition," which is the history of consecutive historical-contextual interpretations of that same shared basic experience. Schillebeeckx's first lesson for modern theology is thus that

7. "Thus this interpretative identification is an intrinsic element of the experience of love" (Schillebeeckx, *Interim Report*, p. 13).

8. "Real love is fed by the experience of love and its own particular ongoing self-expression [. . .]. However, this growing self-expression makes it possible to deepen the original experience; it opens up the experience and makes it more explicit" (Schillebeeckx, *Interim Report*, pp. 13–14).

tradition and the development of tradition are only legitimate when they enable faith experience for Christians today.[9]

It is based on this perspective that Schillebeeckx further elaborates Gadamer's hermeneutics of tradition and arrives at a schema in which he posits the proportional identity between successive relationships of, on the one hand, the expression of faith of a given historical era, and, on the other hand, the socio-cultural context of the same era.[10] The relationship between Jesus' message and Jesus' historical context is fundamentally identical to the relationship between the New Testament message and the historical context within which the New Testament took shape. In spite of the difference between both expressions there is nevertheless identity, continuity — "proportional equality." Such identity continues to be in place in subsequent proportional relationships between the expression of faith and the context in the patristic period, the middle ages, and in the modern period. Schillebeeckx's primary message, however, is the following: the same relationship must also be made concrete today. It is on this point that the category of "experience" finds a prominent place once more in his thinking.

2. For Schillebeeckx, moreover, the category of experience is crucial in order to analyze the *current situation*. Schillebeeckx uses the category of "contrast experience" in order to point — positively — to our ineradicable expectation, persisting in the modern secular context, of a sustainable future for humanity. On the other hand, this experience witnesses — negatively — to the equally persistent distress unsettling all of us because suffering and senseless injustice continue to threaten this future for an overwhelming majority of people.[11]

On saying "No" to suffering and injustice and "Yes" to a better (and open) future, Schillebeeckx writes the following in his *Theologisch testament:* "I refer here to a basic experience common to all human beings, which is thus also pre-religious and therefore accessible to all human beings. It is the experience of a veto, of the indignation that fills one when one looks at the world as it actually is, with its repeated histories

---

9. In the analysis of experience, Schillebeeckx distinguishes three elements: first, an *experiential* element; second, an *interpretative* element which is the expression in concrete images, concepts, and narratives of the experience; and third, a *theoretical* element (a model) which constitutes the framework in which experience and interpretation take place. In his own words: "Consequently what people call a religious experience contains not only interpretation (in the sense of particular concepts and images) but also a theoretical model on the basis of which divergent experiences are synthesized and integrated" (Schillebeeckx, *Interim Report*, p. 26).

10. Cf. Schillebeeckx, *Church*, p. 42.

11. Cf. Schillebeeckx, *Interim Report*, p. 55.

of suffering and injustice."[12] There is, however, a "second, alternative dimension [that] manifests itself in the aforementioned negative contrast experience and in the indignation of all those forced to undergo inhumanity or to watch it happen. This human rejection of the non-human [...] opens up a positive perspective [...]: even when I am unable to imagine what a more human world might look like, the experience of *'enough is enough!'* or *'never again; the world must change and so must we'* persists."[13] Schillebeeckx identifies a fundamental "faith in the humanity of humanity" in this positive dimension together with a sense of hope for a future without suffering, oppression and injustice. "Without this hope, the indignation present as existential experience becomes inexistent, impossible in itself, meaningless and without human content. Without at least a latent positive hankering for human dignity, this human indignation is absurd."[14]

3. It is to this modern context of experience that the Christian faith must relate itself. In order to do so, a *critical correlation between tradition* and the *modern situation* is necessary,[15] which in fact can be rightly referred to as a "correlation between experiences." While concrete contrast experiences help to perceive in the Christian tradition the liberating claim of the God of salvation in a different light. At the same time, the same tradition, as the interpretation history of experiences of salvation, provides perspectives that allow for this modern context of experience to be structured from a Christian point of view. The result is a contemporary Christian faith in which the current situation "is an intrinsic element of the significance of the Christian message for us."[16]

---

12. E. Schillebeeckx, *Theologisch testament: Notarieel nog niet verleden* (Baarn: Nelissen, 1994), p. 128 (translation ours).

13. Ibid., 129–30 (translation ours).

14. Ibid., p. 130 (translation ours).

15. Schillebeeckx later prefers to describe "correlation" as "inter-relation" (cf. his valedictory lecture *Theologisch geloofsverstaan anno 1983*, p. 9). He is even inclined to argue at this juncture that the terminology of correlation is misleading, because authentic theologizing happens in two phases (not three) which together constitute one dynamic whole. In *Church* (p. 36, and earlier in *Christ*, p. 72) Schillebeeckx also speaks of the "interrelation/interrelationship" between Christian tradition and Christian situation, although he still conceives of this interrelation in three steps.

16. Schillebeeckx, *Interim Report*, p. 55. Schillebeeckx continues: "It is therefore striking that the times in which men [sic] refer to their own experiences, individual and collective, with renewed emphasis, are always times of crisis in which they experience a gap between tradition and experience instead of continuity between, e.g., the Christian tradition of experience and their contemporary experience. Of course even old experiences have power to make men question and transform [...]. But even new experiences have their own productive and critical force; otherwise, a reference to "interpretative elements" of old experiences would do no more than solidify and hold back our ongoing history."

For Schillebeeckx, such correlation results today in the claim that "the question of Christian identity is intrinsically connected with the question of human integrity"[17] and thus also implies an ecological, social, and political praxis. It is in this praxis, in actual engagement on behalf of those who suffer, in the struggle for the "Humanum," that the fundamental Christian basic experience can once again take shape. This today is the locus of religious experience, the privileged place where God's commitment to the human person can be experienced: in resistance to suffering and injustice. Being Christian today is therefore a question of intertwining politics and mysticism.[18]

For Schillebeeckx, it is precisely this link between the modern human experience of searching for liberation and the Christian message of salvation that presents the best argument in support of the plausibility and relevance of Christian faith today, both within and with respect to secular society. Christianity and secular society both entail fundamental, thoroughly human experiences of resistance to injustice and longing for wholeness. All people share such experiences. Even though these experiences have to do with life's most profound meaning, however, they do not necessarily call for a religious interpretation. Nevertheless, Schillebeeckx affirms that in order to understand their fundamental character, which so deeply influences human existence, one is *helped by* the word God. He continues: "I say, '[one is] helped by'; [and] not 'gives a better understanding of' this experience than the agnostic explanation.[...] I refer to universally shared experiences that are fundamental to any human existence. By the introduction of belief in God's saving presence, these experiences manifest a distinctive comprehensibility that is not present in other interpretations in which belief in God is not expressed, and which can be understood by others (even if they do not accept it)."[19]

Some conclusions: (1) There can be no faith without experience. A faith that cannot be actually experienced is not worth believing. (2) In historical contextual experiences, the universal significance of the Christian message (the "offer of revelation") continually manifests itself in

17. Schillebeeckx, *Interim Report*, p. 62.

18. "This radical concern for human society indicates a special presence of God. If living man is the fundamental symbol of God, i.e., "the image of God," then the place where people are dishonored, oppressed and enslaved, both in their own hearts and in society, is at the same time the *privileged place where religious experience become possible* in and through a life-style which seeks to give form to that symbol, to achieve wholeness and liberation. Thus real liberation, redemption and salvation always diverge into mysticism, because for religious people, the ultimate source and foundation for the healing and salvation of mankind, living and dead, is to be found in God" (Schillebeeckx, *Interim Report*, pp. 59–60, italics mine).

19. Schillebeeckx, *Church*, p. 84.

concrete particular forms. This was the case with Jesus, and this is once again the case when the narrative of Jesus' life and death "fits in" (or does not "fit in") with our own life experiences. (3) Schillebeeckx is able to affirm on these grounds that for the modern Christian there is an intrinsic bond between a correctly understood modern pursuit of an ethical and just society *and* following Jesus in working for the kingdom of God.[20]

Antoon Vergote: No Faith Based on Experience but Experience on the Basis of Faith

In similar fashion to Schillebeeckx, the increasing importance of experience for faith in the writings of Antoon Vergote[21] has to do with the crisis of faith in secularizing Western European society. Whereas the appeal to experience for Schillebeeckx is an indication and an incentive for the necessary renewal of faith's expression in dialogue with the changed context (aimed at remedying the breakdown in communication between the handed-down tradition and the current situation), for Vergote, such a renewal is *not the solution* to the crisis but rather its *symptom.*[22]

What does not find favor with this philosopher, theologian, psychoanalyst, and emeritus professor of the K.U. Leuven (Belgium) is the way in which an experience-based faith functions. The name "God" is only linked to profound human experiences (e.g., of love, a deep mysterious power, human dignity) *in a second step:* " 'God' becomes a symbolic name-giving, inherited from the religious tradition in order to signify

20. "Christianity has to do with the integration of being human in and through a source experience in which people, confronted with the man Jesus, connect the world, society and the individual with the absolute ground, the living God, our salvation" (Schillebeeckx, *Interim Report,* p. 62).

21. Vergote has written on religious experience in several of his publications: *Religie, geloof en ongeloof: Psychologische studie* (Antwerp/Amsterdam: De Nederlandsche Boekhandel, 1984), 111–86; English trans., *Religion, Belief and Unbelief: A Psychological Study* (Leuven: Leuven University Press, 1996). More general studies on the Christian faith in relation to the modern context include: *Cultuur, religie, geloof* (A. Dondeyne-leerstoel; Leuven: Universitaire Pers Leuven, 1989); *De Heer je God liefhebben: Het eigene van het Christendom* (Tielt: Lannoo, 1999); *Moderniteit en Christendom: Gesprek in vrijheid en respect* (Tielt: Lannoo, 1999); French trans., *Modernité et christianisme: interrogations critiques réciproques* (Paris: Cerf, 1999).

22. With statements such as, "Superficial talk on faith experience leads [. . .] to forms of sheer experience-based faith, faith that is determined by and limited to the immediate experience," Vergote distances himself from what he judges to be an overly facile reliance upon "experience" in faith and theology. See A. Vergote, "Ervaringsgeloof en geloofservaring," *Streven* 52 (1985): 891–903. Also included in A. Vergote, *Het meerstemmige leven: Gedachten over mens en religie* (Kapellen: DNB/Pelckmans, 1987), 16–30. The present discussion makes use of the latter version (for the quote: p. 16, translation ours).

something mysterious, *something* deep, *something* valuable. 'God' becomes an adjective (something divine, or the predicate in a proposition: *the* mysterious, *the* deep . . . that to me is God)."[23] In the Christian tradition, however, God is not a "predicate" Vergote argues, God is a "subject." "After all, love is not divine, but God is love." Profound experiences have less to do with the Christian faith and more to do with basic human disposition, a sort of basic faith or primal trust constituting a part of the human being itself.

The accentuation of the role of experience in faith then runs the risk of reducing Christian faith to this general human "primal faith." Vergote speaks significantly at this juncture of the "sliding of faith into experience-based faith."[24] For Christians, however, faith is not about accepting something based on experience, something secondary; faith rather is a given in its own right. After all, there is nothing in Christianity that would compel people to believe or that would lead them, quasi-automatically, to faith. For non-engaged observers, Christianity is only the accidental product of a series of contingent, historical events, which have no claim on this history whatsoever. The faith Christians enjoy distinguishes itself from that general human primal trust precisely by reading this contingent history as salvation history. It is here, in the wanderings of an insignificant people and especially in the specific person of Jesus that God has been revealed in history. Being a Christian implies this confession: God has come to us in Jesus Christ. Faith then is not the endeavor to hold to a truth (which we cannot know for sure), but rather a performative act: signing up to a reality made open by this confession, entering into a personal relationship with a God who does not merely coincide with our experiences, longings, and motivations: "Recognizing him is not experience"; it is participating in a relationship. "Walking toward God requires a leap."[25]

In contrast to experience-based faith, "faith experience" is not primary. It can only be acquired by fully engaging in the leap of faith one takes in confessing that God has become present in Christ. Thus, faith experience has everything to do with the experience of what it is to be *in* faith. Vergote likewise refers here to the analogy between faith and love. "Love based on experience" can be compared to a spontaneous falling in love and the longing that grafts itself onto that experience. The "experience of love," on the other hand, is the fruit of the surrender

23. Vergote, "Ervaringsgeloof en geloofservaring," p. 17 (translation ours).
24. Ibid., p. 19 (among others).
25. Ibid., p. 26 (translation ours).

of oneself to a very specific person; only after spending years together through good and bad days can people "testify that they know what love is; love becomes the experience of love."[26] Thus, experience does not produce faith, but rather faith produces experience. For Vergote, this happens when people manage to see their own lives and understanding of reality as being in coherence with the message of the Christian faith. It involves an integration between faith and life through which life begins to speak about faith, about "a concrete living of faith which interprets and values the world and one's being human from the perspective of faith." This necessitates the construction of a specific culture of faith, learning to read with the eyes of faith. Otherwise, all that remains is "words, words, words . . . words *without* experienced reality."[27]

Between Continuity and Discontinuity

Both Vergote and Schillebeeckx seek to answer the following question: how can one still be a Christian in a secularizing context when doing so is no longer self-evident? Their discussion thus concerns the way in which Christian faith relates itself to modern secular culture and, related to this, the tension between living out a Christian faith and belonging to a secular context, each of which has its own experiences and interpretative frameworks.

1. Vergote and Schillebeeckx agree that the changed context has caused a crisis of faith and that the modern secular culture arising from this changed context presents a challenge to theology. In this regard, both recognize the universality of secular truth claims — from the sciences, for instance. They also accept as a fact that people are marked with a "natural (religious) disposition," one that can be considered a general human trait. Both consider it meaningful to speak of "profound human" experiences as distinct from Christian experiences.

They disagree, however, on the relationship between what is generally human and that which is Christian. Whereas Schillebeeckx stresses continuity as an opportunity to provide Christian faith with contextual credibility and relevance, Vergote places emphasis on difference. For him, "the generally human" does not equal "the Christian," since the latter requires a leap, a moment of discontinuity that transforms the natural religious disposition of the human being and brings about its own believing rationality. Vergote strictly distinguishes the particularity of the

26. Ibid., pp. 27–28 (translation ours).
27. Ibid., pp. 28–29 (translation ours).

Christian faith from the universality of the generally human: Christian faith does not let itself be reduced to general human religion. Schillebeeckx, however, sees Christian faith first and foremost as a question of linking up with and integrating the generally human, which is then built upon by—and brought to fruition in—the Christian.

2. Both theologians recognize that in Christian religious experiences the intrinsic bond with the Christian tradition needs to be taken seriously. Experiences are not unmediated, rather they are embedded in interpretative frameworks. They are thus not just mere sensations but presuppose rather an initiation in, or at least familiarity with, the Christian tradition, as well as belonging to a Christian community of faith.

Nevertheless, while Vergote presupposes these frameworks as a precondition for speaking of a genuine Christian religious experience in which interpretation precedes experience, Schillebeeckx approaches the matter from the opposite direction. Despite its link with interpretation, experience retains for him a certain independence, allowing it thereby to place certain interpretations under critique. For Vergote, experience has its place in a life of faith when faith has become the key to approaching life and thereby becomes an experienced faith. Vergote thus lays emphasis upon acquiring a specific Christian interpretative framework in which one can then meaningfully speak of a Christian religious experience, and this stresses the dependence of the latter on the former. For Vergote, experience learns from interpretation (even though Vergote does not exclude *per se* a reciprocal dynamic between them). For Schillebeeckx, it is the current faith experience that helps renew traditional interpretations, in order for tradition to be a living tradition. Interpretation learns from experience.

3. Generally speaking, Schillebeeckx stresses the bridging function of theology and thus the continuity between the best of modern culture and Christian faith, over and above the evident differences. Vergote, by contrast, accentuates the difference between the Christian faith option and the general natural religious disposition, which he too recognizes. At the same time, Schillebeeckx also recognizes that discontinuity can occur in the tradition itself owing to the continuity in the critical correlation with current experience (a discontinuity, however, which serves an ultimate desire for continuity with tradition). Vergote, for his part, is inclined to stress once again the continuity between the faith option that is to be made today, and the narratives that one makes one's own through faith experience.

Lessons from a Modern Debate

If, in principle, the difference between Schillebeeckx and Vergote seems unbridgeable, perhaps their mutual disagreement can in fact be somewhat relativized from a contemporary perspective. This is because Schillebeeckx would also argue that there can be no Christian experience without a Christian interpretative framework, i.e., without an actual living of faith within a community of faith. After all, when he assumes a fundamental human experience shared by all, this is never acquired in a commonly shared way as such, but always embedded in particular interpretative frameworks. It is at this point that Schillebeeckx sees the theological-epistemological role of faith experience as offering opportunities for the renewal of tradition. Perhaps here, however, one is obliged to admit that from the outset Schillebeeckx's analysis of what experience is, and certainly of the current context, is already determined to a significant degree by his Christian background and theological input. Non-Christian commentators in particular (but not exclusively), such as the Belgian humanistic atheist Leo Apostel, have maintained this point in their writings.[28] Schillebeeckx presupposes a Christian horizon of understanding when speaking of human (religious) experience. According to Apostel, he leaves the content of religious experience as undefined as possible, while he nonetheless links (or wants to link) experience to tradition. It is precisely for this reason that Schillebeeckx remains trapped in a manner of thinking in which the generally human only attains its ultimate fulfillment in Christianity.[29] In Apostel's option, Schillebeeckx should have emphasized "the autonomy of the prelinguistic moment in religious experience" before linking this to interpretation,[30] but he is unable or

28. Cf. L. Apostel, "Religieuze ervaring bij Edward Schillebeeckx," in E. Kuypers, *Volgens Edward Schillebeeckx*, Rondom filosofen 3 (Leuven/Apeldoorn: Garant, 1991), 91–131.

29. Cf. Apostel, "Religieuze ervaring," p. 118: "According to Schillebeeckx, the struggle against alienation in favor of a sense of wholeness occurs just as fully and authentically (albeit it more heroically and without hope) among atheists as it does among Christians. Nonetheless, he immediately adds so many restrictions that it is only in the Christian struggle for wholeness [. . .] that the true campaign for liberation can be carried out." Furthermore: "Had he portrayed religious experience as such (qualitatively in a class of its own) [. . .], then he would have been able to find it (with different modalities) among the various religions and, at least as concerns the global experience of meaning, also among non-adherents of religion. This would have facilitated genuine dialogue possible, which is what Schillebeeckx wanted, but by tying down the description of experience so tightly to the interpretative frameworks, he prevents himself from reaching his own goal" (translation ours).

30. We find a similar insistence upon the autonomous character of religious experience in the work of Jaak Vandenbulcke, who endeavors to defend Schillebeeckx against Vergote. Vandenbulcke favors a prelinguistic, human depth experience, which "in its fundamental universality" precedes all interpretations (religions) and is at the same time constitutive for them. Moreover, the link to this experience constitutes the touchstone of a religion's claim to authority. Cf.

unwilling to go so far. This explains the ambiguity referred to by Apostel and others. Even though Schillebeeckx holds, in principle, to a universal prelinguistic element in experience, shared by all people as a fundamental basic experience, he nonetheless remains *de facto* entrenched in a Christian interpretative framework — something that relativizes (but does not neutralize) the actual distance between Vergote and Schillebeeckx.

The basic intuitions of Vergote and Schillebeeckx continue to offer interesting points of departure for a present-day reflection on what constitutes experience. At the same time, it is very important to recognize the contextual setting of their discussion and thus the underlying modern epistemological presuppositions in both their positions.

1. Vergote teaches us that there is no Christian experience without faith, that faith becomes experience within an already present and particular Christian horizon of understanding, in the faith community. Ultimately, there is no immediate link between profound human experience and Christian faith-based interpretation.

2. Schillebeeckx reminds us that the credibility, and relevance of Christian faith only emerge in the experience of the faithful and always in relation to context. The interplay of experience and interpretation constitutes the driving force behind the development of tradition. Faith experience thus takes place within the Christian horizon of understanding, but it places the latter under pressure and challenges it at the same time to work toward an interpretative reformulation of the faith. This becomes necessary (a) when long-standing interpretative frameworks no longer adequately express the experience of faith and (b) because the socio-historical context in which this experience manifests itself has changed.

In line with this, much of our current reflection on experience and theology will have to focus on the thorough transformation undergone

---

J. Vandenbulcke, "Geloof op basis van ervaring: Naar aanleiding van A. Vergote's 'Cultuur, Religie, Geloof,'" *Tijdschrift voor theologie* 29 (1989): 270–78. It is this position that has led today to a so-called pluralistic theology of religions in which the latter are understood to be partial, incomplete cultural mediations of a universally shared (mystical) experience. This means that the truth content of a religion stands in relation to this experience and, to the extent that no religion knows how to fully express this experience, no religion can then claim to have the absolute truth. In other words, the particularity of religion is relativized in function of the universality of the (mystical) experience. In its most pointed form, religions are true *in spite of* their particularity. Schillebeeckx finally does not follow as regards this last point and continues to operate within an inclusivist model. See, for example, his "Identiteit, eigenheid en universaliteit van Gods heil in Jezus," *Tijdschrift voor theologie* 30 (1990): 259–75 (amended French translation, "Universalité unique d'une figure religieuse historique nommée Jésus de Nazareth," *Laval théologique et philosophique* 50 [1994]: 265–82).

by a number of modern presuppositions that were still at the background of the debate between Schillebeeckx and Vergote.

2. From the Interruption of Experience to the Experience of Interruption

We will briefly outline the socio-cultural and epistemological shifts that fundamentally shape the context in which theology is being carried out today. In critical distance from this context and modern theological attempts to relate themselves to it, we will then sketch some currents of thought that develop religious experience as a rupture with the context. Despite just criticism, however, such currents of thought survive at the expense of one of correlation theology's most important insights, namely, the intuition that there is an intrinsic connection between faith and context. As we continue our reflection on this intrinsic connection, we will further develop the concept of religious experience as "interruption" in the last paragraphs of this chapter, and demonstrate how it can be understood and function productively from a contextual-theological perspective.

Cultural and Epistemological Shifts

In part 1 we pointed out that the context in which theology endeavors to explain and justify faith has changed considerably on account of important socio-cultural as well as epistemological shifts.

As a result of detraditionalization, the overlap between culture and faith has become too narrow. At the cultural level, profound human experiences can no longer be quasi-automatically interpreted within Christian interpretative frameworks. The frequent result of a non-problematized correlation today, therefore, is *de facto* a horizontal and functionalized reduction of Christianity in terms of cultural Christianity, ethics, or aesthetics. This is what Vergote feared with regard to Schillebeeckx's understanding of experience: *in se* there is absolutely no basis for assuming that a profound human experience will be interpreted as a Christian experience. If the explicit, even the implicit, Christian horizon of understanding (the cultural overlap) in Western societies has been detraditionalized, then the appeal to experience would appear to be counterproductive, were such an appeal not immediately linked to the faith experience of believers standing within a tradition and faith community. This is even more the case when the context is progressively pluralizing. The question of the identity, credibility, and relevance of the

Christian faith thus appears in a completely different light. In short, the current context is no longer that of a culture that has secularized itself away from a Christian horizon, thus with only one recognizable partner to which theology must relate itself; instead, it has evolved into a context of plurality and difference. This naturally has consequences for the way in which Christians account for their faith.

In addition, and related to this shift, postmodern criticism of rationality seriously discredits the modern presupposition that, through reason, a sort of general human standard with a claim to universal truth is developed. It was to this sort of universality claim that Christian tradition and its particular truth claims were to relate themselves. Since the 1980s, however, postmodern sensitivities have undermined the modern presuppositions of universality, objectivity, transparency, and communicability. Having sprung from the lessons learned from the history of the twentieth century — think, for instance, of Lyotard's critique of the "master narratives" — these sensitivities foster suspicion with respect to totalizing intellectual frameworks. Instead, and frequently based on a radicalization of the "linguistic turn," they devise conceptual patterns that take a heightened sensitivity toward radical plurality, historicity, and difference as their point of departure. They point out the limits, contextuality, particularity, and contingency of each construction of meaning. Moreover, they call for a greater awareness of the fact that our ways of coping with plurality and difference perpetually threaten to misunderstand or functionalize them. It is thus from this perspective also that contemporary philosophy and the humanities find fault with an overly simplistic presupposition of consensus, continuity, and harmony. After all, such presuppositions often imply hegemonic mechanisms of inclusion or exclusion. To the extent that modern correlation theology (and frequently also the reaction against it) embraced these modern epistemological presuppositions — whether implicitly or explicitly — it shares in their loss of plausibility. The presupposition of continuity between tradition and context, legitimated by and expressed in religious experience, no longer works and is often considered as a form of Christian recuperation.

How then do we theologically conceptualize the status of religious experience today? Does religious experience ultimately affirm a rupture with the context, an irreconcilable difference between context and faith?

Christian Experience of God: Rupture with the Context?

Similar discussions to those between Schillebeeckx and Vergote have also taken place in the rest of Europe and the United States — and are still ongoing. For some decades now, the problem of correlation theology has been highlighted by the so-called "anti-" and "post-foundationalist" theologies,[31] including the argument for the priority of tradition over experience.[32] Philosophers of religion and theologians — often inspired by Karl Barth — have turned against the modern appeal to experience and reason. In so doing the relationship between religious experience and faith tradition has been reversed: tradition determines experience; narrativity comes first and is confirmed by experience. Those who appeal to the autonomy of experience neglect its irreducible linguistic, and therefore particular, embedding: a Christian religious experience is dependent upon the "cultural-linguistic" context[33] in which it takes place, and cannot be considered without it. Secular experience, therefore, is not simply a neutral experience to which Christians need to relate their faith and tradition, it is also unmistakably embedded in a very specific, non-religious current of thought and lifestyle. It is precisely the different "cultural-linguistic" embedding of both experiences that makes them substantially different. Furthermore, there is no given level at which both experiences can be unified that would escape such "cultural-linguistic" determination. Even those who appeal to a pre-linguistic component to experience already do so from a very specific, context-bound linguistic rooting.

Others still have more recently joined in the chorus of criticism leveled against correlation theologians such as Schillebeeckx and Tracy. They no longer conceive of Christian faith and faith experience as in continuity with context and contemporary thinking, but rather as in a ruptured relationship. Faith and religious experience give rise to difference and open another, even higher, way of perceiving and thinking, which then stands in sharp contrast to current modern and postmodern ways of thinking.

1. In part 1 of the present volume we made reference to the Radical Orthodoxy movement initiated and headed by John Milbank. The

---

31. "Foundationalist theologies" reflect upon the truth of the Christian faith in relation to the context, more precisely the modern context. The term refers to the endeavor to "found" the Christian truth claim according to or upon the (modern) standards of rationality.

32. This debate continues to be vigorously maintained, particularly in the English-speaking world, between the so-called ("anti-foundationalist") Yale school (with proponents such as George Lindbeck) and the ("correlationist") Chicago school (for instance, with David Tracy). See, for example, G. A. Lindbeck, *The Nature of Doctrine: Religion and Theology in a Postliberal Age* (Philadelphia: Westminster Press, 1984); and D. Tracy, *Plurality and Ambiguity: Hermeneutics, Religion, Hope* (Chicago: University of Chicago Press, 1987); and "The Uneasy Alliance Reconceived," *Theological Studies* 50 (1989): 548–70.

33. The term is from G. Lindbeck's *The Nature of Doctrine.*

movement defines religious experience in the context of a reintroduction of neo-platonic Augustinian conceptual frameworks, which it favors as a means to escape the aporias of modernity and postmodernity.[34] Modern secularism, it maintains, led to a world without ultimate foundations, which became all too aware of its valuelessness and meaninglessness in the postmodern context. Cynicism and scepticism now rule the roost, together with nihilism and self-assured superficiality. Secularism has destroyed what it attempted to guarantee: identity, corporality, aesthetics, social and political life, sexuality. Radical Orthodoxy, however, is not merely concerned with a radical-critical exposé of modernity, the scandal of which is revealed in postmodernity. Precisely because postmodern nihilism is the outcome of this secularism, the current context also offers an opportunity for renewal, for a re-introduction of the theological project, since secular claims to truth in postmodernity have lost much of their credibility and been weakened.[35] Because of modernity's failure to ensure value and meaning in the immanent,[36] there is once again room to anchor the integrity of the temporal in the eternal. This requires a radical reintegration of the worldly within a resolute theological perspective. This is the goal of Radical Orthodoxy. "This new project," Milbank writes *cum suis* in the introduction to *Radical Orthodoxy,* "does not, like liberal theology, transcendentalist theology, and even certain types of neo-orthodoxy, seek in the face of this drift to shore up universal accounts of immanent human value (humanism) nor defenses of supposedly objective reason. But nor does it indulge, like so many, in the pretence of a baptism of nihilism in the name of a misconstrued 'negative theology.' "[37] Doing the latter would be to continue the modern theological project, placing the criteria for theological truth outside theology. It is only when the worldly refers to its eternal source, thus only from a profound theological perspective of the temporal participating in the eternal, that the integrity of world and time can be ensured.[38] This participatory relationship — paradigmatically expressed in the liturgy —

34. Cf. section 3 in chapter 2 above, page 37.

35. Milbank, *The Program of Radical Orthodoxy,* p. 42.

36. "Although it might seem that to treat of diverse worldly phenomena such as language, knowledge, the body, aesthetic experience, political community, friendship, etc. apart from God is to safeguard their worldliness, in fact, to the contrary, it is to make even this worldliness dissolve." From the Introduction by Milbank, Pickstock, and Ward, *Radical Orthodoxy,* 1–20, p. 3 ("Suspending the Material: The Turn of Radical Orthodoxy").

37. Milbank, Pickstock, and Ward, *Radical Orthodoxy,* p. 1.

38. "The theological perspective of participation actually saves the appearances by exceeding them" (Milbank, Pickstock, and Ward, *Radical Orthodoxy,* p. 4).

precedes language and experience. "Since God is not an item in the world to which we might turn, he is only first there for us in our turning to him. And yet we only turn to him when he reaches us; herein lies the mystery of liturgy — liturgy which for theology is more fundamental than *either* language *or* experience, and yet is both linguistic and experiential."[39] Hence, religious experience refers to this relationship and places the worldly *sub specie aeternitatis*. Religious experience makes one participate in the harmony of being in relation to God, and reveals diversity reconciled to unity, strongly marking itself off from the contemporaneous cultural experiences of alienation, differentiation, conflict, and intruding alterity.[40] Religious experience thus confirms the ruptured relationship between the theological recapturing of the world and its secularistic and nihilistic reduction in modernity and postmodernity. According to Philip Blond, another member of the Radical Orthodoxy movement, such a secular experience of the world becomes theologically "displaced and exceeded by a religious mode of perception."[41] He describes this form of "perception" (*Wahrnehmung*) as a higher form of "cognition." It requires an active seeing and is therefore more than being passively overtaken by one or another phenomenon that acts as a "vehicle of transcendence" (see, for example Kant's "Sublime," Levinas' "Face of the other" or Marion's "Icon"). When phenomena are perceived from a theological perspective, then what Blond calls "the Trinitarian harmonic" comes into play, "and this harmonic with its focus on mutual joy, solicitude, and love calls human beings to participation in the possibilities that God as the highest reality gives and donates to human life, an activity that is unrecognizable by any mere human passivity in the face of ultimate experience."[42] This higher form of knowledge is at odds with a "secular construal of reality" and opens "the possibility of a greater reality" because reality "always offers more possibilities to sight than any secular attempts to objectify it as a godless materiality. Which is to say that perception sees more than self-sufficient being, because beings themselves show more than self-sufficiency." In contrast to the "secular gaze," which limits itself to the certainty of the visible, "the

39. Milbank, *The Program of Radical Orthodoxy*, p. 44, reference to C. Pickstock, *After Writing: On the Liturgical Consummation of Philosophy* (Oxford: Blackwell, 1997).

40. See, for example, my "(Post)Modern Theology on Trial? Towards a Radical Theological Hermeneutics of Christian Particularity," *Louvain Studies* 28 (2003): 240–54.

41. Cf. P. Blond, "Introduction: Theology before Philosophy," in *Post-Secular Philosophy: Between Philosophy and Theology*, ed. P. Blond (London/New York: Routledge, 1997),1–66, pp. 22ff., here p. 23.

42. Blond, "Introduction: Theology before Philosophy," pp. 23–24.

conjunction of perception and faith discloses a world whose origin lies beyond itself."[43]

2. There are a number of French thinkers such as E. Levinas, J.-Y. Lacoste, and J.-L. Marion, who — at least according to some commentators[44] — have performed a so-called "theological turn" in French phenomenology. They start with the Heideggerian critique of Western rationality, but in a second step they go beyond Heidegger and present a concept of religious experience at odds with modern thought patterns as the starting point for religious thinking.

For Jean-Yves Lacoste,[45] for example, "liturgical experience" breaks off from Heidegger's *in-der-Welt-Sein*. Such an experience, for which the experiences of "repose" (*l'aise*) and "the work of art" are also paradigmatic, is possibly more original than the experience of *Angst* that unlocks *in-der-Welt-Sein* of *Dasein*. For Lacoste, Heidegger's anthropology of *Sein-zum-Tode* fails to adequately express or exhaust the essence of being human. In the liturgical experience, in the Eucharist or in prayer, the closed horizon of the world-without-God is broken open and human existence comes to stand in the light of the dynamic of creation and eschatological fulfillment. By using the images of the hermit and the pilgrim, Lacoste elaborates that the logic of *in-der-Welt-Sein* is transfigured into the logic of the *être-face-à-Dieu* (being-before-God), *esse coram Deo*. The world as world is left behind to make space for an anticipation of the Kingdom.[46] Time and again, Lacoste uses the following terminology to characterize this movement: transgression, conversion, frustration and terror, decentering of the subject, abandonment or surrender of the self, suspension of history, eschatological anticipation. He designates the liturgical experience itself as *non-expérience* (and *non-événement*). As a matter of fact, it concerns an experience that escapes from the experience of and in the world, an experience that does not occur without the world, but at the same time tears it open and reminds

43. Ibid., p. 24.

44. See D. Janicaud, *Le tournant théologique de la phenoménologie française* (Combas: Éclat, 1991); R. Welten, *Fenomenologie en beeldverbod bij Emmanuel Levinas en Jean-Luc Marion* (Budel: Damon, 2001); P. Jonkers and R. Welten, eds., *God in France: Eight Contemporary French Philosophers on God and Religion,* Studies in Philosophical Theology 28 (Leuven: Peeters Press, 2004).

45. See especially J.-Y. Lacoste, *Expérience et Absolu*, Épiméthée (Paris: PUF, 1994); English trans. *Experience and the Absolute: Disputed Questions on the Humanity of Man* (New York: Fordham University Press, 2004), and the study by Joeri Schrijvers, "Jean-Yves Lacoste: A Phenomenology of Liturgy," *Heythrop Journal* 46 (2005): 314–33. This study, incidentally, refers to an evolution in the thinking of Lacoste in which his previous opposition to Heidegger becomes less severe.

46. See, for example, Lacoste, *Experience and the Absolute*, p. 29.

one of the gulf between history and the Absolute.[47] It is here that Lacoste locates the critical potential of the liturgical non-experience: "the fundamentally non-experiential character of liturgy permits us to criticize every theory in which experience governs knowledge [*connaissance*] of God, or in which the relation of man [sic] to God reaches its culmination in the field of conscious experience." Liturgical experience is not simply an experience of God that resonates with our general human world of experience and lends cogency to our religious narratives and theories—an experience to which we can then appeal for religious truth claims. "In the chiaroscuro of the world and of history, liturgy, if we must speak of it in terms of consciousness, is that experience in which consciousness encounters a veiled Absolute and cannot take leave, if not from perpetual ambiguity, then at least from the necessity of a perpetual interpretation that is by no means infallible. No one enters into liturgy without wishing God to visit him. But no one experiences liturgy without comprehending that God is never there present to consciousness in an entirely obvious way."[48]

Research Question: Between Continuity and Discontinuity

Contrary to modern theology, the abovementioned authors and thought currents conceive of Christian experience as a rupture and emphasize its discontinuity with the modern and postmodern context. This has two consequences:

1. First, the Christian faith experience differentiates, conferring a specific identity that distinguishes itself from other forms of identity; it actualizes a specific understanding of reality and living. Christian identity is not just a variation or particular interpretation of a general human religious disposition, which we all have in common and on the basis of which we can come to mutual agreement. This is a powerful response to Edward Schillebeeckx. Despite the importance he places on the connection with the generally human, he still implicitly presupposes Christian identity (*dixit* Apostel). At the same time, however, his method does not explain how Christian identity necessarily follows upon the generally human, or how exactly the leap of faith brings about a particular, powerful transformation of this general human experience (*dixit* Vergote).

47. Cf. Lacoste, *Experience and the Absolute*, p. 43.
48. Ibid., pp. 49 and 63 respectively.

2. Whereas the relationship to the context in modern theology (expressed in terms of the correlation of experiences) contributes intrinsically toward the development of tradition and thereby to a contemporary formulation and conception of Christian faith, to the critics of correlation, however, the relationship between tradition and context is now only considered to be extrinsic. The Christian tradition has little or nothing more to do with the modern or postmodern context, which is mostly critiqued as antagonistic. Faith experience is then foremost the experience of this rupture; it signifies discontinuity. Conversion means turning oneself away from this world. The focus on the intrinsic relationship between tradition and context, and the need for recontextualization at each shift in context, is Schillebeeckx's strong point here: new experiences of faith in a changed context serve to place old forms of the tradition under scrutiny and thereby press for a development of the tradition.[49]

Whatever the case, it is nevertheless plain to see that the conception of religious experience depends crucially upon the way in which one views the relationship between Christian faith and context, be it as continuity or discontinuity, intrinsically bound to each other or merely extrinsically affiliated.

Hence the following research question: if it is correct that the relationship between tradition and context is revealed in the Christian experience (whether as continuity or discontinuity), is it then possible to think of Christian experience as being *both* distinctive *and* maintaining an intrinsic relation between tradition and context at the same time? Is it possible to critique the modern theological presumption of continuity without letting go of the important basic intuition that experience challenges tradition toward recontextualization?

Formulated somewhat differently: is it possible, on the one hand, to conceive of faith experience as that which lends Christians their specific Christian identity thereby allowing this identity to be distinguished and affirmed in relation to other identities? And is it possible, on the other hand, to conceive of this experience as that which puts this identity to the test from within in order to prevent it from becoming closed or totalitarian while remaining open to what is going on in reality? In order

49. Cf. for instance E. Schillebeeckx, "Breuken in christelijke dogma's," in *Breuklijnen: Grenservaringen en zoektochten*, Fs. T. Schoof (Baarn: Nelissen, 1994), 15–49, p. 26: "Even thanks to shifts and breaks in formulations of dogma, the dogma remains true," and further, "An historical break with previous cultural forms of the faith can sometimes then be the only possible way to come to a contemporary reformulation of the dogma which is faithful to the Gospel and the Christian faith tradition. [...] The ever new present enters by redefining the past" (translation ours).

for this identity to be able to define itself anew in relation to the context in which it participates?

In what follows, I would like to demonstrate that conceiving of religious experience as "interruption," thus retaining both continuity and discontinuity, offers a prospective answer to my research question. (a) On the one hand, the specificity of the Christian experience interrupts the all too easily presupposed continuity between tradition and context, between the multiplicity of profound human and religious experiences and the Christian experience of knowing oneself to be in relationship with the God of Jesus Christ. The experience of being Christian refers back to the radical particularity, narrativity, and situatedness of Christian identity, and therefore brings with it distinctness and difference. Interruption, however, is not rupture: Christian experience divorced from what Christians experience as profoundly human becomes esoteric and meaningless. (b) On the other hand, because context and tradition are intrinsically linked, this experience may interrupt the Christian tradition from within. The Christian faith experience occurs amidst a radical hermeneutical process that takes as its starting point the theological awareness that even though God's revelation can only be communicated through language and history, revelation never totally coincides with them. Here too interruption does not mean rupture. Particular language, tradition, narrativity remain revelation's intrinsic conditions of possibility, but time and again revelation forces them to confront their limitations.

Interruption of Experience — Experience of Interruption

We will now further develop this proposal of "experience as interruption" along the following theological epistemological lines, while at the same time summarizing and placing in perspective what we have introduced thus far.

1. Nowadays, the category of "religious experience" is often theologically unproductive and even misleading because of the modern epistemological presuppositions clinging to it. The critique of the modern correlation method has made this clear. The presupposition of continuity between Christian experience and general human experience is not only unable to account for Christian specificity but, at the same time, it finds its context within a modern concept of rationality and truth. When the concept of experience shows traces of the scientific logic of experimental verification, in which the truth of something needs to be established by experience, these presuppositions will only be strengthened all the more.

This implies *a first interruption* to the prevailing modern theological concept of experience, regarding its presumption of continuity between faith and context.

Religious experience, then, primarily refers back to the actual faith life of Christians, a life of being initiated into the Christian tradition and participating in the life of the faith community — thus to a very specific way of living one's life. Religious experience as faith experience, the actual living out of the Christian narrative through becoming experienced in this faith, refers from a theological-epistemological perspective to the density of the concrete, contextually situated faith life, in which narrative, interpretation, *savoir-faire,* perception, praxis, signification, and reflection are interlocked. Typical for faith experience today is that, given the changed context of detraditionalization, pluralization, and individualization, being a Christian increasingly implies a choice, an act of will. To be a Christian means opting for a life that is framed within a well-defined narrative and community, a choice that is often called into question by the confrontation with the current context — even if this choice is experienced and interpreted as a vocation.

2. This does not mean, however, that dialogue or confrontation with the context can only be thought of as extrinsic, as many critics of modern theology contend. Such critics often exclusively use current criticism of the context in order to then immediately present another type of (faith) rationality that rejects the context. Taking postmodern thinkers as their point of departure, they state that Christian correlation theology will never be able to justify itself and that it is therefore destructive for the theological project. They contend, for example, that whoever maintains continuity between Christian faith and the modern context will too easily begin totalizing from a Christian point of view and hence make truth claims that he or she cannot substantiate. Alternatively, such critics explain that correlation theology merely makes Christian faith a reduplication of what humanly spoken is already true, good, or authentic in itself. And precisely these universal truth — and human — claims are suspect in the postmodern context. It is here that dialogue with the context stops for these critics. They then go on to produce a rationality from the depths of Christian tradition itself that opposes the context; for example, they introduce neo-Augustinian models of thought or try to constitute a new type of foundational thinking (in spite of itself) from the "givenness" of reality.

Christians, however, are no less postmodern than their contemporaries. Every manner of identity formation is both shaped and questioned by postmodern sensibilities. It is for this reason that the Christian faith experience necessarily involves the context in its faith life and creates greater awareness of the specific narrativity and reflexivity, historicity and contingency, which define one's footing in the faith, the tradition, and the faith community. In this sense, recontextualization — as the descriptive indicator for the way in which faith and tradition relate to the context — is always already at work. The thought currents outlined above are thus likewise exponents of a certain relationship — or rather the inability to enter into a productive relationship — with the challenges that the current context (in particular, the challenge of otherness and difference) poses to everyone. This implies *a second interruption* to a theological concept of experience, namely, regarding its claim that the breach between tradition and context would become manifested precisely in religious experience.

In addition to this twofold "contextual" interruption of the way in which experience functions theologically, we can also distinguish a twofold "theological" interruption from the perspective of the Christian experience of God.

3. The current critical consciousness, which is rooted in our time in a heightened sensibility toward irreducible plurality, particularity, and heterogeneity, also offers new opportunities for a contextual-theological justification of faith. On this point, therefore, we differ from the critics mentioned above. In fact, it is our conviction that precisely the confrontation with the context makes it possible today for theology to conceive of the status and nature of "religious experience" differently. We do this within the framework of a radical-hermeneutical theology, which takes its primary point of departure from the irreducible and particular narrative character of Christian faith, deeply qualified by radical historicity and contingency. At the same time, this way of theologizing maintains that God's revelation can only be discerned in this all too historical and contingent reality. God appears in history, not in spite of, but thanks to particularity. It goes without saying that the preservation of this radical-hermeneutical tension has serious consequences for considering what the truth claims of Christian faith are (and the various articulations thereof).[50]

---

50. This research theme has been taken up by a new interdisciplinary research project at the K.U. Leuven, under the direction of M. Lamberigts, T. Merrigan, and myself, *Orthodoxy: Process and Product — Church-Historical and Systematic-Theological Study of the Determination of Truth in Church and Theology*. It is important at this juncture that we resolutely distance ourselves from other forms of so-called radical-hermeneutical theologies, which — *à la* J. Caputo

The current contextual consciousness is already at work when we prefer to describe religious experience as *Christian* experience of God, or Christian experience of transcendence, and thereby underline the particularity of the Christian narrative. In their faith experience, Christians are aware that they are part of a historically mediated relationship with the God of Jesus Christ. This experience differentiates Christians from non-Christians, including those who believe in a god, a higher power, something deeper, etc. (the god of the statisticians is not always the "God of Abraham, Isaac and Jacob"), or even the other monotheistic religions. In short, what would seem to unite believers of different religions sometimes leads to extremely pointed differences.[51] The Christian faith experience thus interrupts for the first time, pointing to the irreducibility of the Christian experience of God in relation to other religious and non-religious depth experiences.

The Christian experience of faith is also at work in an interruptive way within the particular Christian tradition itself. We will illustrate this in more detail in the final paragraphs (4–6) of the present chapter.

4. The confrontation with the current contextual critical sensitivity toward plurality, particularity, and otherness, however, also indicates that whoever retreats into his or her own identity is likely to become totalitarian and oppressive. Of necessity, a hermeneutics of contingency must go hand-in-hand with a hermeneutics of suspicion. For this reason, some postmodern thinkers present the confrontation with the irreducible otherness of a concrete other as a new way of breaking identity open without destroying it: a dynamics of appropriation and expropriation prevents identity from becoming totalitarian in such a way that it closes in upon itself and eliminates otherness. These thought trajectories can also be made theologically productive. The Christian experience of transcendence does not simply establish identity, it also problematizes it from

---

and others—endeavor to designate the truth moment of Christian faith as beyond all particularity in a deconstructionist, negative theological movement, with the consequent reduction of particularity. It is only in the all-too-particular that God is revealed and this revelation cannot be dissociated from the said particularity in any way. *Apophasis* does not imply the reduction to nothing of *kataphasis* but rather a radical-hermeneutical qualification thereof. See further my "Christus Postmodernus: An Attempt at Apophatic Christology," in *The Myriad Christ: Plurality and the Quest for Unity in Contemporary Christology*, ed. T. Merrigan and J. Haers, BETL 152 (Leuven: Peeters Press, 2000), 577–93; "The Rediscovery of Negative Theology Today: The Narrow Gulf between Theology and Philosophy," in *Théologie négative*, M. Olivetti, ed., Biblioteca dell' "Archivio di Filosofia," 59 (Rome: CEDAM, 2002), 443–59; and especially my "God, Particularity and Hermeneutics: A Critical-Constructive Theological Dialogue with Richard Kearney on Continental Philosophy's Turn (in)to Religion," *Ephemerides Theologicae Lovanienses* 81 (2005): 305–33.

51. See also chapters 7 and 8 on the relationship between theological truth and incarnation.

within. Within the faith experience itself resides an inaccessibility, an otherness that does not allow itself to be thought of too rapidly as being in continuity with the Christian narrative tradition (and other narratives), even though it can only be articulated within this narrative tradition. Theologians can learn from the current critical consciousness that by appealing to transcendence (or universality), cherished truth claims very often become totalitarian, and that the closed structures of such truth narratives cannot cope with the confrontation with the other (excluding the other or stripping it of its very otherness). At the same time, the current critical consciousness has made theologians aware that a respectful engagement with the "other" of their narrative may provide the critical impetus to critique closing or closed structures and narratives, both inside and outside one's own tradition.

Translated theologically, insights drawn from today's contextual critical consciousness help conceive of faith experience as the experience of being caught up with God in concrete, historically mediated ways. As the Other of the Christian narrative, God withdraws from it, even though it is only in and through this narrative that God is revealed, i.e., comes to speak. The God who ultimately has everything to do with this narrative cannot be grasped by it; instead as the Other of the narrative, God questions the narrative from within, interrupts it, forces it to collide with its borders. Only when faith experience reckons with this interrupting aspect of a God who refuses to be reduced to the Christian narrative (even though God cannot be conceived of without it), can the development of tradition be reflected upon theologically today. It is for this reason that encounters with others, reading texts, reflecting on events, confrontation with joy and sorrow, wonderment and horror, etc. can serve as moments of interruption in which Christian identity formation is paradoxically questioned from within, because for Christians it is precisely in these opportunities that God is announced as the One who interrupts. In the inextricable dynamics of experience and interpretation, which Schillebeeckx saw as the source of the development of tradition, tradition does indeed involve itself with the context, and the critical-practical reevaluation of theology occurs in dialogue and/or confrontation with this context. Nevertheless, this does not stem from a presupposed continuity between tradition and context, but rather from respecting the difference between both—the very difference theology has learned to observe and value as constitutive of the dialogue with the current context. This is the lesson that makes it possible for us to consider the structure of the Christian faith experience from a contextual-theological perspective.

5. This means that new ways need to be found in order to conceptualize Christian experiences of transcendence on the border of what is commonly understood as "experience." In the literature, authors such as Kevin Hart[52] and Denys Turner[53] speak of the experience of God as "irreducible intrusion from elsewhere," "absolute interruption," "experience with experience," "experience of non-experience," "absence of the experience." The question frequently remains unsolved by many theologians, however, as to how this "experience" is to be situated within the Christian tradition and how it can promote reflection on the development of tradition and tradition hermeneutics — which was ultimately Schillebeeckx's concern. Often inspired by their study of the mystics and of negative theology, such theologians present a kind of "experience" that militates against the modern concept of experience (including its autonomy and primacy with respect to interpretation), but they seldom develop how exactly they would allow experience to foster and question living faith.

We are inclined, therefore, to opt for the concept "interruption." Faith experience circles around a God who is made known to us in concrete histories and narratives, a God who cannot be known without such histories and narratives (in other words, a God who is not an object of immediate experience) but who at the same time does not coincide with them, and who frustrates from within every attempt to capture God in word and narrative. An identity informed by faith is, contextually speaking, an uninsured identity. This is likewise the case from a theological perspective. Faith experience places Christians in continuity with the Christian tradition and faith community, while simultaneously questioning and even endangering this continuity because of the radical-hermeneutical structure of the Christian discourse about God. Christian faith experience is both the experience of the interruption by tradition and context and interrupts tradition and context.[54]

---

52. Cf., for example, K. Hart, "On Interruption," in *Questioning God,* ed. J. D. Caputo, M. Dooley and M. Scanlon (Bloomington: Indiana University Press, 2001), 186–208; K. Hart, "The Experience of God," in *The Religious,* ed. J. D. Caputo (Oxford/Malden, MA: Blackwell, 2001), 159–74; K. Hart, "The Kingdom and the Trinity," in *Religious Experience and the End of Metaphysics,* ed. J. D. Bloechl (Bloomington: Indiana University Press, 2003), 153–73.

53. Cf. D. Turner, *The Darkness of God: Negativity in Christian Mysticism* (Cambridge: Cambridge University Press, 1995).

54. The development of such a theological epistemology of interruption is well placed to disarm the present deadlock in the Chicago and Yale school debate, to question recent attempts to re-evaluate the category of experience in terms of pre-modern (neo-Augustinian) schemes (from both Protestant and Catholic sides, cf. "Radical Orthodoxy" and some of the "von Balthasar revival" respectively), and to rectify the hermeneutical weakness of "theologies of revelation."

6. In contrast to (the majority of) correlation theologies (emancipation, political, or liberation theologies), anti-correlation theologies often develop a blind spot toward (or even dismiss) praxis-oriented theology with its sensitivity toward the concrete historicity and materiality of life. It is precisely here that a "theology of interruption" can render its services by holding on to the intrinsic involvement of tradition with context in the interrupting experience of God. It is in very specific encounters and occurrences that God, for Christians, comes interruptingly close, in daily life, in being faced with the poor and with the other, even though for Christians this will often require exceptional attentiveness and hermeneutical care. Interruption thus becomes an interpretative key to assist tradition and context in tracing God's potential manifestations today. Faith experiences remain very particular experiences, bound to concrete histories. In them God does not simply reveal Godself all at once, rather God brings about interruptive intermission, God halts our Christian narratives and throws them open to what is proclaimed therein as the Kingdom of God, which is both realized and promised in Jesus Christ. For this reason, Christians are called to be interrupters, wherever the poor and the other have become a function of totalizing narratives, whether these be Christian or not. The faith experience of interruption causes interruption, and it is here that God is revealed today.

3. To Conclude: Christian Experience of God in a Highly Experiential Culture

Following the cognitive search for the True and the ethical search for the Good, it would appear that, in our present-day context, only an aesthetical sensitivity toward the Beautiful or Sublime has the capacity to offer meaning to the life of men and women. It would seem that these three stages constitute a hermeneutical key, allowing us to explain the recent history of religion in Western Europe. The confrontation between religion and modernity, evident, for example, in the conflict between faith and science, can be analyzed as a struggle between rival truth claims. The ancient and medieval synthesis between reason and faith was shattered in the process. Faith and modernity, however, appeared to reach a point of reconciliation in the domain of ethical praxis. The concrete experience of the good life became a source of meaning. Believers and unbelievers may have disagreed on the ultimate explanation of reality, but they found common ground in the construction of a better society, if not in terms of the eschatological "already and not yet" realization of the Kingdom of God, then in terms of the establishment of a utopic Kingdom of Humanity. When modernity's dream of progress and emancipation collapsed under the weight of its own unfulfilled promises, and postmodern thinkers confirmed the end of the modern master narratives, it appeared that aesthetics alone could be of service in humanity's search for meaning. If the truth about reality (knowledge) and the struggle for justice and a better society (ethics) no longer offered stable points of anchor, then it would seem that individuals are ultimately forced to depend on their own sensitivities: real life then is experience, "sensation." Access to the Beautiful or the Sublime as meaning-giving instances is granted via subjective experience. Moreover, the latter is frequently psychologized, and might be defined as the affective intensification of self-consciousness, of awareness of living, which can relate to experiences of harmony and reconciliation as well as anxiety and rupture.

This search for strongly felt experience, for lived sensation, is an all-present reality in today's world, one which the media and advertising exploit to the full. Clothing, cars, perfume, etc. are not in the first instance merely plain consumer goods but rather well-designed opportunities to achieve authenticity, to consciously create a lifestyle that distinguishes one from another. Today's obsession with emotion and affectivity, illustrated by the "emocracy" of television in informative as well as entertainment broadcasting, serves to illustrate the notion that something is real if it "touches" us in one way or another. "Reality TV" and "soaps" zoom in on life as it is lived by concrete men and women, stimulating profound empathy among their viewers. Other programs allow the viewer to break free from the boundary separating reality and fiction in the search for a more exciting, more spectacular life. In short, a life worth living is a life "experienced" by an individual as interesting and rewarding. Some scholars argue that society today is a "society of experience" (*Erlebnisgesellschaft*), a society geared toward "authentic living" through "enjoying real sensations and experiences." Scholars refer in this context to the "aestheticization of everyday life."[55] Such experiences are enormously varied: the relaxing exertions of a journey on foot through Provence and the respite of an oasis of green in one's own back garden, side-by-side with the excitement of Bungee-jumping in an

55. G. Schulze, *Die Erlebnisgesellschaft: Kultursoziologie der Gegenwart* (Frankfurt/New York: Campus Verlag, 1992). See also W. Welsch, *Ästhetisches Denken* (Stuttgart: Reclam, 1990); "Ästhetisierungsprozesse: Phänomene, Unterscheidungen, Perspektiven," *Deutsche Zeitschrift für Philosophie* 41 (1993): 7–29.

Australian Canyon and the exhilarating anticipation of a one-night-stand on a tropical island.

When meaning and experience are joined together, it goes without saying that the experiential dimension of religion and religiosity also becomes more prominent. For many people today, the word "religiosity" implies in the first instance "religious feelings" or "religious attitudes." In the same way, "spirituality," conceived of as the being "moved" by something beyond us, has gained an enormous popularity, both inside and outside the boundaries of recognized faith communities. This might be illustrated in the context of the Catholic Church by spiritual movements in line with the *Chemin Neuf* community or Jean Vanier's *L'Arche*. The demand for and supply of spirituality outside the Christian communities, however, has enjoyed spectacular growth.

In our current European culture, after the all-encompassing common Christian horizon of understanding has fallen away, an appeal to "religious experience" seems to many to be a final possibility to bring the Christian narrative back into discussion. Holistic experiences of depth, harmony, all-embracing unity, etc., very often lie at the basis of a very general religiosity that frequently acquires concrete form in neo-religious spiritualities or movements in which disparate fragments from older traditions are selectively rehabilitated. It is tempting — in a modern correlation dynamics — to rethink Christian faith in terms of these experiences as something that reveals and explains the deeper layers of these experiences.[56] One has to admit, however, that the Christian faith experience probably does not lend itself to this purpose, presenting rather a distinct experience, which places these movements and spiritualities — as well as its own identity — under critical scrutiny. The Christian narrative of Jesus Christ does not only speak of a God who easily reconciles and who binds in harmonious love. It also speaks of the God of apocalyptic judgement, the God who interrupts time and undermines every endeavor — whether Christian or not — to be self-reliant. It speaks of a God who likewise calls us to be engaged in interrupting those instances in which the least of God's people are despised and oppressed.[57]

The following testimony might serve as a paradigmatic illustration of the productive experience of interruption. Some years ago, during a morning radio show, a woman spoke of an encounter she had had the

56. This represents one of the points of departure for chapter 7.
57. This aspect is further developed in chapter 9.

evening before. As part of a church movement working for a multi cultural society, she was invited by a Moroccan community in a suburb of Brussels to celebrate the "breaking of the fast" with them. The community in question had the practice of holding open house every evening of Ramadan at sundown. The woman recounted that the conversation at table soon took on a profound sense of meaningfulness, certainly when religious themes such as the importance of "fasting" and the relationship between Muslims and Christians were being discussed. During the conversation, the woman was struck by the fact that similarities between Islam and Christianity, with respect to fasting for example, tended also to underline the differences between the two faiths. The encounter did not lead to a relativizing "it all boils down to the same thing in the end," but rather to a respectful recognition of difference and self-worth. The woman then went on to describe how the Christians began to question themselves about the seriousness of their own faith: did they, for example, experience their own fasting as something authentic? Could they explain, for example, what it was about from their own lived experience? Should they not invest more in living up to the specificity of their own faith? And how could this be done then in a relevant and plausible way for today? She concluded that her meeting with the Muslim community was ultimately an unexpected wake-up call.[58] Respect for the irreducible identity of one's own Christian narrative and for the otherness of different religions and other fundamental life options can thus go together — what is more, the encounter made this woman reconsider her own identity and its importance precisely through this encounter with another religion. The experience of the woman in the radio interview can rightly be described as an experience of the productive interruption of one's own Christian narrative by the narrative of the other. Such experiences challenge Christians to reshape and reprofile their faith in a God who is revealed in history and is concerned with history.

58. Taken from Boeve, *Interrupting Tradition*, pp. 97–98.

Chapter Five

The Sacramental Interruption of the Rites of Passage

In addition to religious experience, rituals and religious practices are also significantly present in the contemporary context. Human beings would appear to have rediscovered themselves as ritual beings, beings who structure life through ritualization and give concrete form to life's more profound aspects via all sorts of religious and non-religious practices. Our personal behavior, be it conscious or unconscious, is to a significant degree ritualized behavior. This extends from daily habits — such as getting up in the morning, making coffee, showering, brushing our teeth, getting dressed, reading the morning paper at the breakfast table, the way we do the washing up (first the glasses, then the cutlery . . .), shake hands or kiss when we meet someone or say goodbye — to more complex ritualization — such as the organization of family get-togethers, swearing an oath when we take on an official function in society, academic commencement ceremonies, and so forth. Such rituals are pre-given, provide structure to our existence, create possibilities, and establish boundaries. Rituals live in and from the dynamic interplay between possibilities and boundaries. In the same way that a story is never told in exactly the same way twice, rituals create history and undergo history. The awareness that we are to a considerable degree ritualized beings also functions at the level of religion and other fundamental life options, and concerns the way we deal with important transitions and events in life. The classic Christian rites of passage (baptism, communion, marriage, funeral) appear to have survived the dramatic decline in institutional religious practice, while at the same time new rituals have emerged in both the personal and social existence of many. Rituals have emerged spontaneously in places and instances in which they never existed before (often including elements from existing rituals). Striking examples include the rituals surrounding disaster (the attack on the Twin Towers), the death of important people (Princess Diana, John Paul II), shocking events (racist killings, etc.).

This awareness has ultimately led to the discipline of "Ritual Studies," the interdisciplinary, intercultural, (often comparative) anthropological study of the way in which human beings are shaped by rituals and are inclined to ritualize.[1] In the present chapter we will endeavor to demonstrate that a contemporary theological reflection on rituals and sacraments cannot deny the importance of such anthropological research. At the same time (and more than before), however, our reflection must bear in mind the Christian specificity of sacramental practice, which cannot be reduced to Ritual Studies. We will argue that the latter need not imply the withdrawal of theology from interdisciplinary (and interreligious) dialogue. In fact we will argue that the contrary is the case!

The pastoral situation in which the classic rites of passage have survived provides an interesting case for further exploration. The rituals in question share in the effects of detraditionalization, and participation on the part of the population as a whole has declined considerably. At the same time, however, a remarkable number of people, most of whom are not particularly active in terms of church involvement or consciously committed to their faith in one way or another, still participate in these rituals. Research has shown that the motivation for this participation tends to be enormously varied, and only a minority associate it explicitly with the Christian narrative.[2] In what way should theologians include this reality in their reflection? How can theologians find support in this reality and thereby provide the Christian faith with a contemporary face? What might the ancient adage *lex orandi lex credendi* mean in this situation? Does this evolution bear witness to a new religiosity that might serve as a new locus for theology? Alternatively, does it bear witness to the continued advance of secularization whereby the Christian narrative is reduced to a mere narrative reduplication? What is the most appropriate analysis to be applied at this juncture? What lessons can we learn for both systematic and pastoral theology?

We will begin this reflection with a critical discussion of an article in which Edward Schillebeeckx outlines the contours of a new

---

1. Cf., for example, C. M. Bell, *Ritual: Perspectives and Dimensions* (New York: Oxford University Press, 1997); R. L. Grimes, *Deeply into the Bone: Re-Inventing Rites of Passage* (Berkeley: University of California Press, 2000).
2. Cf. below.

sacramentology.[3] We will then discuss the problems associated with this new sacramentology based on an analysis of the current context. As we noted in the preceding pages, it is important to distinguish between an analysis that takes place in terms of secularization and an analysis in terms of detraditionalization and pluralization. A theology rooted in the latter analysis requires an adapted methodology whereby it is able to conceptualize the paradox of interruption and contextual continuity/discontinuity side-by-side.

1. Schillebeeckx and the Problem of Continuity and Discontinuity in the Relationship between Rites of Passage and Sacraments

According to Schillebeeckx, the split between anthropology and theology has resulted in the fact that Christian rituals no longer relate to the day-to-day life of human beings. In this regard, he considers outdated faith representations to be the main cause of people staying away from observing the sacraments. They leave the church because they feel that it is no longer capable of adequately ritualizing their lives. Here Schillebeeckx sets the focus of his new project: how can we understand the sacraments today as radically related to and involved in human life? To answer this question, Schillebeeckx ties into the human (and natural) sciences' study of rituals and rituality (Ritual Studies). Sacraments should therefore be understood first of all in terms of "ritualization." This is an anthropological category which designates that ritual praxis, whether religious or non-religious, is characteristic of human existence and rooted in a complex interplay of bio-physical, socio-biological, psychological, sociological, linguistic, and cultural anthropological patterns. Schillebeeckx thus stresses the structural anthropological necessity of a Christian sacramental praxis. It is as though he wishes to make clear to those who choose to stay away from such praxis that it is only human to ritualize human life and that — when properly understood — being a Christian includes such participation. In particular, however, Schillebeeckx hopes to find in the disciplines of Ritual Studies

3. Cf. E. Schillebeeckx, "Naar een herontdekking van de christelijke sacramenten: ritualisering van religieuze momenten in het alledaagse leven," *Tijdschrift voor theologie* 40 (2000): 164–87. There would appear to be no available English translation of this article. A French translation has appeared as an appendix to E. Schillebeeckx, *L'économie sacramentelle du salut* (Fribourg: Academic Press, 2004), pp. 545–73: "Vers une redécouverte des sacraments chrétiens: Ritualization de moments religieux dans la vie courante."

the categories with which to re-assess sacraments as the ritualization of life. To this end, he is especially taken by the definition that "ritual is performance."

Schillebeeckx thus accentuates the fundamental continuity between the generally human structural need for rituality and Christian sacramental praxis, and warns against excessive discontinuity. He points a critical finger at liturgists and theologians who "often do not show an interest in what rituality 'in general' is, whereas this, as a structural given, could provide a contribution to their quest for the characteristic significance of their particular ritual traditions."[4] According to Schillebeeckx, a sympathetic but critical investigation of the results of anthropological research is indispensable to a proper understanding of what goes on, or should go on, in the sacraments. Such a dialogue between theology and anthropology takes place in a reciprocal critical correlation.[5] It offers theology the possibility to recontextualize itself anew and to adjust the sacramental praxis of the church where necessary. The question remains, however, whether the specific Christian character of the sacraments can indeed be understood and interpreted on the basis of the general structures of ritualizing. In short, what Schillebeeckx is stressing is the irreducible continuity between the human and the Christian. This becomes further evident when Schillebeeckx illustrates his project and offers a definition of what sacramental praxis means in theological terms: "In the sacraments, therefore, there is always a double dimension, an anthropological dimension and a 'theological' dimension directed toward God, that *merge together.*"[6] He makes this statement more explicit as follows: "For Christians, this ritual complex as such is already mediation by God's grace insofar as it is realized in and through the proper performative power of the liturgical deed inspired by Christian belief, and on a cognitive, emotional, and aesthetic level."[7] Taking insights from Ritual Studies and processing them theologically, the sacraments can then, according to Schillebeeckx, be interpreted anew as "existential-emotive encounters with God."

To Schillebeeckx's credit, he makes clear that theology and anthropology are linked together in the sacraments. On the one hand, generally (and humanly) speaking, they obey the patterns of ritualizing. At the

4. Schillebeeckx, "Naar een herontdekking," p. 174.
5. Ibid., pp. 175–76.
6. Ibid., p. 183 (italics mine).
7. Ibid., p. 183.

same time, however, they express the specificity of Christian belief and are a pathway toward "encounter with God" and "knowledge of God." What is lacking, however, is a further questioning and reflection on the way in which the ritual and the theological dimensions go together. What is the exact relationship between rituality and sacramentality? The answer to this question is precisely what is most essential today. For Schillebeeckx, sacraments are relevant and valuable because they are rites of passage, ritualizing the everyday life of human beings. While we do not dispute this claim, the question remains nonetheless: what is it precisely that transforms rites of passage, when practiced within Christian narrative communities, into sacraments? Furthermore, how can theologians conceptualize this process in the most opportune way for our current context?

2. A Closer Look at the Problem

My question, then, does not pertain to the structural continuity between "ritualizing" as an anthropological category and Christian sacramental praxis. Similarly, I do not contest the fact that theology profits substantially from interdisciplinary research in this regard. On the contrary, it lies at the very heart of the methodological concept of recontextualization underlying our approach. Furthermore, what Schillebeeckx calls the theological dimension (the relation between God and human beings, their communities, and the world) can only become reflexively clear through an interdisciplinary dialogue with a theological finality. It is always as humans rooted in the complexity of our human language and environments that we speak about God and to God. Furthermore, it is precisely on the basis of such an interdisciplinary dialogue — from the encounter between Christian belief and context — that I am inclined to inquire whether the singular stress placed on the continuity between the two is indeed productive as a theological and pastoral strategy for today.

One might argue that the starting point of Schillebeeckx's reflection is the observation that many (borderline) Catholics no longer participate in the Christian rituals because of outdated faith representations and formulas. One might ask, however, whether one of the most prominent pastoral problems today does not consist in the fact that sacraments and other Christian rituals, especially when they still attract significant participation in terms of numbers, appear to function for many participants as nothing more than rites of passage. In such cases, the theological dimension would appear to have almost completely vanished.[8] Only the anthropological dimension of the sacraments would still appear to function, *de facto* separated from their theological dimension, i.e., mediating the encounter with the God of Jesus Christ. In other words, they function rather in a *post-Christian* way.[9] In part on account of the lack of clear alternatives, it would seem that many continue to participate in the sacraments in order to ritualize their lives but not as a means to encounter God. Many not only (or even not in the first place) distance themselves from Christian faith and sacramental practice on account of obsolete imagery and language but also (and primarily) on account of the processes of detraditionalization that are changing Western European culture and society. In these times of individualization and pluralization, resulting from detraditionalization, Christian identity is no longer automatically presupposed by birth; rather it involves a conscious choice to be Christian. Structurally speaking, identity today is constructed rather than pre-given or inherited. Seen from the purely anthropological need of ritualizing, it would seem then that Christian sacraments are perceived by many participants as available rituals for the celebration of lifecycle passages. Together with other rituals — whether profane or from other religious traditions — they are alternatives from which human beings can choose to ritualize their lives.[10]

Pastorally speaking, therefore, an exclusive stress on continuity is counter-productive. Of course, theologically speaking, the Christian sacraments ultimately strive toward encounter with God. The celebra-

---

8. See, for example, K. Dobbelaere et al., *Verloren zekerheid: De Belgen en hun waarden, overtuigingen en houdingen* (Tielt: Lannoo, 2000), p. 119. In 1967, 52 percent of Flemish people (for Belgians as a whole, 42.9 percent) went to church on a weekly basis; in 1998, this was merely 12.7 percent (Belgium, 11.2 percent). In 1967, 96.1 percent of children in Flanders were baptized; in 1998 it was 73 percent. The 1998 figures for Belgium as a whole are more than 8 percent lower at 64.7 percent. The figures for that portion of the population that still opts to wed in church: for Flanders, 91.8 percent in 1967, 51.2 percent in 1998; for Belgium, 86.1 percent in 1967, 49.2 percent in 1998 (see p. 123). Not everyone who participates in the rituals of the Catholic Church is involved with the church in reality. Many participate in such rituals because of the lack of alternatives outside the church for celebrating major transitional moments in one's life (cf. pp. 117 and 136). While virtually all of the church's "core members" and "middle bracket" participate in church rituals at important moments of transition in their lives, 80 percent of those on the margins of the church and no less than 45 percent of the un-churched (42 percent for baptism and marriage, 48 percent for funerals) also participate.

9. Dobbelaere describes these rites of passage as follows: "They are seen as a means available to the public at large that can be used without any specific preconditions. Their specifically confessional nature is thus neutralized" (K. Dobbelaere et al., *Verloren zekerheid*, p. 124).

10. Karel Dobbelaere's "*à la carte* Catholicism" can certainly be explained along these lines. See K. Dobbelaere, *Het "volk-gods" de mist in? Over de kerk in België. Kerk-zijn in de huidige wereld — 1. Sociologische benadering*(Leuven: Acco, 1988).

tions of life in rites and sacraments situate this life, with its joys and sorrows, its ordinary and extraordinary moments, in a relationship with the God who is revealed in Jesus Christ, and in the ever-repeated confession that it is God's love which is the mystery of our life, of the reality we live in. When Christian life rituals no longer testify to the Christian narrative and the God-oriented dimension, however, they have become functionalized from a theological viewpoint, reduced to the function and relevance they have for human life and social existence. Given the fact that Ritual Studies demonstrates the human need for rituality, to neglect this need would then mean to deny one's bio-psychological and socio-biological roots and endanger one's psychological and social life. If we take this a step further then we might argue that ritualizing one's life has a therapeutic impact. While it is true that for good psychological and social balance ritualizing inevitably has a therapeutic effect, the reverse is not automatically true: those who view rites as merely functional deprive them of their effectiveness, and will never be able to evoke their theological dimension.

The latter is also a lesson to be learnt from anthropology: rituals survive on the basis of their particular "incarnation." Others take this a step further and point to the embeddedness of rituality in tradition, over which participants have no control. As a consequence, those who creatively interfere in their constitution and activity run the risk of destroying their pre-given source of sense and meaning. From a theological perspective, such a radicalization, focusing on the pre-givenness and untouchability of our ritual practice, likewise implies a functionalizing of Christian sacramental praxis. Here too this praxis is exclusively legitimated on the basis of the anthropological maxim that human meaning is always "incarnated" in already constituted rituals and practices.

Such an anthropological functionalizing of Christian ritual practice takes on many forms, in Christian as well as non-Christian circles. This applies to so-called progressive trends which state that "we must create rites because we no longer have (good) examples." It also applies, however, to more conservative tendencies which go on to claim that a ritual is something completely beyond our control, something structuring our lives, to which we do nothing but submit. Both these positions move exclusively from the anthropological necessity of ritual in which they situate the Christian sacramental praxis. In both cases, rituals become practices that function within a general human perspective, within "the" anthropological structure of "the" human being. The Christian narrative framework is then merely a particular filling-in of this structure, a narrative framework that does not really contribute to the core significance and relevance of ritual praxis.

It goes without saying that Schillebeeckx cannot be accused of the functionalization of Christian sacramental praxis. Indeed, he explicitly focuses attention on the theological, God-oriented dimension and develops this on the basis of his Jesus research. One is left wondering, however, whether his theological method does not work counterproductively. In addition to his insistence that sacramental praxis should not be alien to our human existence, is his claim that Christians encounter God through human ritualizing sufficiently acknowledged? Can the way in which he combines the anthropological and the theological dimensions ultimately prevent the theological dimension from being forgotten altogether or from being difficult to situate? Indeed, many already consider this theological dimension and its accompanying Christian narrativity as a mere reduplication or narrative filling in of something already present in human terms. This is why the pastoral domain is often faced with questions concerning such rites of passage: must liturgical texts "always" be about God? Must the texts in question come from the Bible only or is it possible to borrow from other sources and traditions?

3. Secularity (the "Generally Human") in a Perspective of Plurality

On this point, our analysis of the problems facing the modern correlation method proves its pertinence once again. In line with many theologians of his generation — both modern and anti-modern — Schillebeeckx engages in the theological endeavor from within the paradigm of secularization. He also interprets the "desecularization hypothesis" (Berger, Cox) from this perspective, namely, from the continuum spanning the extreme of committed "churched" Christians on the one hand to modern secular atheists on the other.[11] New religiosity might incline us to look for a shift in the direction of the first pole and away from the second. Nevertheless, doubts concerning the secularization hypothesis tend to undermine any hope that those who were driven away from the Christian narrative and its community by modernization will almost automatically return to Christianity when they discover that they are

11. Cf. our representation of this continuum in chapter 1, section 4, page 26.

"incurably religious and ritual" — not even if Christianity succeeds in renewing its language of faith, as Schillebeeckx asks (which need not imply that such a request is pointless). It appears to the present author unwise — since it would once again be giving credit to the secularization thesis — to immediately locate the religious renewal again along the "Christianity — modernity" axis, albeit closer to the Christian pole.

The (Western) methodologically atheistic human and natural sciences have an inalienable but nevertheless specific place in the multitude of ways in which we look at life and reality. The secularity within which these sciences function, and which is structurally bound up with Western (and because of globalization, also world) culture, however, no longer has exclusive rights to determine the dynamics of the context to which the Christian narrative is related. Moreover, through the critique brought on by postmodern thinking, the "objective observer position," classically presupposed by science and scientific rationality, has been fundamentally questioned and the hermeneutical circles in which they operate have been unraveled. Nonetheless, in a multiplicity of models and theories they remain constitutive for the way in which Westerners, including the Christians among them, have their outlook on life — not least because they have obtained an almost irrefutable legitimation through their effectiveness and performance.[12] This is why the sciences (in their development[13]) remain of enduring importance for a theology that recontextualizes itself. As we have already noted, however, the context is no longer to be interpreted in terms of secularity alone, nor should the role of the sciences still be conceived of in terms of the secularization thesis.

It follows, therefore, that precisely because the current context denotes itself better in terms of plurality than secularity (and the Christian narrative is then seen as one tradition within this plurality), the most relevant theological question no longer appears to be: how can the Christian tradition be productively involved in a dialogue with modern secularity, resulting in a relevant and plausible modern Christian way of existence? Rather, the question should be: how does the Christian narrative relate to the plurality of religious and non-religious fundamental life options? As

---

12. Cultural sociologist Rudi Laermans (K.U. Leuven) has pointed out in this regard that the modernization process has gone hand in hand with a "proto-professionalization" of the life-world. Popularized scientific knowledge is absorbed and results in a medicalization, juridicalization, psychologization, etc., of the life-world.

13. See, in this regard, Schillebeeckx's reference to the development from a static to a dynamic creative anthropology of ritual and ritualizing. In the former, rites were considered as "not generating" but originating from an irretrievable "grey past" as a result of which ritual creativity was a contradiction in terms (Schillebeeckx, "Naar een herontdekking," p. 169).

we mentioned above,[14] it is significant at this juncture to speak of both an inner and an outer perspective: respectively, the discovery *ad extra* of one's particularity and the examination *ad intra* of what the new pluralistic context, in confrontation with other particularities, means for the development of one's particular narrativity. Even if modern theology did differentiate these dimensions, it clearly did not take them to be essential. The *ad intra* dimension was understood to be the same as the *ad extra* dimension: Christianity allowed itself to be criticized and enriched by secular culture, and thereby become (or remain) acceptable and relevant within the same secular culture. Expressed in modern categories: the particularity of Christianity was formulated in such a way that it became perfectly plausible to, and could even be considered a pre-eminent expression of, the modern person, culture, and society. Not only continuity but also discontinuity, however, can be made productive as a theological category in both dimensions. We already noted too, nevertheless, that thinking in terms of discontinuity alone also endangers the bond between tradition and context that is so essential for the Christian faith.

4. Reassessing Theological Method

Thinking in terms of continuity or even consensus between Christian faith and modern culture and society is no longer plausible, nor does it function effectively in the pastoral domain. When one starts from general human structures, it becomes very difficult to arrive at what is particularly Christian — if one has not already identified the latter with the former. Engaging in theology in a postmodern context, however, does not mean that we should abandon dialogue with the context and, in particular, with the human sciences. Nevertheless, as Schillebeeckx himself has pointed out, it is fitting for the theologian "to be extremely critical from the hermeneutical perspective, and to have a critical eye for what the ethno-anthropological discussion concerning the Christian-specific sacramental inheritance has actually integrated in terms of theological perspectives."[15] Scientific perspectives also function on the basis of presuppositions and paradigms. In the meantime it would serve theology's cause well if it would learn *not to postpone* the theological dimension in its reflection, in the hope that it will be arrived at, as if automatically, through dialogue with the human sciences. Those who place their

14. Cf. chapter 3.
15. Schillebeeckx, "Naar een herontdekking," p. 175.

hopes in such continuity today will be disappointed. The consciousness of the specific particularity of the Christian faith places the faith option of the Christian, the confession that God is involved in human history in Jesus Christ, at the forefront both anthropologically and theologically. Although Christians are human beings (like other human beings), it is this confession that irreducibly qualifies this being human at one and the same time. We do not live according to general human structures, but according to our concrete particularities (in which these structures *a posteriori* can be recognized). As stated above: it is not as human beings that we are Christians but as Christians that we are human beings, irreducibly determined by our own narrativity (just as others are likewise human in their irreducible particularity). We are left with the need to develop patterns of reflection that permit us to conceptualize this irreducible qualification, and it is precisely in this regard that dialogue with the present-day context can also prove to be productive.

To quote the twentieth-century Dutch Protestant theologian Harry Kuitert, "Everything that comes from above, comes from below." From our perspective, this phrase, which can be applied to Schillebeeckx's argumentation, would be better articulated as follows: "everything that concerns itself with what comes from above, comes from below," or "all speech concerning the above, proceeds from below." How should we view the relationship between "from above" and "from below"? Which categories might suit our purposes in this regard? Once again we suggest that the relationship can best be conceptualized in terms of "interruption."

5. Sacramental Interruption of Rites of Passage

The maintenance of a perspective of continuity in our present-day context is tantamount to a celebration of modern secularization, particularly the secularization of the revealed character of the Christian belief in the name of general human religiosity — the human being as a religious animal. In such an instance, revelation can only be thought of as a particular reduplication of what already exists on the generally human level, or as a narrative interpretation thereof. Theologically speaking, however, this is not convincing. For Christian men and women, revelation points primarily to their embeddedness in a relationship with the God who is revealed in history through Jesus Christ. This implies that Christians are involved in a responsive relationship with God, with an Otherness that cannot be reduced to one's own subjectivity (but note: an Otherness that cannot be approached or encountered without one's own subjectivity). This ultimately represents theology's point of departure. Theological dialogue with the context is an endeavor to understand, reflect upon, and explain this relationship.

Our research hypothesis relates thought patterns involving discontinuity with patterns of continuity. This hypothesis rests on the conviction that the stark prioritization of the one over the other is both theologically and pastorally unproductive. The category of interruption can render considerable service in this regard; interruption does not simply imply breach, rupture, or discontinuity opposed to every form of continuity, rather it ultimately presupposes continuity. Interruption always "interrupts" something that continues after the interruption. At the same time, the said continuation is often challenged in the process of interruption, influenced by it, transformed, enriched, taken to greater depths, etc. Interruption also points to the limits of continuity and puts them into perspective. Interruption occurs where discontinuity and continuity encounter one another.

In light of what we have said so far, we provide some indications for further discussion. Once again we take Schillebeeckx's article as our point of departure. In addition to the discernment of a twofold continuity in the sacramental rites of passage, we can also speak of a twofold discontinuity.

1. We begin with the twofold continuity. (a) The first form of continuity is situated in the *anthropological* basis of Christian-ritual praxis, in the aspect of "ritualizing human life" that can be recognized in each sacrament. In this sense, Christian sacramental praxis meets the requirements of what in general anthropological terms is called ritualization. (b) Within this dimension of anthropological continuity we can also discern a Christian, narrative *theological* continuity. Sacraments are completely rooted in the Christian particularity; they are not only expressions of the latter, they are also constitutive thereof. They speak of a God who has revealed Godself in the history of humankind, most fully in the person of Jesus, confessed as the Christ by his disciples. As situated rituals, they incarnate the realization of meaning that takes place through the Christian narrative, and they constitute a specifically Christian symbolical space.

2. This twofold continuity, however, is in need of interruption; otherwise the Christian narrative will become either (a) a mere reduplication or narrative filling-in of the anthropological level, or (b) narrativity for the sake of narrativity — i.e., a closed narrative in which the meaning-giving

reference is trapped within the boundaries of the hermeneutical horizon. At the same time, there is no discontinuity without continuity; otherwise one risks a facile degeneration into escapism. While discontinuity is already present on the anthropological level, inasmuch as rites interrupt and transform everyday life (a celebration, a successful doctoral defense, etc.),[16] the twofold discontinuity that we want to indicate is to be first thought of with reference to Christian narrativity and subsequently (and at the same time) as theological in nature. In the first instance, therefore, we will reflect on the relationship between general human structures and the theological dimension, after which we will move on to theological dimension itself. It is here that the sacramentality of the ritual-liturgical praxis of Christian faith communities is to be situated.

(a) First of all, the Christian narrative interrupts the general human structures that are recognized within it based on the primacy of the particularity. This is best explained from the *ad extra* perspective. Where the generally human points to shared structures and similarities with the Christian narrative, it is often in such similarities that the differences between the various fundamental life options and religious positions become manifest. In short, it is precisely that which different religions and life options have in common that makes them different; or "what binds them, also divides them." Schillebeeckx, for example, locates the source of Easter in an agricultural spring festival.[17] While this may be true for Easter, as a Christian spring festival it nevertheless differs substantively from similar feasts, because it is radically transformed by a non-cyclical perception of history in which history is divinely interrupted. The appreciation of Easter as an originally agricultural feast certainly has the capacity to unlock valuable insights into this Christian feast and perhaps indicate the widespread character of this festal ritual, but it can never automatically refer to the Christian ritual confession that Jesus Christ lives. It is at this point that the Christian particularity gives its own irreducible twist to what are considered to be general human structures. Hermeneutical space opens up a dimension at this juncture without which a sacrament cannot be a sacrament. The same can be said of the practices of prayer, ritual periods (such as periods of fasting), community celebrations, initiations, and so forth. Here too one can claim that what is common to diverse religions makes them at the same time irreducibly distinct.

16. Ibid., p. 183.
17. Cf. ibid., p. 173.

(b) From the theological perspective, the Christian narrative interrupts general human structures, not because the account of these general human structures is untrue or invalid, but because — for Christians — it is not the source upon which the sacraments draw their deepest significance. It is because they speak of God that they are sacraments. Sacramentality is *interruption by God.*

With respect to this theological dimension, Schillebeeckx takes as his point of departure a category that he had already developed in his earlier books on Jesus, namely, the Christian contrast experience: the experience of being confronted with traces of God in one's life, which "are purified into ritual" in sacramental praxis. As contrast experiences, traces of God can be suitably thought of as experiences of otherness, conflict, difference, interpreted against the background of the Christian narrative. Theologically speaking, moreover, such experiences reveal the boundaries of the Christian narrative itself — testifying to God's involvement in human history as its condition and its critical limit. As experiences of otherness, they interrupt ongoing narratives, Christian narratives included. They introduce a God-oriented perspective. God, then, is not thought of exclusively in the first instance as operating within the narrative, but precisely as the One who always escapes this narrative, an escape to which the Christian narrative itself is called to bear witness. The God who interrupts is not a God of premature reconciliation, but on the contrary a God whose trace reveals irreconcilability. Seen from this perspective, recontextualization is not purely an anthropological process characteristic of Christian traditions and narratives, but rather the product of our relationship with the God who inspires our narratives, interrupts them, and yet cannot be captured within them. The same holds true for our sacramental praxis and our reflection on sacramental praxis (for example, on the issue of sacramental presence[18]). Here too, God and God's grace are not tangible or graspable, but are to be thought of in the context of the foundational relationship with the divine Other — a relationship opened within the hermeneutic framework of the Christian narrative, but not reduced to it.[19]

---

18. See L. Hemming on Thomas Aquinas's doctrine of transubstantiation: "After Heidegger: Transubstantiation," in *Sacramental Presence in a Postmodern Context: Fundamental Theological Perspectives,* ed. L. Boeve and L. Leijssen, BETL 160 (Leuven: Peeters Press, 2001), 299–309, pp. 299–303. Thomas preserves Aristotle's physics but at the same time interrupts it, thereby placing it in perspective.

19. See in this regard L.-M. Chauvet, "The Broken Bread as Theological Figure of Eucharistic Presence," in *Sacramental Presence in a Postmodern Context,* ed. Boeve and Leijssen, 236–62.

As incarnations of profound meaning, Christian rituals anchor Christian narrativity in the materiality and corporeality of our human existence. At the same time, they interrupt our human existence rooted in the Christian confession of its creatureliness and the hope of eschatological completion — a confession that in its turn is interrupted by the God it confesses to be the Creator and Savior.

6. Conclusion

We conclude the present chapter with a short summary of its content. We will then briefly return to our discussion with Schillebeeckx found in the two preceding chapters. While differences in methodological perspective are evident, they are grounded nevertheless in the same hermeneutical-theological intuition.

Summary

While these considerations do not pretend to offer ready-made answers to the deep pastoral and theological problems involved in reflecting upon the relationship between rites of passage and sacraments, they may contribute to a clearer perception of the methodological shift to which we have been referring.

It remains our hope, nevertheless, that the reader has acquired some indication of the fundamental theological questions that tend to arise in such a reflection process, of the relative importance for theology of the anthropological and (human) sciences, and of the methodological limits of modern correlation theology when one theologizes in a postmodern context, bearing in mind that it is better to analyze the context in terms of plurality and particularity, than (merely) on the basis of such categories as secularization and general human structures. All these considerations support (and rely on) our research hypothesis: while a current theological reflection on rituals and sacraments cannot deny the importance of anthropological research (or what is collectively known today as Ritual Studies), we must simultaneously (and more than ever before) pay particular attention to the Christian specificity of Christian sacramental praxis. We insist that this does not imply the withdrawal of theology from interdisciplinary (and interreligious) dialogue; it is rather the fruit of such discussion. This shift itself has obliged us to draw the contours of a "theology of interruption" in which continuity is joined to discontinuity and vice versa. Based on the insight that "what binds us, also differentiates us," the phrase "the sacramental interruption of rites of passage" then acknowledges, in the first instance, the irreducibly specific particularity of the Christian ritual praxis, while calling to mind, in the second instance, the theological, God-oriented dimension of this praxis, which can be thought of fittingly as (its) interruption.

Recontextualization of Schillebeeckx's Method, Inspired by Schillebeeckx

The reassessment of the correlation method introduced and illustrated in a variety of ways in the present study may give rise to potential misunderstanding on the part of those who support this modern manner of theologizing, and thereby miss its primary goal.[20] In what follows, we will focus our attention anew and quite explicitly on the differences and similarities between our approach and that of modern correlation theologies and demonstrate that in spite of evident discontinuity there is continuity between both approaches. To be concise, those who take Schillebeeckx's hermeneutical-theological concept of the development of tradition[21] seriously must recontextualize their theological projects — in true *Korrektivtheologie* style.

1. Our first observation in this regard is related to the analysis of the concrete context in terms of detraditionalization together with the theological purpose of such an analysis. For Schillebeeckx, the category of detraditionalization is synonymous with *secularization,* and the present situation challenges Christians to recontextualize the Christian narrative in a secular context: where can the Christian find traces of the God of Jesus Christ in secularity? Schillebeeckx draws particular attention to the so-called "contrast experience" as a means to demonstrate the bond between faith and the secular world. The Christian tradition and faith community are continually called into question by a productive confrontation with the secular context, challenged to justify themselves

20. Schillebeeckx himself presented a critical discussion of *Onderbroken traditie* in "Het gezag van de traditie in de theologie," in *Jezus, een eigentijds verhaal,* ed. M. Bouwens, J. Geel and F. Maas (Zoetermeer: Meinema, 2001), 76–87. He discusses my work as if I contrast tradition "en bloc" with the context and fail to recognize the historical contingency of the said tradition. Critique from anti-modern circles suffers from a similar affliction. See, for example, the commentary offered by the (likewise) Dominican theologian R. Schenk in "*Officium signa temporum perscrutandi*": *New Encounters of Gospel and Culture in the Context of the New Evangelization* and my reaction thereto in the Postscript to my *Beyond the Modern and Anti-modern Dilemma: Theological Method in a Postmodern European Context,* in J. Verstraeten, ed., *Scrutinizing the Signs of the Times and Interpreting Them in Light of the Gospel,* BETL (Leuven: Peeters Press, 2007). Schenk accuses me of the opposite problem, however, namely, that I sacrifice the Christian tradition by forcing it to conform or assimilate to the postmodern context.

21. As presented in *Mensen als verhaal van God* (Baarn: Nelissen, 1989), p. 60.

as potential providers of meaning, as a contemporary response to the questions, crises, and conflicts of the world in which we live. There can be little doubt that the result of this procedure has provided us with one of the finest examples of (late) modern theology, which was justifiably tempting to many. We have already demonstrated why the focus of detraditionalization is broader than that of secularization (since the secularization thesis continues to resound in the background thereof) and that it must be considered today in association with an all-embracing process of pluralization. It is this analysis that constitutes the basis for determining our theological standpoint — and it is here also that critics often miss the point. Indeed, viewed from this perspective, present-day culture can no longer be adequately identified with secularity, with which Christianity is obliged to relate; correlation theologians tend to underline the continuity between faith and world, anti-modern theologians the rupture between the two. For the latter, "our late-modern culture is a source of purely negative aspects" and "the entire Christian tradition past and present *is set in contrast* to contemporary experience." Christian tradition thus becomes a "monolithic counter-culture."[22]

As we have repeatedly argued, however, for those who analyze the current situation in terms of plurality there is no such thing as a singular secular culture to which the Christian faith is obliged to relate (and to the extent that Christians already live in such a culture, they already relate thereto in terms of their experience). Christians today, particularly in the West, are becoming increasingly aware that their Christian faith (as a collective term for a variety of different faith styles) is just one among many in a world of alternative religions and fundamental life options. Confrontation with different positions (Buddhist, Muslim, atheist, etc.) not only challenges Christians to question themselves and engage in dialogue, it also — and immediately — goes hand in hand with a (re)discovery and a (re)profiling of one's own particular position. This does not imply — as some have wrongly suggested — that the tradition is adopted once again *en bloc* and unrevised, and then repositioned over and against the others. Rather, it is precisely at this juncture that the *confrontation with plurality and otherness sets the process of recontextualization in motion.* The question of the uniqueness of Jesus, confessed as the Christ, changes when it is no longer (only) the Jesus of history who enters into the theological discussion forum, but also the truth claims of

22. Paraphrase of Schillebeeckx's words in "Het gezag van de traditie in de theologie," pp. 80 and 84.

other religions and fundamental life options.[23] Understood as such, the Christian faith is clearly not a "counter-culture," but it is also no longer to be identified as a mere partner of an essentially secular culture.

2. It is for this reason that we insist that those who employ Schillebeeckx's hermeneutical method today must radicalize it, because our context has radically changed. Indeed, the modern correlation method is highly contextual and ought to be reassessed from a postmodern perspective. It would be a mistake, therefore, to continue interpreting the position elaborated in the present study along the classical "anti-modern — modern" axis. This axis tends to exaggerate the contrast between tradition and human responsibility/creativity, between the acceptance of authority and the autonomous determination of personal identity, etc. Such antitheses are outdated. It is not a question of "either... or" but rather "both... and." Those engaged today in the search for traces of the God of Jesus Christ would be best advised to do so against the explicit background of the complex and multiform whole that is referred to as the Christian tradition. Christians today who engage in reflection on autonomy, responsibility, and creativity, in the experience of which they infer traces of God, confess the "gift" character of these three values rooted in their faith in creation. The latter's faith is not diminished in the process; rather it is enriched with a sense of perspective, content, and promise.

3. A final consideration is related to the place of the tradition and the faith community in theology. For Schillebeeckx, tradition would appear to be a unified conglomeration of truths and practices handed down to us from the past and thus not in the first instance (although not excluded as a possibility) an historical-particular reality that continues to function in the present. One might indeed argue that tradition and church still tend to exude paternalism and alienation, lack of liberty and authoritarian power structures, etc. It goes without saying that the tradition's most vulnerable and enriching dimensions run the greatest risk of perversion. In the last analysis, however, those who belong to the Christian tradition and the Christian community bear witness to the fact that Christians are already in a responsive relationship with God — although they may not be fully aware of how and indeed where they should listen to God. Insofar as tradition and community (sacramentally) mediate this relationship, they make it clear that being human is a gift (and as such also a task). People do not generate their own identity *ex nihilo*: autonomy,

23. Cf. chapter 8.

responsibility, and creativity are gifts. Tradition and the church community bear witness to the God with whom they form a relationship. This need not imply that tradition and church must be accepted *en bloc,* take it or leave it. On the contrary, it is for this reason that a continuing methodical hermeneutics is absolutely essential — precisely because of their sacramental character. It is, e.g., not because the over-exclusive link between the determination of the truths of faith and the Vatican magisterium has been called into question and subjected to criticism that the faith community no longer has a role to play in the search for the said truth — once again, there is no "either ... or." The personal search for one's faith identity is given form by tradition in community, contributes to both, and is also subject to their critique. Tradition and community are not obstacles in the search, but rather the anthropological and theological precondition thereof. In the postmodern context, Christians continue to inherit and bequeath, the latter being impossible without the former. Bearing this in mind, we would therefore argue that those who still wish to put Schillebeeckx's hermeneutical-theological concerns into practice must radicalize his hermeneutical theology on account of the changed context to which Schillebeeckx himself was responsible for drawing our attention.

Chapter Six

Narratives of Creation and Flood

A Contest between Science and Christian Faith?

Religious revival and the critique of modern, often scientific rationality are also evident on other fronts. Indeed, for some the relationship between religion and the natural sciences is once again open to debate. Discussion on matters such as creationism and intelligent design is rooted in the incapacity to ascribe an independent place to the specific way in which the methodologically atheistic sciences inform us about ourselves as human beings and the world in which we live. At the same time, scientism, which imposes an atheistic fundamental life option on the basis of the methodological atheism of the sciences and reduces religion to genes or memes,[1] has not disappeared. In its turn, however, this approach has been unable to ascribe a place to the specificity of the religious discourse. In the present chapter, we will explore this thoroughly modern debate. It will become evident that thinking in terms of difference rather than harmony or opposition can be a potentially productive alternative.[2]

---

1. See, for example, the application of "Darwin's dangerous idea" on culture and the generation of meaning by the neo-Darwinian Daniel Dennet: just as genetic vicissitudes explain biological evolution, Dennet argues for the existence of "memes" to explain cultural evolution. Cf. D. Dennet, *Darwin's Dangerous Idea: Evolution and the Meanings of Life* (London: Penguin, 1995). Dennet also applies his arguments to the phenomenon of religion in *Breaking the Spell: Religion as a Natural Phenomenon* (New York: Penguin, 2006).

2. In 2005, the Department of Geology at the Catholic University of Leuven organized a high-profile exhibition entitled "Life in Stone" (cf. *www.artesleuven.be/site2006/en/leveninsteen.htm*). With a display of fossils varying from four billion to ten thousand years old, the exhibition told the story of life on our planet. At the opening of the exhibition, the organizers explicitly referred to the rise of creationism and intelligent design theories severely criticizing the scientific value of the theory of evolution. On the same occasion, a book was published in which the emergence and evolution of life on our planet was explained and illustrated from a variety of different approaches within the domain of the natural sciences. Because of the creationism-evolution debate the organizers of the exhibition explicitly wanted to involve a theologian in their discussion. The present contribution offers a chronicle of our involvement in the debate.

1. Creation or Evolution?

Giant Oysters in the Andes

From time to time, geologists discover fossils of aquatic animals at great altitudes, or in layers of sediment or sand deposits. Scientific explanations tend in this regard to point to the collisions between the continental plates that caused mountain ranges to rise up out of the oceans, thereby illustrating why it is possible for fossils of giant oysters to be discovered at an altitude of 4000 meters, high in the Andes Mountains (200 million years old). Alternatively, they presuppose that floods took place 500 million years ago in which octopuses were trapped under massive amounts of sand and ultimately fossilized, thus explaining why digs in Wisconsin can reveal traces of such invertebrates 500 million years later.

A website entitled *Answers in Genesis*, intent on "respecting the authority of the bible from the first verse to the last," offers an alternative explanation, however. The surprising presence of fossils of aquatic animals high in the Andes is the result of a global flood over which the bible speaks in the book of Genesis chapters 6–9: "Noah was six hundred years old when the flood of waters came on the earth . . . all the fountains of the great deep burst forth and the windows of the heavens were opened. . . . The waters swelled so mightily on the earth that all the high mountains under the whole heaven were covered with water. . . . And all flesh died that moved on the earth, birds, domestic animals, wild animals, all swarming creatures that swarm on the earth, and all human beings. . . . Only Noah was left, and those who were with him in the ark" (from Gen. 7:6–24 — NRSV). The Bible not only explains why so many aquatic animals are to be found in silt deposits and sedimentary layers but also why they are to be found at such an altitude. According to the same website, we read in the eighth verse of Psalm 104 that after the flood "the mountains rose up and the valleys declined." The entire process, therefore, is not the result of evolution over a period of millions of years but rather a relatively recent event that took place roughly forty-three hundred years ago. The website concludes, "So next time you hear of fossilized aquatic organisms high above sea level, you can confidently say, 'Yes! Yet more evidence that all the world was once covered with water in a global Flood, not millions of years ago but relatively *recently* — just as the Bible says.' "[3]

---

3. Quoted from the website: *http://answersingenesis.org/creation/v24/i2/oysters.asp* (accessed January 1, 2007).

Another website, appropriately entitled *The Evolution Irritation Site*, offers the following brief explication concerning the flood:

> The Flood was more than just bad weather! The cloud/water-covering over the whole Earth came down and all the "waters which were under the earth" erupted in great fountains. (There is evidence of this along the floor of the Pacific Ocean, but that's another subject!). Within 40 days an unimaginable amount of water forcefully moved into place and then only slightly slower drained to its present locations. It's not far-fetched to assume that most of the animal & plant life wasn't just drowned but swept about, along with tons of rock and soil, and in many places formed great piles and were covered by countless tons of debris, thus forming today's land-based oil fields. Neither is it unreasonable to understand how this massive movement of water could account for many unique things we see today, not the least of which is the Grand Canyon! This would all make a great disaster movie with computer graphics stretched to their limits! But it is a far better example of a scientific theory than Evolution! It takes into account as much information as is available, it puts it all together in a justifiable scenario and it doesn't contradict any laws of physics or nature. You'll see in some of the following examples, that the drastic effects of the Flood explain away a lot of minor points that evolutionists use to claim that the Earth is not 6,167 years old. Sorry, they can't even stretch it to 10,000! The Bible is not a science book, but when it deals with science (geology, archaeology, etc.) it is accurate.[4]

Is the Earth Young or Old?

The use of fossils as evidence for the truth of the bible is only one way in which creationists promote the biblical creation narrative as a reliable explanation of the beginnings of the world in contrast to conventional geological and biological evolutionary theory. The world as we know it is not the product of an evolution that took place over a few million years; rather it was created by God between six and ten thousand years ago. According to creationists, the "young earth theory" is no less scientific than what they call the "old earth fiction." On the contrary, all the presuppositions of evolutionary theory are unmasked either as hypotheses that cannot be substantiated or as falsifications, or are undermined on the basis of counter examples or alternative explanations. Reference

4. Quoted from: *http://home.pages.at/slush/evol/youngeart.htm* (accessed January 1, 2007).

is made, for example, to the accelerated processes of fossilization (the earth need not be as old as is commonly argued to support the creation of fossils); to the many presuppositions or interpretations evident in the theory of evolution that continue to lack genuine substantiation (such as the "missing links" in the biological theory of evolution); to the contingency margins related to the so-called C14 carbon dating method that ultimately make its results implausible. . . .

Moreover, creationists not only defend the "young earth theory" with reference to so-called scientific arguments, they also appeal to the fact that creation and flood narratives occur in several cultures all around the world. While errors may have found their way into the majority of the said narratives down through the centuries, the biblical story still offers a reliable representation of the origins of the earth.

Although there are various different kinds of creationist, all share the common conviction that the physical beginnings of the earth can be traced back to a creative deed on the part of God. Where some creationists will take the biblical narrative very literally ("young earth" creationists), others allow for a degree of flexibility and accept that the six days of creation may be metaphors for a significantly longer period of time ("old earth" creationists), and in some instances leave considerable space for evolutionist ideas ("theistic evolutionists"). Some of the latter group translate the belief in a creator God into the proposition that the world was given form according to some kind of "intelligent design," arguing that complexity at the micro level (cell biology) and macro level (cosmology) is so enormous that it could not have come about on the basis of "accidental" evolution. The first group — the "young earth" creationists — is commonly identified with "creationism" as such and is most vocal in the United States.[5]

The discussion instigated by the Viennese Cardinal Schönborn in the *New York Times* on July 7, 2005, however, demonstrates that the relationship between creation and evolution is also a source of tension elsewhere. The cardinal suggested that accidental evolution could not be reconciled with faith in a creator God and, so doing, was immediately declared a protagonist of intelligent design.[6] The Vatican's senior astronomer reacted promptly, reminding the public of the declaration of the International Theological Commission of 2004 on human persons

---

5. For more links and information see *www.talkorigins.org*.

6. For more information on intelligent design see, for example, L. Witham, *By Design: Science and the Search for God* (San Francisco: Encounter Books, 2003).

created in the image of God.[7] Under the leadership of the then Cardinal Ratzinger, the Commission insisted that there was "no incompatibility between God's providential plan and the results of a genuinely contingent evolutionary process in nature."[8]

Rival Theories Concerning the Beginning

For creationists, the entire discussion with the proponents of evolutionary theory is not simply a matter of "biased religious creationists" *versus* "objective scientific evolutionists." Rather, it is an ideological struggle, the defense of the Christian image of the human person and the world against the prejudices of secular humanism. For creationists, two radically different interpretations of the same scientific data are at stake. According to some, evolutionary theory is an atheistic conspiracy against the Judaeo-Christian belief in creation. It is for this reason that a number of US states have included creationism side by side with evolutionary theory on their high school curricula.

However, one may legitimately pose the question whether it is correct to reduce the whole discussion to a black and white choice between evolution and creation, between a reality with or without God. Are we obliged to choose between a "godless" world that has been left to its own devices and to the vagaries of accidental evolution, on the one hand, and, on the other, a world intended by a supernatural God, created according to God's plan? It is true that some defenders of the theory of evolution also approach this debate from an analogously polarizing perspective. For them, the scientific theory of evolution has become an argument against belief in God, and scientific evolutionary thinking offers — so they claim — sufficient grounds to justify an atheistic materialist worldview.

Debates of this sort between rival declarations run the risk of descending into little more than a pointless game of "yes it is" — "no it isn't." One example of this game is the search for the so-called "religious gene." If the gene that is responsible for the human person's religious sensitivity can be isolated and — as a consequence — be removed, some maintain, religion would cease to have a future because it would have been proven

7. Cf. *www.vatican.va:* International Theological Commission, *Communion and Stewardship: Human Persons Created in the Image of God,* released on July 23, 2004.

8. Cf. George Coyne, "God's Chance Creation," in *The Tablet,* August 6, 2005, 6–7, p. 6. Coyne implicitly alludes to §69 of the ITC declaration: "it is important to note that, according to the Catholic understanding of divine causality, true contingency in the created order is not incompatible with a purposeful divine providence. Divine causality and created causality radically differ in kind and not only in degree."

that religion, like so many other things, is simply genetic. Opponents of this approach, on the other hand, argue that, even if such a gene were to be located, it would not necessarily substantiate the claim that religion is a genetically determined illusion. Indeed, who could have placed a gene responsible for human religious sensitivity in the human genome? A game of "yes" and "no" with no way out.

2. Christian Faith and Science: Three Models

The question remains, therefore: must we choose between evolution or creation? Is science an argument against faith in God and religion? Are they competing theories, each other's rivals? What we know for sure is that since the emergence of the sciences, ideas on the relationship between the Christian faith and science have been the source of considerable commotion.[9]

In the modern period, Christian faith found itself not infrequently at loggerheads with the sciences and in particular the natural sciences. After an exhaustive and lengthy learning process, Christian theology — and, following in the latter's footsteps, magisterial utterances — discovered the specific uniqueness of the scientific discourse and the uniqueness of the discourses of faith and theology.[10] From the historical perspective, we can distinguish three models that have been employed to conceptualize the relationship between faith and science.[11]

---

9. For a general introduction see, for example, A. E. McGrath, *Science and Religion: An Introduction* (Oxford: Blackwell, 1999); see also W. B. Drees, *Religion, Science and Naturalism* (Cambridge: Cambridge University Press, 1996); J. Wentzel van Huyssteen, *Duet or Duel? Theology and Science in a Postmodern world* (London: SCM, 1998).

10. In the encyclical *Humanae generis*, which appeared on August 12, 1950, Pius XII, for example, still continued for the most part to uphold the historicity of the biblical creation narrative, particularly the notion of monogenism (humanity can be traced back to one single set of parents), in an effort to secure the theological notion of original sin. As a matter of fact, he even went as far as to forbid research into the notion of polygenism by Catholic academics. Cf. G. Minois, *L'église et la science: Histoire d'un malentendu. II. De Galilée à Jean-Paul II* (Paris: Fayard, 1991), p. 366: "Monogenism is the only theory which is in accord with the dogma of original sin, a personal sin committed by Adam. What is even worse is that the pope in this case forbids Catholic academics to continue their research in the direction of polygenism. A theory which already possesses a significant degree of truth is declared *a priori* false because it would contradict a religious truth" (translation ours). A little further, from p. 370 onwards, Minois provides details of the resistance of the Catholic authorities to the ideas of Teilhard de Chardin.

11. For an alternative account see, for example, I. Barbour, *Myths, Models and Paradigms: A Comparative Study in Science and Religion* (San Francisco: Harper and Row, 1976, repr. 1991).

The Harmony Model: The Metaphor of the Two Books

In the theology of the Middle Ages, in part under the influence of Bonaventure, the metaphor of the two books was employed to give shape to the relationship between faith and nature, and between theology and the natural sciences (not yet the modern natural sciences). "The will of God can be read in the book of nature *and* in the Sacred Scriptures. Given that God [as Creator of heaven and earth] is the author of both the book of nature and the Sacred Scriptures [as revelation of God], conflict or contradiction is in principle out of the question. [. . .] Knowledge concerning nature and the heavenly bodies fits into an all-embracing synthesis."[12] God is not only the highest fulfillment of the human person, of history and society as a whole; God is not only the end of all human reflection (metaphysics), but also the one who set the entire cosmos in motion and who inspired it with creative energy. Every correct understanding of nature ultimately leads to God as the beginning, the driving force, and the end of all things. Living, thinking, and being all lead to God. Medieval theologians such as Thomas Aquinas envisaged a far-reaching convergence between theology (nourished by revelation) and natural science (nourished by experience [not yet the "empirical experience" from the experiments of modern sciences]), whereby both were presented in a single synthesis. The Ptolemaic and Aristotelian worldviews, which understood movement in the world as being based on underlying causality or causation, were integrated in a Christian theological synthesis. The unmoved mover who ultimately set everything in motion was identified as the biblical God. The various heavenly bodies were animated with spiritual powers (angels) that derived their dynamism from the first mover and in their turn set the lower creatures (the earthly) in motion. The entire cosmos was thus understood as one single thrusting movement from above downwards. The cosmos constituted "a harmonically ordered whole in which all things had their proper place in a universal system of causes and effects. God — the *causa prima* — was the Unmoved Mover [. . .] and the things He set in motion, the heavenly spheres [the seven known planets (including the sun and the moon) above which two or three heavens],

12. J. Van der Veken, *Een kosmos om in te leven: Het nieuwe gesprek tussen kosmologie en geloof* (Kapellen: Pelckmans, 1990), p. 15, with reference to the study of Max Wildiers, *Kosmologie in de westerse cultuur,* Kapellen: Pelckmans/Kampen: Kok Agora, 1988. Wildiers demonstrated in his book how evolutions in worldview, under the influence of modern natural science among other things, partly determined cultural and theological reflection.

are the instruments, the *causae secundae*, which He employs in order to accomplish his will on earth and achieve his plans."[13] Based on such a perspective, it is quite understandable therefore that Thomas Aquinas suggests in his writings that the study of created things, the cosmos, is very useful, illuminating, and even necessary for teaching the faith (*Summa contra Gentiles*, II, 1).[14]

The figure on the following page provides an apposite representation of the harmony model.[15] The earth, God's creation, can be found at the bottom, functioning as the linchpin of a geocentric worldview around which the moon, the sun and the planets revolved. We can observe a threefold division, each with seven subdivisions (three and seven are sacred numbers): the "sublunary" with the four elements — earth, water, air, fire — which are further subdivided in order to arrive at seven (this territory belonged to the material world); the "superlunary," structured according to the seven known "planets" that revolved around the earth: the Moon, Mercury, Venus, the Sun, Mars, Jupiter, and Saturn (this territory belonged simultaneously to the material world, the planets, and to the spiritual world, the powers that drove the planets in perfect circles round the earth); the "celestial" that is structured in the first instance according to the four higher spiritual capacities (will, reason, intellect, and mind), followed by the Trinity: the Holy Spirit, the Word (i.e., the Son, Jesus Christ), and God the Father. The third level is exclusively spiritual, offering us a perspective on God as God is familiar to us. A fourth level can also be seen above the third where God is referred to as God, God as God knows Godself, since God is greater than that which we know of God from revelation and creation. The given cosmological structure is thus in perfect harmony with the God revealed in the bible. Furthermore, the anthropological world, the world of human beings, is also located within the structure. The structure of the macro-cosmos is also the structure of the human person who consists of (a) matter, symbolized here by the lower body, (b) an intermediate level of matter and spirit, represented here by the upper body (with the intestines and the heart as the location of the emotions and the aspirations), and (c) the spiritual level, with the four higher capacities and the location of the encounter with the Triune God.

---

13. See in this regard M. Wildiers, *Kosmologie in de westerse cultuur*, pp. 70–71.

14. Ibid., p. 63.

15. The illustration is borrowed from: *Mores. Pedagogisch tijdschrift voor morele problemen* 42 (1997): 372.

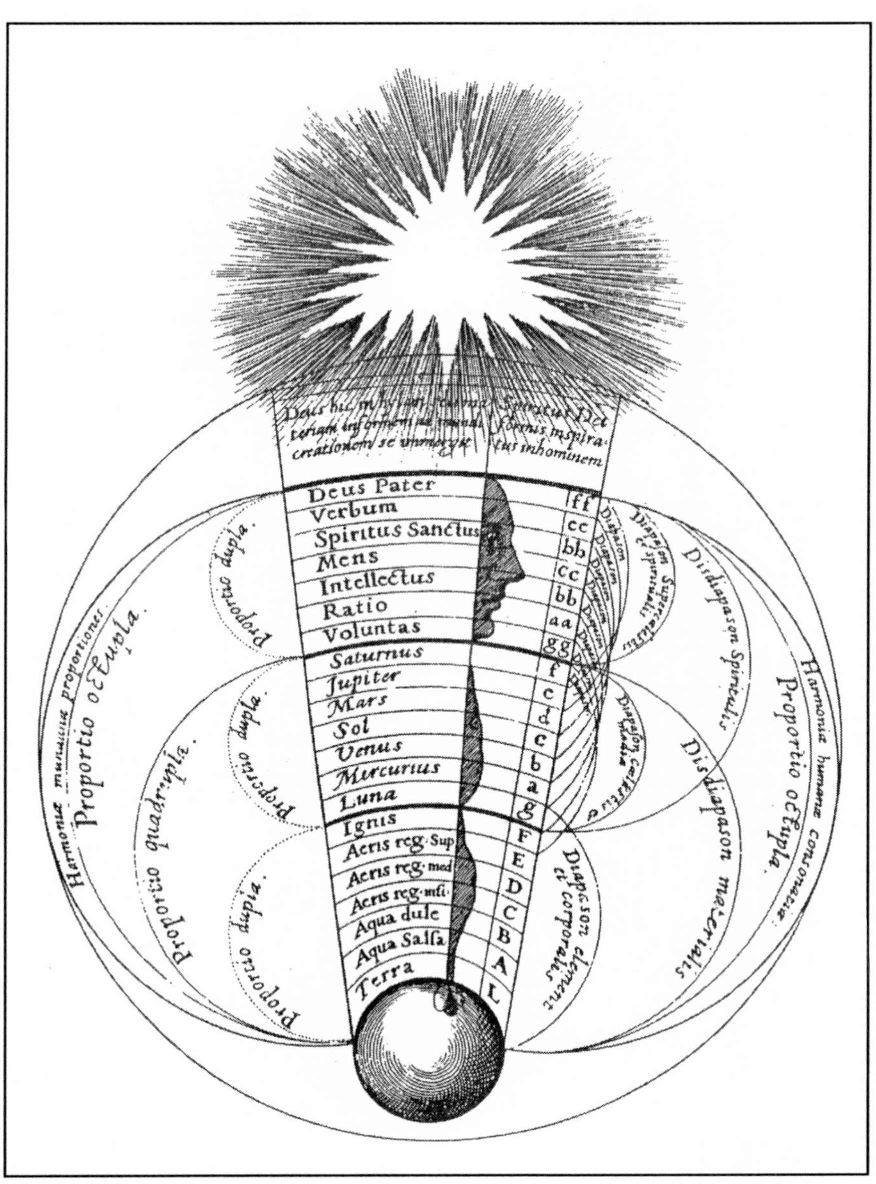
Deus Pater
Verbum
Spiritus Sanctus
Mens
Intellectus
Ratio
Voluntas
Saturnus
Jupiter
Mars
Sol
Venus
Mercurius
Luna
Ignis
Aeris reg. Sup
Aeris reg. med
Aqua dulc
Aqua Salsa
Terra
ff
cc
bb
cc
bb
aa
gg
f
e
d
c
b
a
g
F
E
D
C
B
A
Proportio dupla.
Proportio dupla.
Proportio dupla.
Proportio octupla.
Proportio quadrupla.
Disdiapason Spiritualis
Disdiapason materialis
Proportio octupla.

Transition: Initial Conflicts and the Emergence of Deism

While the emergence of the modern sciences put an end to the medieval synthesis we described above, this did not imply the immediate demise of the harmony model. The condemnation of Galileo Galilei, who defended the heliocentric position maintained by Copernicus, serves to illustrate this fact.[16] The suggestion that the sun no longer revolved around the earth, however, had consequences stretching far beyond the cosmological: it ultimately contravened classical thinking on God and humanity. In the last analysis, Galileo also conceived reality according to the two-book model. The only differing presupposition he started from was that in matters of dispute, one should no longer consider the bible (revelation) to be the norm but rather the natural sciences, since the book of nature was written in a much clearer manner, according to mathematical patterns. The bible, however, was frequently obscure. Moreover, Galileo maintained that the bible was not in the first instance about "the course of the heavens" but rather about "how one gets into heaven."

Other natural scientists were likewise not inclined to exclude God immediately from their understanding of the cosmos. While they may no longer have given God a "localizable" place in the scientific worldview, scientists such as Isaac Newton nevertheless envisaged God's hand behind the laws of nature that had been discovered and mathematically established. To an increasing degree, they were able to combine a mechanical worldview with belief in God. For them, God was the one who first pressed the button of the world as we know it, after which this God withdrew and the mechanism of the world continued to function. The Deistic God was the great architect of the world, the divine watchmaker (Voltaire). On closer inspection, however, Deism continues to fit within the harmony model, to be distinguished nevertheless from the classical medieval variant thereof since faith no longer constitutes the starting point (the harmonization of our knowledge of nature with what is given in biblical revelation) but precisely the opposite: belief in God is made to fit within the results of the new natural sciences.

It is worth mentioning as an aside that many people at the beginning of the nineteenth century accepted the thesis of the mechanistic worldview

---

16. For the transitional role of the "Galileo Galilei case," cf. J. Van der Veken, *Een kosmos om in te leven*, pp. 15ff: "The myth of the conflict between faith and science." In 1992 Pope John Paul II reinstated Galileo Galilei (1564–1642, condemned in 1633) after three and a half centuries.

in one form or another, among them Deists, many Christian believers, and many unbelievers. Deists and unbelievers were thus able to exclude God from history (the cosmos at work); believers, however, envisaged miracles as supernatural interventions on the part of God against the natural laws of the mechanistic cosmos. Indeed, for many believers such miracles were evidence of the correctness of Christian teaching (in more or less the same way as experimentally acquired empirical data supported scientific theories: supernatural evidence for supernatural knowledge). In this sense, it would appear that the influence of science on faith was a significant one, in spite of the fact that faith had long disputed many of the results of scientific research.

The Conflict Model: Faith versus Science

As time passed, however, the various points of conflict between faith and science could no longer be reconciled; they became rival explanations. The conflict model was nourished from both sides. In each instance, it was a question of crossing boundaries. On the one hand, conflicts arose because believers contested scientific theories that evidently ran counter to positions traditionally understood to be rooted in the faith and its sources: geocentrism *versus* heliocentrism, creation in seven days *versus* the theory of evolution, the independent creation of human beings *versus* human beings as descendents of the ape, divine interventions in the world (wonders, miracles) *versus* the world confined by a mechanical straightjacket. In all these instances, faith crossed the boundary and intruded on the domain of science in an effort to explain the physical world on the basis of its own traditions. On the other hand, practitioners of the scientific method — rightly — called into question faith's authority to make dogmatic statements in such instances. However, they also frequently crossed the boundaries of their own scientific domain in order to adopt ideological positions against specifically religious truth claims. In so doing, science became an argument against religion and belief in God.

Precisely because of its success and in part because of its promising technical applicability, scientific thinking acquired for some an inviolable and unique status; positive scientific thinking was then considered the only trustworthy way to seek the truth. Auguste Comte (1798–1857), the father of positivism, for example, preached the end of the theological (mythological) and metaphysical era, and announced an era in which truth claims of whatever sort could only be substantiated on the basis of positive scientific methods.[17] Science, it was claimed, would ultimately make it possible for humanity to discover everything there is to know about the world, human society, and the human persons. Whatever did not fit within the methodological parameters of science — religion, for example — was to be banished to the realms of fable. Society and ethics, therefore, were to be determined exclusively on the basis of scientific criteria. This led to the emergence of human sciences such as psychology and sociology, proposing empirical explanatory models for human behavior (such as behaviorism, socio-biologism).

Such a positivist position ultimately led to scientistic materialism, which set about "not only to sidetrack religion but also [other] non-scientific insights and convictions from everyday life and to replace them with 'scientifically justifiable' ways of thinking (and acting) [. . .]. Thus it was not only religious ideas that had to disappear, other categories from the everyday world in which human persons lived, such as self, soul, idea, person . . . were considered to be fictions created by the human imagination: the brain and its process were all that really existed. This materialistic vision of reality ultimately had to result in a conflict with every form of belief in such fictions. Materialists were only allowed to address their activities to that which really existed and were obliged to adapt their moral principles on an ongoing basis to new scientific insights."[18] A similar shift was also evident in philosophy, resulting in a movement away from metaphysics toward a "scientifically justifiable" philosophy. For "logical positivism," for example, a movement that emerged in the philosophy of language and developed its theories in line with Comte's positivism, only descriptive language — i.e., propositions that describe something demonstrable and verifiable — was considered acceptable and meaningful, since only such language was able to distinguish between truth and untruth (*Wiener Kreis,* ca. 1930–36). All other language was thereby designated as meaningless. Indeed, from the perspective of logical positivism, the creedal formula "I believe in God, creator of heaven and earth" was simply nonsense. To use the words of Wittgenstein (I) (1889–1951) from his *Tractatus logico-philosophicus:* philosophy should be concerned with saying "nothing except what can be said, i.e., propositions of natural science [. . .], and then, whenever

17. Comte saw the same development he had proposed with respect to the cultural evolution of humanity as a whole in the process of growing up into adulthood. Children believe in fairy tales, adolescents rationalize, and adults have learned to think according to positive science.

18. From H. De Dijn, "De toekomst van een illusie," in *Mores. Pedagogisch tijdschrift voor morele problemen* 42 (1997): 391–99, p. 395.

someone else wanted to say something metaphysical, to demonstrate to him that he failed to give a meaning to certain signs in his propositions"; "What we cannot speak about we must pass over in silence."[19]

In a nutshell, the conflict model emerges from the transgression of boundaries, from faith to science and vice versa. Conflicts thus arise on the basis of an incorrect assessment of the domain, scope, and truth claims of the Christian faith, on the one hand, and the scientific discourse on the other. This observation leads us directly to the third model: the difference model.

Faith and Science Differ Profoundly: The Difference Model

Sensitivity for the specificity of religious language was later developed within the same philosophy of language, however. Religious language was then no longer described as meaningless but rather as "different." Religious language had to do with evoking profound human emotions rather than with descriptions. According to Wittgenstein (II) in his *Philosophical Investigations,* the discourse or language game of religion "has nothing to teach us about reality, but about the attitude we adopt toward reality."[20] Conflict between faith and science was thereby avoided. The intention of both discourses was different: science provided cognitive information about reality as it is; religion made no claim to being cognitive, rather it dealt with our experience of reality and our existence therein.

Against a background of conflict and the crossing of boundaries, it gradually became clear that science and religion were not simply competing discourses, struggling against each other on the same ground. A position held in one domain did not have to be reconciled or disputed from the perspective of the other. The claim that "the more scientific one is the less religious" and vice versa was no longer self-evident. Furthermore, the awareness grew that science and religion differ too much from one another to be in conflict: their language registers serve different goals and are determined by different points of reference. Only those who are not able to consider — or do not accept — the specificity of both language registers are likely to generate conflict between the Christian faith and science.

---

19. L. Wittgenstein, *Tractatus logico-philosophicus: Logisch-philosophische Abhandlung,* with a new translation by D. F. Pears and B. F. McGuinness (London: Routledge & Kegan, 1961), p. 151 (nos. 6.53 and 7).

20. J. Van der Veken, *Een kosmos om in te leven,* p. 28.

In its more acute form, this position gave rise to the *rupture model*, holding that the difference between religion and science is a deep and unbridgeable void, making interaction, let alone conflict, between both impossible (and thus also undesirable).[21] The rupture model advocates a strict separation between meaning-giving (and thus also religion) and science. In this model, scientific knowledge is a form of knowledge that concurs with reality, and this concurrence is not accidental but can be demonstrated in an empirical-methodological way. The scientist is an observer of reality who describes it in communicable, transparent language. Religion, by contrast, is first and foremost a praxis, a familiarity with values and attitudes, an experience of meaning and tradition (thus not a collection of dogmas or theoretical insights expressed within a particular worldview). One can only gain insight into the "truth" of a tradition and speak its language as a participant. Science is about solving problems, religion is about respecting a mystery. It is neither possible nor desirable, therefore, to realize reconciliation, integration, or even consider interaction between knowledge and religion, between science and life; the contrast between religion and science is not a contrast between rival or complimentary theories, but a qualitative contrast. Science and religion are just too different to be in conflict with, to complement, or to interact with one another.

A rupture model of this kind, however, is too radical. In spite of the fact that there is no direct link between both language registers — and there is likewise no shared common language with which both religion and science can speak about reality — it is nevertheless "the same reality" that we desire to know and within which we live. Moreover, historically speaking, scientific statements have had an influence on the Christian faith, just as the Christian faith points to the boundaries of science and technology. It is evident that Christian faith, from within its own dynamics, intends to be more than a praxis in the exclusive service of the maintenance of habits and values. From of old, it has always aspired toward cohesion and thus toward comprehending the place of human beings, history and society in this world, in the cosmos. When rupture is too radical, how then should we conceive of the difference between Christian faith and science?

---

21. The rupture model is represented in the Low Countries by Herman De Dijn. Cf. H. De Dijn and A. Burms, *De rationaliteit en haar grenzen: Kritiek en deconstructie* (Leuven/Maastricht: Universitaire Pers Leuven, 1986) and H. De Dijn, *Kan kennis troosten? Over de kloof tussen weten en leven* (Kapellen/Kampen: Pelckmans, 1994).

3. Taking Stock

A Shift from Rival Theories to Different Language Registers

The way in which the difference model distinguishes between faith and science at least introduces more clarity into the discussion between creationism and scientific evolutionary theory, precisely because it allows us to point to the boundary transgressions committed by creationism. Creationism crosses the boundary from religion to science and forces the latter to embrace its specifically religious worldview. Every form of scientific theorizing that takes evolution as its point of departure and excludes a divine act of creation is contested. In the process, creationism reduces science at the methodological level to knowledge of facts and scientific methodology to empirical verification. In terms of content, it reduces science to those facts that do not contest creationist presuppositions. The ultimate goal of creationism is the realization of a harmony model, taking a literal reading of the bible and the subordination of science as its point of departure. Such an endeavor, however, results in a conflict model because it rejects, on the basis of unscientific arguments, scientifically tested knowledge and theory formation. The opposite may also be true. The claim that the theory of evolution can serve to provide the grounds for an ideological atheism transgresses the same boundary, but in the opposite direction. Scientific methodological agnosticism is then mistakenly considered to be the foundation for ideological atheism and scientistic materialism. Ideological conclusions are thus drawn from scientific presuppositions and knowledge, of necessity, without mediation, and without taking into account the difference in terms of language register between science, on the one hand, and religious and ideological discourses on the other. In both the cases of creationism and scientistic materialism, the fundamental difference between religion and science is no longer respected. It should be added at this juncture that the way in which intelligent design endeavors to bridge the gap between science and religion also suffers from the same weakness; both from a scientific and a sound theological perspective, it should be unmasked as a boundary transgression.

Following the line proposed by the difference model, however, science and belief in creation are not simple alternatives to one another and thus cannot be rivals. The difference between them is more fundamental. To paraphrase Galileo: science teaches us about the world in which we live, religion teaches us how to live in the world. We can compare the difference between both with the difference between a biological description of the phenomenon of people falling in love and a poetic description of the same. The first will analyze this phenomenon in terms of the pheromones that are released in the process. The second is concerned with giving expression to the lovers' feelings for one another and for the world around them. The poetic description is not more true or less true than the scientific description, although its truth is clearly not of the same nature. Both discourses are dealing with the same "falling in love," yet both have their own place which they cannot exchange with the other, unless science, for example, should lapse into socio-biologism and cross its own boundaries from within its own language register, imposing itself as the only truth about reality and condemning the rest to the world of illusion.

Is there still a place for discussion between science and faith? Is the gulf indeed too deep? Is every attempted rapprochement simply another boundary transgression?

Dialogue between Science and Faith?

As we have already suggested, Christian faith is not only a matter of trust, a praxis, a way of engaging reality, it is also about reflecting on life, history, and society as rooted in praxis and engaging reality. In relation to the surrounding context, Christians of every era have sought to establish a plausible image of humanity and the world, often in interaction with the philosophies and other cultural traditions of their day. The medieval harmony model is an excellent and concrete example of the construction of such a Christian worldview in interaction with the surrounding conceptual patterns. In the first part of the present volume, I endeavored to demonstrate that it is part of the nature of Christianity to search for a contextually anchored self-understanding, to be constructed in relation to its contemporary critical consciousness (as expressed, for example, in the philosophies of its time). Such contextual self-understanding, which can be coined the "theological moment" in Christian faith, neither precedes Christian faith nor replaces it, but is an inherent part of faith, entering into an exchange with the praxis of faith. Precisely because of its endeavor to arrive at a Christian understanding of the world and history, Christian faith over the last few centuries — and up to the present day — has been challenged by the rise and impact of modern sciences and has struggled to account for the specific and irreducible nature of the scientific language register. Because of this dynamic, intrinsic to Christian faith, a dialogue between faith and science is thus necessary once again, not with a view to re-establishing a harmony model, but aiming at better mutual understanding and self-understanding.

In order to engage in this dialogue, it should be clear that, from the Christian perspective, the past has taught us a number of lessons. (a) No more harmony model. Christian faith does not look in the first instance to science in order to have its own discourse confirmed, nor does it submit itself to science. Neither the book of nature nor the bible offers a discourse within which the other can also be given its rightful place. (b) No more conflict model. Christian faith enters into dialogue with the natural sciences and, as far as possible, respects the specificity of the latter's language register by, for example, not forcing the conclusions of the scientific discourse unmediated into the service of the discourse of faith. (c) No radical rupture between science and faith but a constitutive difference. Christian faith sees science as a challenge to be dealt with from within its own discourse. Science is neither an enemy nor a competitor, nor something alien that is completely irrelevant to Christian faith. Science is a partner in the endeavor to better understand humanity and the world, in spite of the fact that science and faith speak a different language and the results of the scientific endeavor belong to a different language register.

In what way can Christian faith engage in such a dialogue with the scientific discourse, for example, on the question of evolutionary theory?

4. Back to the Question: Creation and/or Evolution?

Science and Evolution

More than before, the scientific discourse on evolution has become aware of its theoretical boundaries, especially in the wake of studies in the field of the philosophy of language and linguistic analysis. In general, the sciences have become aware that they do not simply mirror reality; rather they offer mathematically structured models to deal with reality in an understanding and efficient way. Evolutionary science, for example, distinguishes moments in human history in which populations were obliged to adapt in the face of threatening circumstances in order to survive. Whatever did not adapt ultimately found itself on an evolutionary sidetrack leading to extinction. Some adaptations were insufficient. Indeed, certain mutations or variants were unfavorable and led to the extinction of entire species — million years of processes of "trial and error." All the while, organisms were becoming more and more complex. A (provisional?) final leap in this process of development was the emergence of the *homo sapiens.*

Explanations?

Some refer to the process of adaptation as one driven by a dynamic at work in reality itself. Such individuals make use of either a weak or a strong anthropic principle. This principle maintains that evolution took place in such a way that the human person could be its result. The strong variant argues that this fact is explicitly built into the concept of evolutionary history; the weak variant that while it was not explicitly built in to the concept as such, a series of opportunities made it possible. Others declare that the evolutionary process was purely accidental. Whatever the claims made in this respect may be, the scientific discourse can do little more than observe that mutations took place in such a fashion that organisms became capable of surviving under certain circumstances, that unpredictable changes took place making survival possible, and that it is possible to determine *post factum* a real tendency toward increasing complexity. The evolutionary processes within which "something" happened are then described as contingent, accidental, unpredictable — the process could have taken a different course or even have come to an end. Nevertheless, it did not come to an end nor did it take a different course. Moreover, according to some, it is reasonable to claim — after a thorough examination of the facts — that "everything on this planet conspired together *as if* life was its intended result. The expression 'as if' points to the impossibility of saying more on the basis of our current scientific knowledge alone."[22]

Scientists and other thinkers would appear to have enormous difficulty living with such an element of contingency and indefiniteness in their conceptual world. Indeed, they endeavor, not infrequently, to explain the scientific data — the established leaps in the evolutionary process and the "as if" of the previous paragraph — in broader constructions and narratives, which often exhibit religious (in the broadest sense of the term) connotations.

The Temptation of the Believer

Believers would seem to be quick to see the hand of God behind such processes and to identify the presupposed dynamics that lead reality as

22. Cf. J. Van der Veken, *Een kosmos om in te leven*, p. 105.

a creative process toward every increasing complexity (with the human person as its result) with God's providence and active guidance. With process philosophy (Whitehead) as their partner, for example, many theologians have argued that God draws toward the appropriate, creative option and that evolution should be read as the actual history of such God-drawn creative and viable options and their unfeasible counterparts. Other, more fundamentalist creationist positions envisage the biblical narrative of creation (understood literally) as a sort of counter-discourse in competition with the scientific discourse.

Both endeavor to undermine the scientific discourse as a specific discourse in its own right, either by including it within the larger narrative of faith, or by excluding it on the basis of the faith narrative.

An "Open" Dialogue on the Basis of Constitutive Difference

How then can one engage in productive dialogue concerning the constitutive difference between science and faith? Generally speaking, such a dialogue requires four steps:

1. In dialogue with the scientific discourse of evolution, believers should begin by exploring the results of scientific research. In so doing, they should be critical of elements within their own discourse that still bear the traces of earlier dialogues with (older forms of) science. An example in this regard might be certain creation theologies, in as far as they ruthlessly forced the scientific discourse into a subordinate role.

2. In the second instance, believers should resist the temptation to identify what science refers to as unpredictability and accident with God's plan, thereby attempting to correct or to supplement the scientific discourse. After all, in such procedures, God runs the risk of being no more than a stopgap, filling in the (provisional) holes in the theories provided by science. Taking both of these steps into account will ensure that believers do not to fall too quickly into the trap of creationism (in its many forms) and other boundary transgressions.

3. In the third instance, believers should have the courage in the course of the dialogue to point out where scientists themselves are inclined to go beyond the boundaries of their own language register, when they would propose unverifiable interpretative principles to deal with their data (running the risk of trespassing on the religious or ideological domain). This third step explicitly involves a theological criticism of atheistic and materialistic perspectives that appeal to the sciences without mediation in order to sustain their ideological positions.

4. In the fourth and final instance, and bearing in mind that the faith of Christians is nourished by its openness toward otherness and the unexpected, believers could be intrigued by the wonder and amazement to which many scientists (among others) testify in the course of their research. Believers may also be curious about that element of the scientific discourse that scientists designate as contingency and unpredictability because they are unable to grasp it completely or locate it within one or other theory. Referring to this sense of amazement thus evokes a kind of "unity in tension" that characterizes both faith and science, i.e., a fundamental passivity, openness, receptivity, which drives both faith and science forward, each from the specificity of their own language registers.[23] It goes without saying that believers are at liberty to associate this sense of amazement with faith in creation and God as the good creator — as long as they maintain the difficult tension with science and avoid the temptation to transform this same Creator God into a factor of, or agent in, the scientific discourse. Closely related to this first observation, one can determine a second structural similarity between faith and science, namely, *pathos,* longing for truth, the urge to search for meaning and understanding. The scientific endeavor is also an "ethical matter, grounded in the human person's awareness of being addressed on a personal basis [. . .] Knowledge is not a loose-leaf folder full of facts. Knowledge rather is responsibility for the integrity of what we are, in the first instance what we are as ethical creatures."[24]

The dialogue between faith and science is probably unable to go beyond this, despite considerable reciprocal influence evident between the two, such as the mutual exchange of metaphors and conceptual models. A higher synthesis into which both science and faith are united and in which their specificity and incommensurability are dissolved — as the proponents of certain holisms would support (including intelligent design theories) — is likely to collapse into one or other hegemonic master narrative, at odds with the structural analogies which we hinted at above (receptivity, *pathos* for truth, etc.). Such grand, unifying master narratives fail to do justice to the multiplicity of language registers and approaches with which we understand and experience reality, precisely one of the treasured discoveries of our time. A nuanced difference model, which is able to situate the independence of both language registers while seeking structural affinities, however, will help in avoiding futile conflict

23. Cf. J. Haers, "Geloof en wetenschap," *Hoogland Dok* 27 (1985): 159–92.
24. Ibid., p. 188.

and forced unity. On the contrary, it will inspire us to reflect further on what it means to be a human person in today's multifaceted world.

5. Creation and Flood Narratives

How should we deal, then, with the biblical creation and flood narratives? What do they mean in the language register of the Christian faith? Of course, it will already be clear that they do not offer a literal description of the origins of the world and life on earth.[25]

A Multiplicity of Creation and Flood Narratives

Many parallels in Mesopotamian literature exist to the biblical narratives found in the first chapters of the book of Genesis and many of them are considerably older than the biblical narratives. With respect to the flood, for example, we have an ancient Babylonian narrative at our disposal concerning a certain Atramhasis who, like Noah, had to build a boat in order to escape the devastation of the flood (written version circa 1650 BCE). The clay tablets containing the Gilgamesh Epic in which Utanapishtim played a similar role are dated around 1200 BCE. In the Gilgamesh Epic (tablet XI) we read the following:

> Gilgamesh spoke to Utanapishtim: . . .
> The hearts of the Great Gods moved them to inflict the Flood . . .
> Ea, the Clever Prince (?), was under oath with them;
> so he repeated their talk to the reed house: . . .
> "Man of Shuruppak, son of Ubartutu:
> Tear down the house and build a boat!
> Abandon wealth and seek living beings!
> Spurn possessions and keep alive living beings!
> Make all living beings go up into the boat!" . . .
> All the living beings that I had I loaded on it,
> I had all my kith and kin go up into the boat,
> all the beasts and animals of the field and the craftsmen I had
> go up . . .
> The stated time had arrived . . .
> I watched the appearance of the weather,

25. For the following paragraphs see, among others, L. Boadt, *Genesis*, in *Internationaal commentaar op de Bijbel*, ed. E. Eynikel et al., Band 1 (Kampen: Kok/Averbode, 2001), 392–452; E. Noort, "The Stories of the Great Flood: Notes on Gen 6:15–9:17 in Its Context of the Ancient Near East," in *Interpretations of the Flood*, ed. F. García Martínez and G. Luttikhuizen, (Leiden: Brill, 1988), 1–38.

the weather was frightful to behold!
I went into the boat and sealed the entry . . .
All day long the South Wind blew . . . ,
blowing fast, submerging the mountain in water,
overwhelming the people like an attack . . .
The gods were frightened by the Flood,
and retreated, ascending to the heaven of Anu . . .
Ishtar shrieked like a woman in childbirth,
the sweet-voiced Mistress of the Gods wailed: . . .
"The olden days have alas turned to clay,
because I said evil things in the Assembly of the Gods!
How could I say evil things in the Assembly of the Gods,
ordering a catastrophe to destroy my people!
No sooner have I given birth to my dear people
than they fill the sea like so many fish!"[26]

It can be reasonably assumed, however, that the oral tradition behind such narratives stretches back to 1800 BCE and earlier. The biblical narratives are younger, dating from the first millennium BCE, the youngest layer from as late as 550 BCE. Many specialists are thus of the opinion that the biblical narrative is indebted to a significant degree to the older Babylonian narratives. In contrast to Palestine, Mesopotamia was not unfamiliar with catastrophic floods. While the Nile was known to flood with particular regularity, the floods of the Tigris and the Euphrates tended to be unpredictable. In addition, storms from the Persian Gulf heading inland form the south were known to be dangerous and often devastating.

Creationists argue that the extensive distribution of flood narratives, even beyond the cultures of the Ancient Near East, provides evidence of the historical basis of a global, devastating flood that destroyed everything that existed. Given the fact that human settlements tend to be located close to water and on the banks of rivers, men and women have been aware from ancient times of the potentially destructive powers of water. The *tsunami* in East Asia on December 26, 2004, which cost thousands of lives and wreaked havoc and destruction on a massive scale, is a powerful reminder of this fact.

---

26. See online *www.ancienttexts.org/library/mesopotamian/gilgamesh/tab11.htm* (accessed August 12, 2006).

Creation and Flood Belong Together

Whatever the context in which the biblical flood narrative evolved may have been, in addition to many agreements it is important to be aware of the significant differences between the biblical narrative and its Mesopotamian counterparts. In such Near Eastern cultures one can only understand the present when one has an awareness of the roots thereof, when one sees how the present still bears the imprint of the beginning, of creation. The dramatic narrative of primeval times, mentioning the activities of the gods, offers a penetrating portrait of the present. It is a legitimate presupposition that the biblical authors became familiar with the Mesopotamian narratives via trade and diplomatic relations as well as with the association these narratives underlined between creation and flood according to the standard plot: creation (of humanity), gods are disturbed, flood, restoration. It comes as no surprise, therefore, that the biblical narratives concerning the beginnings of the world follow the same sequence. The narrative content, however, was thoroughly adapted to the Bible's specific cultural-religious perspectives. With respect to its creative reception of older narratives, therefore, the Bible was not really an exception in the Ancient Near Eastern context. The many points of similarity between narratives relating to a variety of different periods in time lead one to presume that the narratives in question hark back to ancient traditions that were later supplemented and enriched with new elements and interpretations. The work of the Babylonian priest Berossus who lived in the third century BCE also deals creatively with older narratives, writing and rewriting them, and represents a further, relatively young example of such a flood narrative stemming from the same region. Without a knowledge of the cultural-religious context in which such creation and flood narratives were composed, it is extremely difficult to grasp their precise meaning. This is also true for the biblical variant thereof.

The Flood: Creation Reversed

The connection between creation and flood is also evidently present in the biblical version — or better, versions, bearing in mind that exegetes distinguish two layers in the first chapters of Genesis, an older narrative tradition referred to as the Yahwist (J — circa 950–850 BCE) and a younger Priestly source (P — circa 550 BCE), brought together by a later redactor. It is for this reason that the flood narrative in Genesis 6–9 contains a significant number of irregularities and repetitions. The younger layer presents the flood unreservedly as the reversal of creation. The flood was caused by the fact that the division between the waters of the primeval sea and the waters of the heavens (i.e., the work of the second day of creation — Gen. 1:6–8), was breached; the fountains of the primeval sea and the floodgates of the heavens were opened. The order of creation, imposed on the primal chaos by the divine creative word, was revoked.

While the association in question is not unique for the bible, the reason why the association is made is distinctive. In contrast to the Mesopotamian narratives, the biblical flood is not sent over the earth to restore the rest of the gods and rid the earth of noisy human beings. The bible, in the first instance, speaks of one single God and not of the many gods referred to in the Babylonian narrative. At the same time, it is not because of overpopulation that God sent the flood but because human beings had become wicked and this grieved God and made God regret having created humankind (Gen. 6:5–6). The reason motivating the flood is therefore the serious disruption in the relationship between humankind and God. Noah is spared, because he, in contrast to the others, "was the only one in his day who lived an exemplary life, closely united with God" (Gen. 6:7). The differences with the Mesopotamian narratives immediately clarify what the biblical documents relating to the creation and the flood are all about: the quality of the personal relationship between the one God and humankind.

The God of the Covenant with Humanity

God's relationship with Noah, and through Noah with the rest of humankind, is confirmed after the flood in the covenant God entered into with Noah, his descendents and all living beings. After the repetition of God's blessing over the creation of humankind (Gen. 9:1–2, cf. Gen. 1:28), God promises: " ... never again shall there be a flood to destroy the earth. ... I have set my bow in the clouds, and it shall be a sign of the covenant between me and the earth" (Gen. 9:11–13). In like fashion to the narratives relating the creation of humankind, including the fall, the flood narrative thus speaks of the unique relationship between God and humankind. The God of the bible thus reveals Godself as a God of human beings, concerned with human history and human society — a God of fidelity and promise, a God of the covenant. Later in the book of Genesis, from chapter 12 onwards, the covenant between God and humankind is specified in the covenant with Abraham. It is ultimately the same God the first Christians confessed so many centuries after the authors of the Genesis narratives as the God who revealed Godself in the human person named Jesus of Nazareth — a confession that was written down in what was later to become the New Testament. God has established a new covenant in Jesus, confessed as the Christ. In this same Jesus, Christians have come to see that the mystery of reality is Love — a gift and a task at one and the same time. This, in the last analysis, is the message the biblical documents intend to pass on to humanity.

Part III

GOD INTERRUPTS HISTORY

Narratives on God, Incarnation, and Time

The fact that religious experience and religious rituals are enjoying renewed attention in our present-day post-secular context testifies to a so-called religious revival that some have claimed to be characteristic thereof. In the present chapter, we will discuss three themes related to this so-called revival. In each instance, we will be able to illustrate the radical-hermeneutic character of the theology of interruption proposed in the present volume. Chapters 7 and 8 will focus in the first instance on the theological-epistemological consequences of such a theological approach and chapter 9 will turn its attention to the political-theological consequences thereof.

In chapter 7, we offer a study of so-called "something-ism" and explore the relationship between this new religious phenomenon and the Christian faith. The loss of plausibility facing modernity's master narratives of rationality and science has created space for a new type of religiosity, which tends to be vague by nature and not particularly bound to one or another specific tradition or institution. Moreover, the idea that there is "something more" or "something higher" is left undefined by preference, averse to the constraints of language. We will analyze this "something-ism" as a sort of culturally motivated negative theology, as a characteristic way of dealing with detraditionalization and pluralization. We will then explore the differences between this new perspective and Christian negative theology, bearing in mind that the latter does not speak in vague terms about God but rather of a very concrete God, a God to whom narratives and practices bear witness, yet a God who cannot be contained by such narratives and practices.

Chapter 8 is dedicated to religious plurality and the way in which it challenges our traditional propositions for reflecting on religious truth. We will focus in this regard on the following question: does the confession that God is revealed (made incarnate) in Jesus in a definitive and incomparable way not constitute an insurmountable stumbling block for the unprejudiced participation of Christians in interreligious dialogue? Based on an analysis of three classic strategies we arrive at a reconfirmation of the constitutive value of the incarnation for the way in which Christians reflect on religious truth in a multi-religious context. In summary, the truth of the incarnation for Christians consists in the incarnation of the truth. It is only in the concrete and the particular that God makes history with humanity, and Jesus Christ offers Christians the hermeneutical key to discover traces of God therein. Those who endeavor to eradicate this reality ultimately violate the core of the Christian faith.

In chapter 9 we will turn our attention to the apocalyptic sensitivities that tend to raise their head from time to time in the uncertain times in which we live. Biblical images would appear to serve as metaphors for a rootless culture and an endangered world, in spite of the fact that apocalypticism has faded into the background of Christian faith and theological reflection (on account of its radical and mythological character). These contextual sensitivities provide an occasion to rediscover the pertinence of apocalypticism as a contemporary theological concept. The confession of God as the boundary of time leads to theological self-critique and critique of the world.

Chapter Seven

"I believe that there is 'something more'!"

Religious Revival and Negative Theology

Recent inquiries concerning religious belonging, often reported in the popular media, indicate that "God is not dead in Europe." Secularization did not lead to the expulsion of religion. The nature of religion and religiosity, however, appears to have changed significantly: it is less institutionalized and thus more individual and indeterminate. A recent poll revealed, for example, that many young people in Europe, a large proportion of them well-educated, would appear to believe in "the spiritual." It would seem that the demythologization of the world has left people unsatisfied, leading them to search for "something more."

In recent years, a number of Dutch atheists offered considerable critique of this so-called desire for "something more," which they styled "something-ism," claiming it to be a remnant of religion that had almost been completely wiped out by modernity. They lamented the unwillingness and lack of courage exhibited by secularized men and women to take the final and logical step toward atheism. On closer inspection, however, the belief in "something more" and the search for the spiritual would indeed appear to be the result of processes that have thoroughly reshaped the European religious landscape in the last fifty years. Both detraditionalization and religious pluralization have stimulated the evolution of a wide-ranging and vague religiosity, both inside and outside the Christian churches.

In the present chapter, we will analyze this so-called "something-ism," appearing in our contemporary world as a kind of "*cultural* apophaticism." We will argue that cultural developments in the wake of the processes of detraditionalization and pluralization have fostered the development of a religiosity that does away with some particular beliefs of Christian faith and is open to alternative expressions.[1] Traditionally, apophatic or negative theology warned against an excessively cataphatic or positive theological naming of God, and fostered the consciousness that God is always greater than what one can say of God. In this regard — as a prominent representative of the negative theological tradition — Denys the Areopagite stated that negative statements about God are "more true" than affirmations.[2] With "cultural apophatic tendencies," therefore, I intend to indicate a culturally motivated reserve or uneasiness to name God or the divine, or to link God or the divine in definitive ways to a particular tradition.

The leading questions of this chapter read as follows: How should theologians analyze this development? In what way does something-ism pose a challenge to Christian faith and theology? (1) Should theologians welcome this religiosity as a new opportunity, a "re-enchantment" of the world with which Christianity can enter into dialogue again after years of secularism and anti-ecclesial atheism? Perhaps something-ism could serve as the perfect sparring partner for a new "joint venture" between theology and culture. Or, better still, as a result of the transformation of religion in Europe, something-ism might serve as a sort of culturally motivated apophaticism offering the Christian faith an attractive and easy opportunity to reconnect with its own apophatic theological traditions. And why not: perhaps something-ism is even the future of Christianity, in line with the socio-cultural transformation of the religious and of God in Europe. (2) Or is the opposite the case? Should theologians despise these cultural apophatic tendencies as a weak and superficial remnant of secularization? It is then analyzed as merely a hollow religiosity, parasitic of traditional religion and providing religious comfort for a world in which the major dreams of modernity and traditional religious narratives have been left behind. In this sense it furnishes the perfect solution for those who are not daring enough to be full-blooded atheists and not receptive and courageous enough to engage in Christian faith.

---

1. A good example of this is the belief in a personal God: only one fifth to one third of the Western European population still maintains this belief, in almost all cases outnumbered by those believing in God as a spirit or life force. The least one can say is that the word "God" has become polysemic in character, and that a univocal horizon of signification is no longer a given. Another belief under pressure is the belief in life after death: although roughly half of the Western European population still maintains this belief, the way in which they conceptualize it tends to place reincarnation in serious competition with resurrection. Cf. L. Halman, *The European Values Study: A Third Wave. Source book of the 1999/2000 European Values Study Surveys* (EVS/WORC/Tilburg University 2001), resp. 94, 87, and 92.

2. For a short introduction, see Boeve, *Interrupting Tradition*, chapter 8.

It is probably too early to fully embrace or bluntly reject this phenomenon in the context of a theological reflection. Indeed, something-ism appears to be a characteristic feature of the present-day Western European religious situation and as such it cannot be disregarded. It offers expression to a tendency in our contemporary culture that has drastically transformed the way in which people — including Christians — view religion and religiosity. Something-ism does not stop at the doors of the church; rather it has a direct influence on the way Christians experience and explain their faith. Theological critique, therefore, should err on the side of caution and pay due attention to the complexity of this religious phenomenon. In the following pages we hope to demonstrate that something-ism does indeed present a fundamental challenge to the contemporary understanding of the faith, although it does so in a manner different than that outlined above. We must bear in mind that there is in fact a fundamental difference between this *cultural* negative theology and the way in which *Christian* negative theology challenges Christianity from within. Cultural apophasis can lead the Christian faith to rediscover its own specificity — including its own negative theological tradition — and facilitate a new relationship between faith and the present-day context.

1. Detraditionalization and the Longing for "Something More"

"Something-ism" and the Transformation of the Religious

It should be clear by now that the processes of detraditionalization have not lead to the disappearance of religion in Europe, but rather to its transformation.[3] The continuing institutional and mental de-Christianization of Europe have not led to a secular culture and society but to a new kind of vague religiosity. As we have noted, some have termed this phenomenon "something-ism," referring in general to a rather indeterminable acceptance that "there is something more" to life than facts and figures. Some claim that this religiosity is not an infantile waste product of contemporary secular culture, but a new shape of humanity's religious consciousness. It results from our disenchantment with secular rationality and utopia, and reacts against the deep-seated nihilism

3. Cf., for example, Y. Lambert, "A Turning Point in Religious Evolution in Europe," *Journal of Contemporary Religion* 19 (2004): 1, 29–45; and further H. Cox, "The Myth of the Twentieth Century: The Rise and Fall of 'Secularization,'" in *The Twentieth Century: A Theological Overview*, ed. G. Baum (Maryknoll, NY: Orbis, 1999), 135–43. See also chapter 1.

of post-secular society.[4] Confronted with the contingency and meaninglessness of their existence, people develop a new type of religiosity with special attention to personal experiences and responsibility, while being averse to traditional orthodox religions. It is the expression of a religious longing, adequate to the contemporary context, of the hope that there is more to life than what scientific worldviews maintain. The vivid and profuse religious imagination, perhaps best understood as the reverse side of something-ism, has given rise to new religious movements borrowing from Eastern religions, the renaissance of ancient Celtic religion, all kinds of syncretisms, etc.

The evacuation or "deconstruction" of specific Christian beliefs, rituals, and practices is not only visible among those who have taken leave of Christianity, but also manifests itself within the Christian churches. In a weekly column entitled *The Prodigal Son*[5], a Flemish newspaper published the following testimony of a Roman Catholic youth minister under the title "everyone a bit divine":

> As to the question of the meaning of life in general, I would not even presume to have the answer. I can only speak for myself. All my life I have regularly wondered why I am on this earth. I have since come to believe that there is something very powerful and pure residing in every human being. You can employ all kinds of words for this: essence, passion, inner strength. I prefer to use the word "divine," because it actually concerns something ineffable. The divine — that is what this life is about. In my many contacts with young people, I see that they often wrestle with pain, sorrow, disappointment. As a youth minister, I then try to help them search for that divine power within them. Whoever is able to tap into this source will be better able to cope with life's hurts.[6]

The statement of this youth minister bears witness to an unfathomable God, or better, the inexpressible divine. The latter is presented as the

4. Cf. S. W. Couwenberg, "Onttovering van het geloof en het 'ietsisme' als eigentijdse uiting van religieus verlangen," *Streven* (January 2004) 10–20; G. Groot, *Geloven en geluk: over het krediet van een religieuze cultuur* (Alfrinklezing 2004; Vught: Radboudstichting, 2004), 5–22.

5. This column is another expression of the so-called "transformation of religion" in contemporary society: religion has become a trendy item again in newspapers and magazines, especially when it is individualistic and in some way exotic or extravagant. See also the introduction in the British edition of the women's magazine *Cosmopolitan* of a new rubric "Spirituality and the City," focusing on alternative forms of religion (and definitely not on organized religion), practical tips and techniques, on the religious trends of celebrities.

6. G. Van den Broek, "Iedereen iets goddelijks," *De verloren zoon*, *De Standaard* 19.11 (2003).

deepest empowering core of the human being, which can be mobilized by people to cope with their pain and failures.

Empirical research, according to Hans van der Ven (empirical theologian in Nijmegen in the Netherlands), would appear to confirm the wide-spread presence of such spiritualities. Recent Surveys indicate four characteristics of the current transformation of belief in God.[7] (1) People no longer believe in an interventionist God, who rules and controls everything. Hierarchy, monarchy and patriarchy, images of divine omnipotence, divine will and predestination are hindrances to believing in God because they too easily invoke corresponding faith attitudes of submission, obedience, and guilt. Moreover, they give rise to an image of competition between God and human beings. (2) Van der Ven also notes evidence of polycentric images and presentations of God's presence and activity in the world. God is no longer presented as the one and only source from which everything is derived and toward which everything is moving. This tendency goes hand in hand with a certain polytheism. Research has shown that devotion to anonymous powers and spirits as well as a belief in the role of coincidence and fate, or the existence of providence or a master plan, are far from unusual. The combination of both also occurs with frequency: coincidence as the plan of a kind of higher power, to which one has access through astrology, horoscopes, and other spiritual approaches. It is as if the three Fates are ruling again: Chance (*Tychè*), Fate (*Moira*), and Necessity (*Anankè*), weaving the threads of life, and helping people to cope with suffering, death, and evil. (3) The third characteristic referred to by van der Ven is the observation that the majority of people understand God as non-personal (which is not the same as the more negatively laden "impersonal"), as "the divine." Images of breath, power, spirit, drive, impulse, or inspiration indeed bear witness to the preference for seeing God as a non-personal divine power and energy. (4) Closely related to the third characteristic, van der Ven concludes by referring to an evident reticence when it comes to explicit images of God. Many have problems with the biblical-Christian image of a personal God who speaks, knows, loves, judges, and rewards. Those who are more attracted to non-personal images of God, by contrast, tend to prefer what van der Ven calls the *aniconicity* of God: the renunciation

7. Cf. J. A. van der Ven, *God Reinvented? A Theological Search in Texts and Tables*, Empirical Studies in Theology, 1 (Leiden: Brill, 1998), 14–19; "Faith in God in a Secularized Society," in *Bulletin ET* 9 (1998): 21–45; *Contemporary Theology in a Secularized Society*, in *Bulletin ET* 9 (1998): 199–219; "Gegenwärtige christliche Konstellationen: Säkularisierung und Desäkularisierung?" in *Chrześcijaństwo jutra*, ed. M. Rusecki, K. Kaucha et al. (Lublin: Towarzystwo Naukowe, 2001), 181–228.

of images and representations of God. Put in a slightly paradoxical way: the avoidance of images and representations of God belongs precisely to the current representation of God. According to van der Ven, moreover, such sensitivities should not be too quickly dismissed as ignorant or vague, since they constitute an important aspect of the transformation of present-day belief in God.[8]

On the basis of these findings, and in order to restore the plausibility of Christian faith for people today, van der Ven consequently pleads for an adaptation of traditional theistic doctrine. Theology should challenge itself and stress more the immanent transcendence of God. It should dare to refer to the polycentric character of the divine, to promote nonpersonal images to refer to God, and to set limits to an overemphatic imaginative representation of (a personal) God.

What is apparent in these strains of spirituality and theology is a kind of negative theology, which is inspired and motivated by contemporary culture. It strives at relativizing elements of the Christian tradition, especially those aspects it denounces as its dominating and oppressing tendencies. The result is a spirituality with more room for diversity, freedom, power, energy, positive feelings, and so on. Religiosity then becomes a source of joy and happiness, and at the same time a source of strength to cope with life's shadow side.[9] This *cultural-apophatic* drive, one could say, prompts a scrapping of cumbersome old religious images and ideas in order to start afresh, making room for new and more fitting religious images and ideas, giving shape to a religious longing for harmony, cohesion, etc.

Solution and Symptom

This brings us to some observations and a thesis. Something-ism appears to be a significant aspect of the contemporary quest for meaning, happiness, and harmony. As such, it offers an implicit criticism of the meaninglessness of modern society, the erosion caused by secular rationality, demythologization and disenchantment, now inverted into a re-enchantment of the world. However, it also reveals the precariousness

8. "Though some claim that such views are a matter of religious agnosm (cf. Houtepen 1997, 53ff.), it could also be that we have arrived at a structurally different cultural phase in which it is necessary to emphasize God's aniconicity, alongside and in connection to His iconicity." See J. A. van der Ven, *God Reinvented,* p. 19, in reference to A. Houtepen, *God: een open vraag: Theologische perspectieven in een cultuur van agnosme* (Zoetermeer: Meinema, 1997); English trans., *God: An Open Question* (New York: Continuum, 2002).

9. See also the analyses made by A. van Harskamp in *Het nieuw-religieuze verlangen* (Kampen: Kok 2000).

of identity formation today, in a world in which guiding narratives have become implausible and suspect. Individuals are left with a magnitude of religious "products" on offer and almost no guidance or structure to accompany them in this process. The detraditionalized individual is thrown back onto itself. The subject, proclaimed as the center of its own meaning, experiences a serious decentering, especially when confronted with contingency experiences. It copes with this decentering by framing it within a movement from the self to the divine, not infrequently being located within the deepest kernel of the self. To put this thesis more technically: the self-divinization of the modern subject-centeredness seems to have evolved into the postmodern self-divinization by way of decentering the subject.

This vague religiosity would then be both the symptom of, and the solution to, the crisis of the modern subject, which is no longer its own master. In its search for identity, meaning, harmony, stability, security, the human subject engages in a movement of self-transcendence toward something other, the divine. This movement both reveals the limits of the subject and enables it to cope with these limits. The growing number of those who believe in a kind of life after death reinforces this line of thought. Because of the fact that meaning is located in the autoconstruction of the self, people cannot locate their own death as the unmasterable end of this self.[10] Religion, as "self-divinization by way of decenteredness," again seems to be first and foremost a mastery of contingency, the opening of a comforting and hospitable horizon in which everything finds its legitimate place, and everything is related to everything else. This would explain why this cultural apophasis sometimes swings in the direction of an overabundant religious imagination fed by the diversity of the religious market, surprisingly leading to belief in angels, miracles, paranormal powers, and other phenomena, which in modern times as well as in Christian theological circles have been abandoned and demythologized.

It is, I suppose, a legitimate question to ask why people in their search for religion are not returning to the institutional churches, especially when one acknowledges that many of them are still nominally Christian (since the majority are still baptized). Some partial answers can be suggested at this juncture. On the cultural level, first, because of the ever-growing detraditionalization, there is no longer an immediate link between this religiosity and Christian faith: the factual overlap between

10. Cf. Lambert, "Turning Point," p. 43.

the Christian horizon of meaning and contemporary culture has faded away. Moreover, it would seem that the institutional churches still suffer on many occasions from their own cultural-hegemonic past, and in this regard are called to account for seemingly still unsettled bills. Others, for example, van der Ven, finally argue that Christianity has become too alienated from contemporary culture, which makes it unattractive for new religious searchers. The language of the Christian tradition, the structures of Christian churches, etc. are outdated and need to be renewed. One may wonder, however, whether the latter is really the whole answer to the question. Perhaps there is something about Christian faith itself, which is hampering the smooth return of those who experience religious feelings.

2. Pluralization and the Relativization of Christian Particularity

In addition to detraditionalization, the pluralization of religion, both from an intra- and interreligious perspective, represents the other aspect under which the transformation of religion in Europe should be discussed. The consciousness of this pluralization is first and foremost the result of contacts with other religious traditions and growing interreligious contacts. Nevertheless, it would seem that this consciousness of religious diversity reinforces the culturally motivated apophatic theology, already hinted at in the preceding paragraphs. In the prevailing cultural consciousness, there seems to be a widespread assumption that above, or underlying, the many forms of religiosity and spirituality resides the same religious longing, the same relationship with the divine (or whatever name this transcendent reality is given). Religious plurality, then, results from the fact that this one religious desire is expressed in manifold ways, according to time, place, and traditions. This assumption is frequently present both in Christian and non-Christian circles.

In the same column of the Flemish newspaper, a month earlier, one could read the testimony of a lay chaplain of one of the major Flemish Roman Catholic women's movements.[11] In her youth she studied theology and was very much engaged in pastoral activities in her parish:

> After [my theological studies] I actually became weary with all this theoretical knowledge and the Western image of a God above and

11. G. Van den Broek, "Een inwonende God," *De verloren zoon, De Standaard,* October 29, 2003.

> beyond us. Young as I was, I had already had experiences that made me look for what was essential. The fact that I was able to visit India on a doctoral study trip was a pleasant coincidence. Whilst there, reading the ancient texts of the Bhagavad-Gita, that hoped-for world of depth and meaning suddenly opened to me. In these centuries-old scriptures I found written what I had been contemplating for years: that God was an indwelling God. God and humanity could be in collaborative partnership.
>
> For me God encompasses far more than just a person or the figure of Christ. At the moment, I prefer to use such descriptive perspectives of space, openness, and uninterrupted calling forth. When I awake, my first thought is: what awaits me today? And, how can I do all this in such a manner as to be an instrument of God? All that I do is after all nothing more than assisting in God's work. For this you don't have to be pious and neither is it a lofty role to play. It is an essential feeling that at the same time makes me relativize and let go of many things. [...]
>
> I experience a greater sense of oneness. [...] I remember a wonderful moment when, at the foot of the Himalayas, I visited a library specializing in books on all the religions of the world. As our diverse group watched the sun go down, everything at that moment came together for me. It suddenly became clear to me that there was only one experience. All the rest is just form. You could call this experience God or oneness. Everything is linked to everything else. Or, to employ a typically Hindu image: he who strips away layer after layer of himself will arrive at a harmonious center. The rest simply falls away. [...]
>
> To find the depths of myself in the depths of another and in this way to be a meaningful person for society, that is what it is all about.

Together with detraditionalization, pluralization seems to foster an apophatic theology that evacuates the Christian tradition, its conceptuality, narrativity, etc. Taken on its own merits, this kind of apophasis relativizes that which makes Christianity a particular, specific religion, and thus that which distinguishes it, even separates it, from other religions. In as far as the specific Christian particularity obstructs the underlying, original experience of harmony and unity, and its interpretation, it should be wiped out, put between brackets, or neutralized as only one way to refer to the divine. The shared feelings of religious authenticity, of longing for wholeness and harmony make people do away with what brings separation, conflict, and difference: particular truth claims, specific practices and imagery, etc.

Likewise in theological circles, the same procedure can be diagnosed in thinking patterns concerned with the relationship between Christianity and other religions. Many images and metaphors hint at the unity underlying religious plurality: religions are paths to the same mountain top (mystically veiled in clouds); they are the many sides and limbs of the same elephant, the different perspectives one can take in looking at the same dew drop glistening at the break of dawn[12], the many colors of the same rainbow, and so on. So-called pluralist thinkers, such as John Hick and Paul Knitter, would advocate such a position; religious plurality is the other side of religious unity, and even functional to an encompassing learning process toward religious harmony and peace.[13] Therefore, incarnation is to be considered a myth or a metaphor, a Christian way to express our being related to the transcendent ("The Real"). Incarnation should definitely not imply a historical claim, or a claim to uniqueness and unrepeatability.[14]

In his contribution to the proceedings of the LEST IV-conference on religious experience and theological epistemology,[15] Sebastian Painadath, an Indian Christian theologian working at the Center for Indian Spirituality (Kalady, India) formulates a similar point. He proposes that we adapt the classical scheme of Paul Tillich, distinguishing between "religion" and "culture" ("culture is the form of religion; religion constitutes the substance of culture"),[16]) in order to analyze and resolve religious plurality. Painadath, however, substitutes "spirituality" for "religion" and "religion" for "culture." Religions then are particular symbolic expressions of spirituality, whereas spirituality constitutes the uniting kernel of cultural-historically differentiated religions. "The

12. For an account of the first image, see chapter 8; for the second and third image, see *Interrupting Tradition*, pp. 164–66, 168–69.

13. Cf., for example, J. Hick, *An Interpretation of Religion: Human Responses to the Transcendent* (Basingstoke: Macmillan, 1989), 299–315, 380; P. F. Knitter, *One Earth, Many Religions: Multifaith Dialogue and Global Responsibility* (Maryknoll, NY: Orbis, 1995), 35–37.

14. See, for example, J. Hick, *The Metaphor of God Incarnate* (London: SCM, 1993).

15. LEST stands for "Leuven Encounters in Systematic Theology," a biannual international congress organized by the research department of systematic theology, K.U. Leuven. For more information: *www.theo.kuleuven.be/lest/*.

16. Cf. P. Tillich, *Kirche und Kultur, in Die Religiöse Substanz der Kultur: Schriften zur Theologie der Kultur,* Gesammelte Werke, band IX (Stuttgart: Evangelisches Verlagswerk, 1967), p. 42; further: *Über die Idee einer Theologie der Kultur,* pp. 21–22; further in derived form: *Systematic Theology* (Chicago: University of Chicago Press, 1951–64), 3 vols., 1:76.

universal spiritual experience finds concrete expression in the diversity of religions."[17] Spirituality, rooted in a mystical involvement with the transcendent is, as a consequence, that which binds the various cultural-historical religions. Those who are unable to reach through and beyond religion to this more profound spirituality run the risk of reducing religion to fundamentalism.

One may wonder, however, whether the Hindu metaphor being referred to here (as well as above), that of the nut from which one has to strip layer after layer in order to arrive at a harmonious kernel, is appropriate to imagine what the nature of religion and religious plurality is, and to qualify the apophatic-theological strategies the latter would seem to instigate. It might be more appropriate, perhaps, to use the metaphor of the onion in order to imagine the outcome of such an apophatic move. After all, when one strips layer after layer of an onion, it is not a kernel one obtains; one is merely left with the skins. Those who set out to discover the universal core of religion by abandoning religious practices, rituals, narratives, and convictions are likely to return with empty hands.

3. Ambiguities and Opportunities

These culturally motivated negative-theological tendencies teach us something about the contemporary context in which Christians, including theologians, are situated and in relation to which they are challenged to reflect upon their faith. Moreover, these tendencies are also evident within the Christian churches and are not averse to questioning Christian faith from within. The fact that the two testimonies referred to above stem from professional Christian pastors is evidently telling in this context.[18]

17. Cf. S. Painadath, *Diversity of Religions, Unity in Spirituality,* in *Religious Experience and Contemporary Theological Epistemology,* BETL, 188, ed. L. Boeve, Y. De Maeseneer, and S. Van den Bossche (Leuven: Peeters Press, 2005), 141–51, 144–45.

18. The position maintained by the Dutch protestant theologian Gijs Dingemans is an analogous one. As far as he is concerned, the question mark following the title of his recent essay *Something-ism — A Basis for Christian Spirituality? ("Ietsisme" — Een basis voor christelijke spiritualiteit?* [Kampen: Kok, 2005]) might just as well be left out. For Dingemans, something-ism bears witness to the fundamental religious relationship between human persons and Something greater than themselves, given form in different cultures via different religions. Christianity is therefore to be understood as our historically determined incarnation of this relationship, just as other religions are "relief networks . . . in which people have endeavored down through the centuries to come to terms with that Great Mystery, the One, the Unnameable, or God" (p. 71). Dingemans thus takes a fundamental continuity between something-ism and Christianity as his point of departure, whereby the former makes new modes of church formation and spirituality possible in our present context of detraditionalization. He refers in this regard to new faith communities ("flowers in the desert"), all of which must at least display an openness toward the Great Mystery that stands incomprehensibly at the background of our

We have our doubts as to whether both approaches are to be considered as adequate theological responses to something-ism's challenge to the Christian faith. In order to clarify the matter we will first endeavor to analyze something-ism more explicitly by describing it in relation to the Christian understanding of God and then raise some aspects of ambiguity as well as opportunity raised by the phenomenon.

Comparing "Something-ism" with a Christian Understanding of God

Perceived from a Christian horizon of understanding, something-ism, in all its diversity, takes leave of the Christian God. It appears to generate a twofold discomfort with God as the Other who makes concrete history with human beings. This discomfort concerns both (a) God's otherness, and (b) the way in which we come to know about God in the particularity and contingency of history. Something-ism would seem to be ill-at-ease with (a) what is revealed, and (b) the concrete way in which this is revealed.

(a) First, our contemporaries do indeed experience difficulties with the *otherness of God,* of a God who, from God's difference with history, comes toward history and engages it. They seem to be unable to conceive of (and accordingly believe in, or surrender to) a transcendence that is really distinguished from and anterior to the human subject. This inability only becomes stronger when conceiving of this transcendence implies the belief in a personal God who makes an appeal to people, challenging, perturbing, judging, loving them, etc. This discomfort thus concerns the structure of faith and the inability to come to faith, as an answer to an anterior and provocative appeal.

(b) As we have noted, however, this discomfort does not only concern God as Other vis-à-vis history, but also the way in which this God is concretely manifested in the *particularity of history.* Christian knowledge of God is intrinsically linked with an interpretation of concrete events and stories, embedded in particular histories of interpretation, and lived by specific communities of interpretation. Many contemporaries appear to have significant difficulty with the irreducible link between revelation and particular history, with a faith tradition that makes concrete history

existence and must be bound profoundly with the primal sources of religion" (p. 151). From the theological perspective, Dingemans barely distinguishes between cultural negative theology and Christian faith. The attractiveness of something-ism for him lies in the very fact that it allows Mystery to be mystery: "it is good that we can throw old ballast and fabrications concerning God overboard in order to be able to look at the phenomenon of religion in a new way" (p. 71). Elsewhere, Dingemans coined the slogan: "better something-ism than nothing-ism."

and remains indissolubly bound to it. Christians do indeed profess that God reveals Godself in a definitive and unique way, unrepeatably, in specific events on particular occasions. The culmination point hereof is the profession that the concrete human being Jesus of Nazareth is the Christ and that in this Jesus Christ, God has become known to us in an incomparable way. From the perspective of history, however, these events and occasions are as contingent and particular as any other historical material.[19]

Today, this farewell to the "too-Christian" God of history has become more manifest than ever because of the continuing contraction of the overlap between the traditional Christian horizon of understanding and contemporary culture. Because of this, vague religiosity can no longer be easily recuperated through theological correlation strategies. It is no longer feasible to establish a link with any degree of ease between this cultural, vague religiosity and the Christian faith.[20] Instead of postulating continuity between the two, this religious revival calls for an analysis that is attentive to the elements that distinguish them. Three aspects present themselves at this juncture: (a) The god, or the divine, which surfaces in cultural apophaticism does not originate from a constitutive difference between the transcendent and history, but is rather *holistic* in nature. The supporting experience is one of immanent deepness, unity, and harmony. The divine is everywhere, in everyone; no particular image or expression can determine or limit the divine. It is not bound to and defined by specific places and times, but all around. This religiosity has to do with a deeply felt relationship with a divine primal source, which is precisely *not* linked to time and history. This explains why such religiosity often goes hand in hand with a circular conception of time rather than a linear one. (b) Second, and closely related to the first point, vague religiosity leads to an immanentization of the divine, often resulting in a kind of pan(en)theism, in some cases even colored with neo-animistic features and so-called paranormal phenomena. (c) Finally, from an epistemological viewpoint, truth in this type of religiosity is conceived of in terms of the general, the one religious mystery, the original source, which escapes determination. The concrete and the particular may be its face or form, but these must be left behind when one wishes to proceed to the kernel, to the depths, to the truth. Confronted with such an approach to

---

19. This is further explained in the following chapter.

20. Although, as we have demonstrated, this is precisely the strategy proposed by Dingemans in his *"Ietsisme"—Een basis voor christelijke spiritualiteit?*

God and religion, those who are used to conceiving of God from Christian particularity and narrativity are increasingly rediscovering today the specific profile of their faith in the God of Jesus Christ.

Opportunities

As we already mentioned, this cultural apophatic trend instructs us on the contemporary context, and the way in which this context perceives Christian faith. For a theology that is involved in a process of recontextualization, it makes sense to examine both the opportunities and ambiguities generated by this trend. We will first explore the opportunities. (a) Cultural apophaticism unmistakably expresses a criticism of religion, opposing an overly transcendent and dominant God and authoritarian religion that enslave people and alienate them from themselves. (b) Moreover, this trend ventilates a criticism of modernity; it is an expression of the consciousness of the limits of human knowledge and power. A horizon of meaning merely built on rationality and secularity ignores the deeper layers of human life, both at the individual and the social level. (c) Lastly, it reveals a will to reconciliation between religions, favoring of a peaceful society of people of different religions and fundamental life options—a longing for unity, harmony, and fulfillment.

Ambiguities

In addition to these opportunities, one can also detect some ambiguities, both from a cultural and a theological perspective. I present them here in four clusters of questions. (a) First, questions arise concerning the nature of the god or divine surfacing in cultural apophaticism. One might ask whether this is not, in the last analysis, a god of the self, a divinized self (as we said above, a kind of self-divination via "de-centeredness"). Another question along the same lines concerns the inherent view of divinity that ultimately remains so indeterminate that it no longer means anything, that it can no longer "make a difference." It would seem to be all about my or our divinity. What is being projected here? What desires are being taken for real? (b) Second, there is a link between this religiosity and what in classical terms is defined as superstition and idolatry: magic, paranormal phenomena and powers, etc. This leads to questions about whether there are still criteria available to distinguish between good and bad religion, apart from the exigency that religion should reconcile human beings with the contingencies of life, the boundaries with which human beings are confronted. (c) Third, taking this a step further, one might ask about the reconciliation, fulfillment, harmony wished for:

for whom? and how? Does this kind of religiosity not lead away from concrete history? Does it not create a splendid isolated space of uninvolvement for the one who can afford it, in order to be able to survive in history? Is this not a facile utopia in the midst of all the lack of reconciliation, conflict, suffering, injustice, and death surrounding us today? For Johann Baptist Metz, the answer is clear: "Religion today appears to be only Dionysian, as the striving after happiness by shunning suffering and sorrow and by putting at ease erring fears. Religion has become a mythical spell of the soul, a psychological-aesthetical assumption of innocence for people who have stopped all eschatological upheaval in a dream of the return of the same, or [...] in the newly rising fantasies about transmigration of souls and reincarnation."[21] (d) A final cluster of questions: Does religion really function as a provider of happiness? Can it function this way? Are people really comforted by it when they clash with or are overcome by the contingencies of life? Insofar as this culturally motivated negative theology is also present within contemporary Christianity itself, is this the way in which Christian religion functions, or should function? More specifically, is such a vague and holistic religion that takes leave of its indissoluble bond with history, narrativity, and particularity an alternative to the Christian faith or is it, for believers today, its newest form? Is this something-ism the future of Christianity?

A positive answer to this last question would imply that the transformation of religion in Europe is bringing about the transformation of Christian faith; the relativization of Christian specificity would then have resulted in a kind of general religiosity. The theological question therefore runs as follows: Is such culturally motivated apophaticism also for Christians the new religious way to deal with the contingencies and particularities of life? Is it the contemporary modus or appearance of Christian faith, even its fulfillment? Or is it rather the expression of a post-Christian attitude of life?

4. The Rediscovery of Christian Negative Theology in the Heart of Radical Theological Hermeneutics

At this point, the reader will hardly be surprised that I tend to opt for the last answer. Cultural apophaticism is an exponent of a post-Christian religiosity rather than the future of Christian faith itself. Indeed, as already

21. J.-B. Metz, *Religion, ja—Gott, nein,* in J.-B. Metz and T. R. Peters, *Gottespassion: Zur Ordensexistenz heute* (Freiburg: Herder, 1991), 11–62, p. 24 (translation mine).

developed above, I fear that the two intrinsically interwoven constitutive elements of Christian faith are underrepresented or absent in it: first, faith in God as the Other of history, qualified by the constitutive difference between God and humanity; and second, the inscription of the involvement of God with human beings and history, an involvement that can only be concretely shaped and read in the very particularity of history. It is to these two elements that the living Christian tradition bears witness, in narratives and praxis, prayers and rituals, doctrines and reflections. Combined, they give rise to a specifically Christian critical-hermeneutical consciousness. Christian faith does not primarily concern the human search for God, but is ultimately a human answer to God in search of human beings. Faith, then, is the option (made from a complex interplay of initiation, will, and intellect) to look at history and society from the perspective of this God and to interpret them accordingly. It is faith in a God who reveals Godself as and in concrete love — faith in the God who, as Love, becomes the key for reading the very particularities and contingencies of history.

This precludes a too-facile identification between cultural apophaticism and Christian apophatic theology. According to some, however, an opportunity is presented at this juncture to make a close connection between culture and tradition once again. They consider something-ism as a new opportunity to anchor contextually the relevance and plausibility of Christian faith. Cultural negative theology then constitutes a point of departure for a new correlation of the Christian tradition with the postmodern context, in order to reach a culturally plausible and theologically legitimate Christian faith. However, in line with what we have demonstrated above, because of detraditionalization and pluralization, recontextualization today should be wary of such unproblematic postulations of continuity. Cultural apophaticism does not challenge Christian theology in the first instance in order to recuperate it on account of a presupposed familiarity with its own apophatic consciousness. On the contrary, cultural apophaticism leads Christian theology to rediscover anew the specificity of its own position, including its apophatic-theological dimension. In a Christian radical hermeneutical consciousness, apophasis does not do away with cataphasis, but is intrinsically at work in it. I will endeavor to clarify this point further in what follows.

Christian critical-hermeneutical consciousness is a resolutely theological consciousness, which aims at a continuous radical hermeneutics of history rooted in faith in a God at work in it. This hermeneutic originated in the Old Testament, where for the Jewish people the exodus event became the theological key for reading God's activity in history. The continued theological interpretation of the exodus event functioned both in an aetiological ("because then, therefore now") and in a paradigmatic ("like then, so also now") perspective. In the theological hermeneutics of the present for the Jewish people, the exodus event formed the structuring pattern for new experiences of God's salutary involvement in history, experiences which simultaneously gave new shape to the exodus-God-experience.[22] The transmitted past informed their reading of the present; the lived and interpreted present re-actualized the salutary experiences of the past. It is precisely in this kind of hermeneutic that the Jewish-Christian apophatic-theological consciousness is to be situated. Revelation of God in history and the prohibition to make images of God go hand-in-hand: the revelation of God to Moses at the burning bush, "I am there for you" (Exod. 3:14), leads to the "You shall not make images" on Mount Sinai (Exod. 20:4), for "I am the Lord your God, who has brought you out of the land of Egypt, out of the house of slavery" (Exod. 20:2). The negative-theological critical consciousness, then, does not distract from history, separating God from the historical and particular, rather it qualifies the way in which history is theologically interpreted. The God active in history cannot be contained by history. Everything pointing to God's activity in history, every witness to it in narratives and praxis, is therefore subject to an uninterrupted hermeneutics.

The same critical consciousness is at work in the New Testament. Here, from the very start, the Christological interpretative key underlying the theological hermeneutics of history is radicalized in apophatic theological terms. Likewise here, this radical hermeneutic does not lead God and those believing in God away from history — on the contrary. The transfiguration story (Mark 9:2–10 par.), for example, in which Jesus is presented as the glorified Christ in dialogue with Elijah and Moses, is revealing in this regard. Mark writes for instance that Jesus' clothes became so white "as no fuller on earth could whiten them" (Mark 9:3). The glorified Christ is not to be grasped in earthly categories. When Peter full of awe, however, suggests that they build three tents, he does indeed not know what he is saying (Mark 9:6). The evangelist, who resorts

22. For a clear presentation, see D. Sattler and T. Schneider, *Gotteslehre*, in *Handbuch der Dogmatik*, ed. T. Schneider (Düsseldorf: Patmos, 1992), 51–119, pp. 54–75.

to using this narrative to express something about Jesus, then lets God typify Jesus, after which he suddenly concludes the event: when Peter and the other disciples looked around, they saw no one except Jesus and themselves. They had to go down from the mountain again, into the world. Further, the fact that the risen Christ is not to be grasped in his earthly form — although, at the same time, inseparable from his earthly form — is expressed in an exceptional way by the narrative of the disciples on the road to Emmaus (Luke 24:13–32). The two travelers to Emmaus meet a stranger who, in the course of the encounter, reveals himself in word and deed to be the Christ. Upon recognition, however, he immediately withdraws from them. The risen Jesus reveals himself in the reading of the Scriptures and the community gathered around the table. The evangelist indicates at this juncture, moreover, that it is precisely in the concrete word and meal that the relationship with the risen Christ can be realized.

The Christian apophatic-theological reserve rises to the surface at this point: only in the all too concrete, in the all too historical, in the all too contingent — and in an interpretation thereof — does God engage history in an irreducible and definitive way, without, however, coinciding with it. Incarnation never implies the neutralization or cancellation of the historical-particular in terms of the universal, or of the contingent-historical in terms of the absolute. The latter is always irreducibly inscribed in the former, without discrediting the former, but at the same time, without isolating the latter from the former. Only in the all-too-human is God revealed, not without it — only in the all-too-historical can Christians read God's presence and activity.[23]

God's ineffability, therefore, has nothing to do with vagueness, nor with something that leads away from the concrete. On the contrary, it leads immediately back to history itself. God as the Other of history is involved in it as determinate Love, as prophetic challenge to all to make visible God's invisible presence and activity. In this regard, it is like the love between two human beings. Such love is not an indeterminate given. It is only realized and can only survive as something very concrete, tangible, life giving, inscribed in particular events and stories, even when the language of love cannot find the words to express it, and even when all determination ultimately falls short and never succeeds in grasping its mystery.

23. See chapter 8.

5. Particularity, Negative Theology, and the Language of Faith

The renewed interest in the particularity of Christian faith could easily be understood as a plea for more attention to be given to the specific language of faith as it is transmitted by tradition in narratives, practices and doctrines. Insistence on the very particularity of the Christian faith tradition, however, should not result in particularism.

Indeed, faith has to do with a particular language and becoming a Christian means getting acquainted with this language. However, this need not necessarily lead to blind and stubborn particularism or a kind of dogmatic literalism with regard to narratives and doctrines, precisely on account of the apophatic-theological critical consciousness that is at work in this particular traditional language. We will explain this point in more detail in the following paragraph.[24]

On the border between church and society, at least two problems occur with which theologians (and pastors) are confronted. (1) The first of these problems arises from the awareness of the irreducible particularity of Christian language. Currently a lot of people in Western Europe, even Christian people, do not become familiar enough with this language, the vocabulary and grammar of faith. Moreover, in line with cultural apophatic tendencies, many of them consider this language to be too particular, and an excessively limiting determination of the religiosity or spirituality for which they are searching. For some theologians, the inability to deal with this particularity, handed down from the past, serves as the reason to call for a profound revision of the (outdated) language of Christian tradition. Being too determined, it prevents people from experiencing a more original religious sensibility. (2) The other problem concerns virtually the opposite position. Because of the rediscovery and heightened sensitivity of Christian language, some theologians and church leaders have warned against any adaptation of Christian language, and stick to a quasi-literal continuation of the transmitted narratives and doctrines. They do not allow for a legitimate theological hermeneutics to take place: any adaptation is considered treason and loss from the outset.

In both cases — for the wrong reasons — a sound recontextualization of Christian faith and tradition is short-circuited. (1) In the first case, the call to adaptation under the influence of the cultural apophatic

24. For the distinction made here see chapter 3.

drive leads away from one of the main features of Christianity, that is, its "inscription" in particular history and language. There can be no negative theology without positive theology, no apophasis without cataphasis. In spite of the fact that negative theology calls every positive statement concerning God's involvement in history into question from within, positive theology remains a necessary precondition for negative theology. An example in this regard may be the difficulties some people have with the Christological claim of Christianity: Jesus is not a prophet as many others, but God incarnate in history. (2) In the second case, the argument of the intrinsic particular features of Christianity (often ventured as a critique of the first case) limits all space for a legitimate theological hermeneutics of tradition. As such, the apophatic-theological dimension is downplayed. For in its continuous dynamic relationship with the cataphatic dimension, apophasis nurtures a radical theological hermeneutical consciousness. Continuing the Christological example: such an attitude would obstruct any tentative attempt to construct new images of Jesus Christ in relation to the contemporary context, testifying to this same Christological consciousness, and thereby keeping it alive, plausible, and relevant, if not to the public at large, then certainly to contemporary Christians. In short, a contemporary recontextualization of Christian faith does indeed lead to a heightened sensitivity to its intrinsic particular nature (to be theologically motivated by a further elaboration of the theological category of incarnation), but also of its no less intrinsic radical hermeneutic nature. As a matter of fact, the consciousness of the latter is part of the particular grammar of the Christian tradition, and it only becomes operative through a deep familiarity with that tradition.

6. Conclusion

The theological rediscovery of Christian particularity, and of the radical hermeneutics which resides in the heart of this particularity, results in at least two challenges for contemporary theology. First, because of cultural apophaticism, it warns against a culturally quite acceptable and rather facile relativization of the differences between convictions and religions, because in the end, beyond differences and conflicts, "it would all boil down to the same kernel of religiosity." Second, this rediscovery also warns, on theological grounds, against rigid particularism, because such self-enclosed positions forget the radical hermeneutical dynamics at work within all Christian discourse on God's involvement in history. It indeed forecloses from the outset any fruitfully challenging dialogue or encounter with religious others. It is precisely this radical hermeneutical consciousness that makes it possible for us today to be on the lookout for traces of this involvement in our concrete historical circumstances. And in our contemporary context, it is for Christians probably in these concrete dialogues and contacts with other religions that God, and God's universal salvific will, may become visible. Such a theological interpretation of current history then does not result in relativizing the historical particularity of the respective religious traditions (with a view to establishing a consensus behind or above such particular traditions), it acts rather as a starting point from which to continue this history, and indeed, for Christians, to make the invisible God more visible today. We will explore this possibility further in the following chapter.

Chapter Eight

Jesus Both God and Human

Incarnation as Stumbling Block or Cornerstone for Interreligious Dialogue?

There is nothing in Christianity that forces people to believe: no awe-inspiring events, no ironclad logic, no exceptional religious experiences. On closer inspection, the fact that some Christians read narratives and events as the history of God's relationship with humanity would appear to be little more than accidental. There is nothing to compel such a reading, certainly not with respect to the most important element of the Christian faith, namely, the confession that Jesus is the Messiah, the Christ, God and human being at one and the same time, God's Word made flesh, God's incarnate son. Wasn't Jesus the son of Mary and Joseph, the carpenter from Nazareth? Wasn't Jesus a marginal Jew, caught up with God, perhaps, but not to the extent that people were immediately compelled to recognize him as God? Did the earth really quake, the rocks really break asunder, the graves burst open and the dead rise up at the crucifixion of Jesus as Matthew narrates it in his gospel (Matt. 27:51–52)? It would seem that even the resurrection was not the earth shattering global event it has been portrayed. If it had been so, then all of Jesus' contemporaries would have been able to do nothing other than believe in Jesus' divinity. According to the High Priest and the elders, the disciples removed Jesus' body from the tomb (Matt. 28:13). Is it possible to prove that the empty tomb was a result of Jesus resurrection? In spite of the many unanswered and unanswerable questions, however, the first Christians and many generations thereafter claimed and continue to claim that this very Jesus is the risen Lord and that God came close to humanity in an unforgettable and unparalleled way in this concrete human being of flesh and blood. Believe if you can!

The situation is no different today. For many, Christians and non-Christians alike, the idea that God became human in Jesus is difficult to swallow. Today, as before, there is nothing to force such a confession:

no awe-inspiring events, no ironclad logic, no exceptional religious experiences. Few would be inclined to deny that the Christian faith has to do with a collection of meaningful Christian values. Many would even subscribe to the suggestion that the Christian faith is still entirely plausible when it speaks of a loving God, of the deepest mystery of reality, of the "something more" than we can see, a profound core to which our experiences of joy and pain, of amazement and dependence point us. The claim that such a message is dependent in its entirety on one single human being who lived two thousand years ago, however, remains for many a serious stumbling block.

Moreover, at the level of both theoretical and practical concern, the ongoing defense of Jesus Christ as the ultimate expression of the core of the Christian faith remains a problem for continuing dialogue with other religions and convictions. Many are of the opinion — both Christian and non-Christian alike — that the "Christ claim" already stands in the way of every form of rapprochement. The idea that Jesus was a prophet, a religious genius, a wise spiritual master, is acceptable for many, but at the same level as Moses, Mohammed, and Buddha, or divine in the sense that Brahman, Shiva, and Vishnu are divine. There can be little doubt that Jesus Christ has taught us a great deal about the meaning and purpose of being human and the path we should follow in order to live together in happiness. Jesus, however, is not unique in this regard. Is it not reasonable to argue that the goal of every religion is human salvation, happiness, or redemption? Other religious figures have made an equal contribution in this regard, and may even have accentuated elements that supplement if not complete the Christian message. Why then should we continue to uphold the idea of Jesus as the Christ, a man who lived two thousand years ago and was brutally put to death (crucified like so many others) at thirty-three years of age?

In the present chapter we will argue that, difficult to believe or not, the entire Christian faith nevertheless stands or falls on the premise that God became human in Jesus. The person who desires to understand the Christian faith cannot avoid this premise. At the same time, the person who seeks to understand the truth claim of Christianity will, sooner or later, have to deal with the "dogma" of the "incarnation." Indeed, the truth of faith (the truth Christians live by) and the way this truth functions are revealed therein.

We will begin with a reference to the question of interreligious dialogue, examining how our understanding of the truth is challenged thereby and how we can stress the distinctive features of the truth of faith maintained by the confession of Christ in a new way. At the end of this exercise, we hope to have made clear that the Christian understanding of the truth is perhaps closer to the actual context than we had first presumed. Based on this understanding, moreover, it would even seem to be possible that Christians, rooted in their particular Christian critical awareness, have a genuine contribution to make to contemporary discussion in culture and society. We will turn our attention in the first instance, however, to a brief sketch of the way in which men and women of every age have wrestled with "Jesus—the divine human."

1. The Revelation of God in Jesus Christ: A Continuing Challenge for Theology

For the Jews Offense, for the Pagans Foolishness

Christians believe that God revealed Godself definitively in Jesus Christ. They have endeavored to give expression to this belief in a variety of different ways up to and including the present day. They confess that Jesus Christ is the Son of God, according to the Council of Chalcedon (451 CE): at once both God and human, unchanged, undivided, without separation. He died on the cross for our salvation and God raised him up and glorified him. It is in his Spirit that Christians know themselves to be united with one another in the church. Every age has borne witness to this confession in words, images, music, and gesture.[1] It contains a truth claim that reaches to the core of Christianity and characterizes it most fundamentally. The God of Christianity is a God who participates resolutely in human history, in such a radical fashion that this God actually became a human person, actually became part of human history. "And the Word became flesh and lived among us" (John 1:14a). It is only through this Word made flesh, this "incarnate" Word, that we have access to God: "I am the way, and the truth, and the life," states the evangelist John, "No one comes to the Father except through me" (John 14:6). God does not only reveal Godself therefore in an unsurpassed way in Jesus Christ, it is only through Jesus Christ that we can encounter God.

Since time immemorial, this Christian truth claim has been a source of difficulty, misunderstanding, and even conflict, both within the Christian community and in its relationship with the world outside. Christians

1. See, for example, P. Schmidt, *In handen van mensen: 2000 jaar Christus in kunst en cultuur* (Leuven: Davidsfonds, 2000).

argue that God involved Godself in history in an extremely concrete fashion by becoming human — a Jewish man from Nazareth in Galilee, born during the reign of Emperor Augustus who, heaven forbid, died on the cross and rose again on the third day. Paul is aware that this is unacceptable for Jews and gentiles alike (1 Cor. 1:23). The turbulent history of the early church is likewise characterized by a search for the appropriate way to give expression to this belief — that God came close to humanity in a unique and definitive way in Jesus — in the language and thought of the day. According to the Christian community, key moments in this search are represented by the Councils of Nicea (325), Constantinople (381), Ephesus (431), and Chalcedon (451). Confronted with people who found it impossible to believe that it really was God who had identified Godself with Jesus, the Fathers of the early church emphasized the divinity of Jesus Christ. In discussion with those who endeavored to minimize Jesus' humanity and reduce it to mere appearance, they insisted that Jesus was truly human, a man of flesh and blood, like us in all things (except sin). In the period of the early church, it was ultimately and primarily the humanity of Jesus Christ that people found difficult to combine with his divinity, which in the Hellenistic context of the day was much easier to accept as the point of departure for the theological significance of who Jesus Christ was. The Church Fathers and theologians of antiquity, on the other hand, sought in the first instance to conceptualize the real humanity of Jesus Christ from the perspective of his divinity.[2]

This approach changed dramatically in the period of modernity. The Enlightenment challenged religion before the court of reason, where reality and the conceptualization thereof are subjected to critical research in full freedom and autonomy. Whatever fails the test of reason loses its plausibility. The fact that Jesus was a human being, perhaps even an extremely special human being, did not emerge as a cause of concern for the modern woman or man. The idea that this same human being was also God and thus that the meaning of all humanity and the history of the world had been revealed in him in a decisive way, however,

2. This ultimately represents the point of discussion with the Arians, which turns, in essence, around the divinity of Jesus; not so much that Jesus would thus be too human but rather that he would be less divine, a lesser god. Arius (circa 318) considered Jesus Christ to be a sort of divine intermediary between God and creation. The disputes between the so-called Alexandrian and Antiochian schools, expanded into Monophysitism and Nestorianism (first half of the fifth century), turn around the question of the divine Logos becoming human: did he merely take on humanity in a general sense (Alexandria), or was he indeed very specifically human (Antioch)?

was beyond modernity's capacity to comprehend. God as universal God, reality's deeper foundation and logic, were acceptable thus far; Jesus as a concrete, albeit unique, human being was no significant problem. The idea of binding God in a definitive and irreducible manner to an extremely concrete human being with an extremely concrete history as "*the* way, *the* truth, and *the* life," "salvation for the world" (incarnation) was simply out of the question.

This the problem with which modern theologians such as Edward Schillebeeckx and so many others wrestle when, having taken Jesus' humanity as their point of departure, they point to traces of relationship with God, his Father. These traces then inspire Christians to confess this Jesus as the Christ, God's definitive revelation as "a God intent on humanity." Schillebeeckx refers, for example, to Jesus' intimate experience of God as "abba" (Aramaic for "daddy"), which was very unusual in those days. He alludes further to Jesus' boundary-breaking words and deeds that set him apart from Jewish society, and to the disciples' extraordinarily profound resurrection experience, an experience of ultimate forgiveness articulated in expressions such as "He is alive," "we have seen Him" — an experience that set them on the path toward forming community in Christ.[3] Rooted in Jesus' humanity, an effort is made to work toward what it means to confess this human being as the Christ. According to Schillebeeckx, this procedure allows Christians to arrive at a better and contextually appropriate understanding of their faith. At the same time, non-Christians are taught to understand that the faith of Christians is not some outdated and irrational obsession with mythological (illusory) images. As long as modern western culture continued to be sufficiently marked by the Christian conceptual horizon, this strategy was often successful in making the Christian faith "believe-able" for people of today.[4] The social processes of secularization and detraditionalization, however, have eroded the overlap between the Christian conceptual horizon and contemporary culture to a significant degree. The challenging step from "Jesus the extraordinary human being" to "Jesus the divine human" has certainly not been made easier by this erosion.

---

3. Cf. E. Schillebeeckx, *Jezus het verhaal van een levende* (Bloemendaal: Nelissen, 1974); English trans. *Jesus: An Experiment in Christology* (New York: Seabury Press/London: Collins, 1979).

4. We discussed this theological strategy — often referred to as the correlation method — in chapter 2.

Christology Challenged by Religious Plurality

Christians today are no longer only challenged to reflect on their faith in discussion with the (secular) modern context, marked as it is by an emphasis on the autonomy and rationality of the human subject, the methodological atheism of the sciences, the separation of church and state, and the atheistic fundamental life option of, among others, the free-thinking humanists. The secularization process ultimately pulled the carpet from beneath the unquestioned givenness of the Christian faith in large parts of Europe. The Christian faith, including its understanding of humanity and the world, its ethical perspectives and attitudes, in short, Christianity's entire conceptual horizon, serves for fewer and fewer people as the (explicit and even implicit) ultimate point of reference when they seek to give meaning to their lives and to society as a whole. Those for whom this remains true frequently no longer understand their Christian identity as something inherited from the past, but rather as an option in faith that calls for continual confirmation in word and deed and in dialogue with society.

As we have indicated above, however, secularization did not succeed in expelling religion from modern society.[5] A secular culture did not simply take the place of the Christian religion; rather a multitude of religious and other fundamental life options filled the vacuum. This pluralization of religious and other fundamental life options, which is even more visible at the global level, also has to do with the transformation that has taken place in the way contemporary men and women relate to such matters. Just as some consciously or unconsciously opt to be (or remain) Christian, others have turned to other religions and other fundamental life options, both in their classical, institutionalized forms (the so-called world religions) and the new religious movements (New Age, Wicca, etc.).

All of this has significant consequences for those who reflect on Christianity today. It is no longer (only) the secular, modern culture of science and emancipation that challenges Christians to renew their understanding of what it means to believe in Jesus Christ. To an ever growing degree, it is instigated by the encounter with the diversity of religions and fundamental life options that forces them to reflect on this faith. Indeed, the current context, described by some as postmodern, is one of religious plurality, of multiple fundamental life options, and it is from within this new situation that Christians ought to search for a

5. Cf. chapter 1.

contemporary understanding of the faith. How does the Christian faith relate, for example, to Buddhism? Can we draw comparisons between Jesus and Buddha? What does it mean to recognize that other religions are also able to inspire men and women to live authentic and happy lives?

When we endeavor to address these questions, it becomes clear that the encounter or confrontation with other (world) religions presents Christians with a twofold challenge. (1) In the first instance, questions arise with respect to the *relationship* between the Christian faith and the other (world) religions. In the last decades, three now classical theological "schools" of thought were developed as a means of dealing with this question: exclusivism, inclusivism, and pluralism. We will investigate the problems surrounding the discussion of these three models in the following section. Suffice to say, for the time being, that none of the three conceptual strategies appears to be subtle enough to formulate an adequate and plausible answer to the question, given the fact that a delicate balance is required in maintaining, on the one hand, the Christian identity and truth claim and, on the other, establishing a fundamental respect for other religions, including their own truth claims. (2) At the same time, the confrontation with (someone adhering to) a different religion forces Christians to reflect on their own *identity:* what does being Christian mean exactly? What distinguishes Christians from those of different faiths? What does the Christian truth claim consist of and what does it mean in practice? How can we justify this claim against the background of religious diversity, and more concretely, in interreligious dialogue?

A response to the first series of questions cannot be given in isolation from the second series and vice versa. Strangely enough, the Christian response begins and ends with an answer to what it means to believe in Jesus Christ. It is precisely in the theological reconsideration of such faith that we are able to clarify the Christian truth claim while simultaneously opening a way to reflect on this truth claim in relation to other religions.

2. The Pitfalls of Exclusivism, Inclusivism, and Pluralism

We briefly alluded above to the three classical theological strategies that have been enlisted in an effort to conceptualize the relationship between the Christian faith and other (world) religions: exclusivism, inclusivism, and pluralism.[6] We now present a brief sketch of each strategy according to its primary features. We will then examine the theological-epistemological role they play as regards faith in the incarnation, the confession that God has made history in a unique and incomparable way in Jesus Christ.

The Limits of the Three Classical Strategies

1. *Exclusivism,* with *extra ecclesiam nulla salus* ("there is no salvation outside the church") as its motto, maintains that there is no truth or salvation to be found outside the Christian faith, outside the Christian faith community. Those who do not accept Christianity as the way to salvation are not saved. Those who adhere to a different religion should convert to the true faith, certainly if they have already come into contact with Christianity. This strategy bears witness to a deep sense of trust in the redemptive truth of the Christian faith, on the one hand, and the gravity of the Christian truth claim, on the other. God's universal salvific will is strictly bound to the saving mediation of Jesus Christ and the salvific necessity of the church. The strategy is not quite as rigid as it might seem: those who adhere to a different belief system yet desire implicitly to be baptized and thus to belong to the church can still be saved.

2. *Inclusivism* argues that while the Christian faith is the true religion, this does not exclude the possibility that elements of truth and salvation may be found in the other religions. As a matter of fact, God's salvific will extends to all people. All those who seek God and live according to their own conscience can be saved. Some theologians, notably Karl Rahner, speak in this regard of "anonymous Christians." The fragments of truth and salvation apparent in such men and women, however, only acquire their fullest significance and ultimate completion in the light of the gospel. The Christian understanding of truth and salvation provides the key to the appreciation and evaluation of the elements of truth and salvation present in other religion. Religions that encourage their adherents to charity in their interaction with others, certainly with respect to the poor and the alienated, ultimately lead their adherents to, albeit implicit, Christian discipleship. The fullest significance and scope of such behavior only become explicitly manifest in the Christian faith. The Second Vatican Council thus stated that the church "did not reject anything

6. For a comprehensive, paradigmatic survey see P. F. Knitter, *Introducing Theologies of Religions* (Maryknoll, NY: Orbis, 2002).

true and sacred found in other religions," even though "the fullness of religious life is to be found in Christ."[7]

3. A *pluralist* perspective maintains *grosso modo* that all religions are to be considered particularizations or concrete cases of a universal religion or religiosity, distinct witnesses to a universal religious experience or different historical-contextual representations of one and the same religious desire. Taken together they give form to (often complementary) perspectives on a truth (or parts thereof) that is richer than anything that can be contained by one single religion. The salvation promised in Jesus Christ, therefore, cannot be presented as unique, irreducible, or complete, because the Christian perspective constitutes only one single part of a more inclusive religious reality. Other religious geniuses and figures such as Moses, Mohammed, Buddha, Shiva, etc., reveal an equal measure of worthy aspects of this ultimate reality. Religions are facets, as it were, of one and the same diamond, which no one is able to see in its entirety.

It is primarily this third conceptual strategy that tends to weaken the constitutive character of the Christological confession for the Christian faith. Each in their own fashion and in their own historical context, every religion and every religious leader (Buddha, Jesus, Mohammed . . .) has opened a pathway toward the fulfillment of religious desire, which is a universally human phenomenon. Pluralist Christian thinkers endeavor to give expression to this reality in theological terms. They mostly begin with the presupposition that God is, in principle, unknowable and that Christians cannot claim to have privileged access to such knowledge. Such a perspective calls, in the first instance, for a review of the central role of Jesus Christ, the man in whom Christians confess God has been revealed. Some do so by designating the incarnation as a myth or a metaphor, or by describing Jesus as one of the many faces of God. Others separate the second and third persons of the Trinity, the Son/the Word and the Spirit, from the concrete figure of Jesus Christ and ascribe to them a more elaborate salvific role, remote from Christ. Other religious figures likewise refer to the second person of the Trinity or are inspired by the third. As a consequence, the revelation of God in Jesus, and thus also his salvific role, is considered to be limited, incomplete, or imperfect. In short, in order to ascribe a role to other religions, the theologians in question radically relativize the Christian truth claim. At the most, Jesus Christ *represents* God but he does not incarnate God. Jesus is a human

7. Second Vatican Council, *Nostra Aetate*, no. 2.

example of God, but no longer God made flesh.[8] The awareness of religious plurality thus leads to relativistic pluralism, whereby it becomes difficult to take truth claims and identity seriously, let alone uphold them. If everything has the same truth value then nothing is ultimately true.

The question remains, of course, whether one would be better off with the other two conceptual strategies. Exclusivism tends to have extremely totalitarian features, and has enormous difficulty in ascribing a place to the good things encountered outside Christianity. Incarnation, as God's concrete intervention in history, is both absolute and limiting at one and the same time: since salvation is complete in Jesus Christ, there is no room for salvation elsewhere. The step toward Christian fundamentalism is but a short one, especially in an inimical environment that lacks any level of sensitivity toward the Christian confession. Moreover, such an exclusivist approach is problematic at a time in which the encounter with believers of other faiths teaches Christians that religious identity, profound spirituality, authentic praxis, and deep-rooted rituality are no longer the monopoly of Christians.

When it comes to respecting the "seriousness" of other religions, inclusivism is much better placed. It allows for the presence of truth and salvation outside Christianity, albeit always in a fragmentary form that can only achieve completion within Christianity. The incarnation of God in Jesus Christ is ultimately the deepest realization of the fragments of salvation and truth to be found in other religions. Upon closer inspection, however, inclusivism does not succeed in ascribing a worthy place to other religions, including their truth claims, in relation to the Christian faith. Whatever way one looks at it, Christianity is always more true, more good, more authentic. Such an, often latent, sense of superiority has the evident capacity to undermine every form of interreligious communication in advance, because it remains in essence just as totalitarian as exclusivism (although not quite so in practice![9]).

Each of the three classical strategies intended to facilitate our conceptualization of the relationship between Christianity and other religions must inevitably come face to face with its own limitations. Pluralism fails

---

8. Cf., for example, J. Hick, *An Interpretation of Religion: Human Responses to the Transcendent* (London: Macmillan Press, 1989); P. F. Knitter, *One Earth, Many Religions: Multifaith Dialogue and Global Responsibility* (Maryknoll, NY: Orbis, 1995), and esp. J. Hick, ed., *The Myth of God Incarnate* (London: SCM, 1977); id., *The Metaphor of God Incarnate* (London: SCM, 1993). The same critique of pluralism is expressed in *Dominus Iesus*, the Declaration of the Congregation for the Doctrine of the Faith on the unique and salvifically necessary universality of Jesus Christ (and the church).

9. Cf. P. F. Knitter, *Introducing Theologies of Religions*, pp. 103ff.

to maintain the identity and gravity of the Christian truth claim; exclusivism and inclusivism find it difficult to ascribe a satisfactory place to other religions and their truth claims. In interreligious dialogue, pluralism is required in advance to relinquish a core element of the Christian confession of faith as a self-imposed condition, in order to be able to participate in the said dialogue in the first place. Exclusivism and inclusivism take the veracity of their own convictions as their point of departure and leave little if any room for any kind of otherness that does not square with their own convictions. How then do we move forward?

Incarnation between Universalization and Particularization

All things considered, the three conceptual strategies can ultimately be reduced to two ways of resolving the question of the relationship between the Christian faith and other religions. In the first instance — with respect to exclusivism and inclusivism — Christianity is *universalized:* the Christian faith is the one and only truth, for all times and places and peoples. It is thus from the perspective of this truth that Christians perceive other religions as either completely lacking in truth or sharing only in a part thereof. The person of Jesus Christ is considered primarily from the perspective of his divinity. The fact that Jesus Christ is God incarnate makes the Christian faith superior to or at least more comprehensive than other religions.

In the second instance — with respect to pluralism — Christianity is *particularized:* the Christian faith is (only) one perspective on, or part of, a greater truth. It is one specific (particular) truth that is contained in or surpassed by a higher (universal) truth. The divinity of Jesus Christ becomes relative in the incarnation. Jesus was certainly an extraordinary human being, characterized by a profound relationship with God, capable of inspiring people and leading them to the knowledge of God, but he is not *the* incarnation of God, qualitatively incomparable, unique and definitive. In a best case scenario, Jesus is certainly a splendid representative of God, but not necessarily the only one.[10]

Exclusivism and inclusivism generalize the confession of Christ, and because of this, the religious truth claims of other religions are denied or forced to fit within the Christian truth claim. Pluralism, on the other hand,

10. For a philosophical-theological elaboration of this dynamics of universalization and particularization, see my "The Particularity of Religious Truth Claims: How to Deal with It in a So-called Postmodern Context," in *Truth: Interdisciplinary Dialogues for a Pluralist Age*, ed. K. De Troyer and C. Helmer, Studies in Philosophical Theology 22 (Leuven: Peeters Press, 2003), 181–95.

relativizes the confession of Christ by subordinating it to a transcendent, more comprehensive truth, to which other religions also contribute as partial truths or perspectives on the truth. In more technical terms: in the first instance, the historical-contingent particularity of Christian revelation is immediately positioned within a virtually meta-historical Christian frame of interpretation. Concrete narratives and histories, people and events are taken up into an all-inclusive vision of history; they stand face to face with *the* truth, *the* salvation, and are thereby deprived in principle of their historical accidentality. In the second instance, the Christian truth claim is relativized in function of a more general religious truth, precisely because it is *merely* a product of an overly historical-particular and contingent history of tradition. Precisely because it is rooted in an accidental convergence of circumstances, an historical conglomeration of narratives, events, and rituals, Christianity cannot lay claim to the truth and the Christian claim to the truth is unjustified. The concrete particularity of the Christian faith narrative is thus used as an argument in support of relativizing Christianity's truth claim; the particular can never be identified with the truth.

In both instances, "incarnation" is understood as the absorption of the historical-particular into the universal or the reduction thereof into the universal. Truth thus comes to equal universality. This also explains the way in which the three strategies in question evaluate "incarnation": for exclusivism and inclusivism, incarnation is the cornerstone of the truth claim that universalizes Christian particularity; the human Jesus becomes the vessel of a universal, all-embracing divine truth. For the same reason, by contrast, incarnation is the stumbling block par excellence for pluralism. Precisely because the dogma of the incarnation universalizes the historical-particular Christian truth claim, thus making it totalitarian, a respectful approach to other religions becomes impossible. It is only when the fullness of truth is not identified with the Christian faith that it becomes possible for other religions to claim the truth (however partial). The truth in both instances is not to be found in the specific particularity of the Christian faith but rather in either a universalized Christian faith or a universal religion, of which particular Christianity is but one single form. If truth exists then it does so *in spite of* particularity.

It remains a question whether the truth of a religion (understood as the truth one lives by rather than in terms of scientific truth) is best conceptualized in general, universal terms to which concrete religious traditions are related in as far as they are particular, contingent, and historical instances thereof. Do we not do an injustice to the specificity of theological truth by capturing it in an asymmetrical opposition between particularity and universality? Furthermore, is it not possible to understand incarnation in the opposite sense, namely, by insisting that, if truth exists, it is to be found in the concrete, the historical and the particular? Is this not the ultimate meaning of incarnation: that the "all-too-human" speaks for God, without diminishing God in the process and without assimilating humanity into God? In order to complete our line of inquiry we now return once again to the theological reflection on interreligious dialogue, to communication between different fundamental life options.

3. Truth and Incarnation

Truth in Interreligious Communication: Toward an Alternative Form of Inclusivism

We already noted above that contact and confrontation with other religions not only forces Christians to reflect on the relationship between Christianity and the religions in question but also to think about the Christian faith itself and the truth claims for which it stands. An encounter with a Muslim or participation in a Hindu ritual can confront Christians with questions about what they themselves stand for, how they themselves experience their faith. In contrast to pluralism, which maintains that one's own truth claims and one's own identity have to be relativized in, or with a view toward, interreligious communication, we contend that the dynamic is precisely the reverse: in one's contact with other religions and the dialogue that ensues therefrom, potential points of mutual kinship emerge side by side with reciprocal difference and an awareness of the uniqueness of the dialogue partners.

A discussion between Christians and Buddhists on the topic of mysticism and contemplation, one suspects, would reveal significant points of agreement. At the same time, however, it also attests to the difference between both. It truly makes a difference if one contemplates the mystery of reality as "love" or as "emptiness."[11] For the Christian believer, the ultimate truth of reality was definitively revealed in Jesus Christ as the mystery of love. Living one's life according to this reality makes one a Christian and ultimately serves as the measure of one's Christianity. It is

11. See e.g., the biographical reflections of J.-M. Verlinde in *L'expérience interdite* (Versailles: Editions Saint-Paul, 1998), chapter 9.

thus rooted in such an identity — which is not acquired automatically — that Christians approach the plurality of other religions and enter into dialogue with them. Their endeavor to follow Christ in their lives does not only lead Christians on a path that brings them into contact with others, it also forms the background and interpretative key of the way in which they engage in such contacts. For Christians, the recognition of goodness and truth in other religions takes place of necessity in reference to Jesus Christ, precisely because they engage in contact with others as Christians. Does this mean that Christians necessarily enter into every dialogue in an inclusivist way? In a certain sense: yes! How then do we deal with the objection that inclusivism leans in the direction of totalitarianism?

Perhaps we are dealing with a *different* type of inclusivism in such instances, an inclusivism that does not bear the universalizing tendencies we noted above. Indeed, interreligious dialogue teaches us in practice that there is no neutral place or neutral language in which to speak about the multiplicity of religions, and that the Christian discourse also consists of a highly specific grammar and vocabulary rooted in its own background and traditions. This Christian discourse cannot simply be translated into the discourses of other religions and vice versa. Non-Christian dialogue partners are often unable to recognize themselves in the language employed by pluralist theologians, for example, to conceptualize the multiplicity of religions (because it often contains a significant residue of the Christian discourse). There is no such thing as a religious Esperanto into which every religion can be translated. We have no standard religious language, neither philosophical nor anthropological, at our disposal that allows us to make the uniqueness of every religion — as it is sensed by their faithful from within — transparent and understandable to all. We do not possess a conceptual framework in which a sort of unified religion can be designated or constructed of which the various religions of the world are concrete representations. Christians engage in dialogue with people of other beliefs and other fundamental life options as participants with their own background and horizon side by side with other participants.

As a matter of fact, interreligious dialogue itself confronts inclusivist theologians with their own particular points of departure and makes them aware that they participate in such dialogue from a Christian perspective. Christians are already located, have already adopted a position in the plural domain of interreligious communication, and it is from this position, in the midst of other positions, that they should assess their necessarily inclusivist dealings with others. Christians do not have a bird's eye view that allows them to survey religious plurality as detached observers and grant it a place in light of its own truth. Indeed, Christianity's own place in the midst of plurality is part of the picture. The "different inclusivism" to which we refer is conscious of the particularity of the Christian faith and brings it into the dialogue, not in order to relativize its own position but rather to determine it in the plural, interreligious world. In the context of interreligious contacts and communication, Christians will ultimately be confronted with their own specific way of speaking about reality. Unable to distance themselves from their particular options, presuppositions, terminology, and conceptual schemes, Christians ultimately approach others with their own "baggage." An example thereof is the universal salvific will of God, which explains why Christians tend to be so highly motivated in their engagement in interreligious dialogue.

Probably the (modern/rational) notion that Christian believers can abstract themselves from their concrete rootedness in a tradition lies hidden behind the opinion of certain theological pluralists that Christians can adopt the position of detached observers, allowing them to make statements above and beyond the plural religious reality to which they then adapt their theology. In such a scenario, the truth of the Christian faith becomes dependent on a coordinating rational scheme that enables it to locate all religions. Incidentally, an atheistic variant of such pluralism also exists. A number of atheistic scholars in anthropology or religious studies, certainly those still profoundly impregnated with the ideals of the Enlightenment, likewise see themselves as observers located at a meta-level, elevated above the plurality of religions, which they maintain they are free to judge. They forget, however, that as self-declared children of the Enlightenment, they are also a part of the plurality over which they judge, and that their atheistic position does not grant them the right to pretend otherwise.

We can use an image to explain what we mean. Some pluralists present the various religions as a variety of different paths that lead to the same mountaintop engulfed in clouds. How can we verify such a hypothesis, however, if we only follow one of the said paths, namely, the Christian one? Without a bird's eye perspective on the religious reality it is impossible to legitimate the image. There's the rub! Only from a "helicopter" perspective one could be sure that all paths lead to the same top. A further elaboration of this image therefore leads to the opposite conclusion. The experience of religious plurality and interreligious dialogue reveal that the observer's position is in fact unsustainable. We are all participants. We all follow our own path. We are aware that other paths exist that cross our own from time to time or run parallel with our path for a while only to go off in their own direction. Walking on our own path, however, it is impossible for us to confirm that all these paths actually lead to the same mountaintop. Indeed, it is equally possible that one or another path, which disappears beyond the horizon and into the clouds, might lead to a different mountaintop. It is impossible to confirm this from the perspective of our own path and likewise impossible to deny it. We simply do not know. Nevertheless, we climb the mountain using our own path and from time to time other paths cross our own. It is thus from our own experiences as mountain climbers that we enter into dialogue and that we are able to exchange thoughts and customs, joys and concerns with others, rooted in our experience of the journey. A particular role is set aside in this endeavor for the imagination. Aware of the fact that we are participants, and learning about the other inform our contacts with the other, we are capable, to a degree, of changing our perspective, without revoking however the irreducible otherness of the other in the process.

An inclusivist perspective is thus — epistemologically speaking — unavoidable. Nevertheless, the question posed by pluralist theologians with respect to the relationship between Christian truth claims and the other religions remains a pressing one: how do we couple an explicit Christian identity to a fundamental respect for other religions? The practice of interreligious dialogue would appear to show that there is room for both, but how can we conceptualize this reality in theological terms? Is a sort of "pluralist" inclusivism conceivable?

In contrast to the classical inclusivist position, this would at least imply that Christians approach religious plurality from the perspective of participants. For us as Christians, the mystery of Christ constitutes the perspective from which we speak about religious salvation and truth, because we live in and from this truth. Just as the universal salvific will of God, which is revealed to us in Christ, provides the Christian point of cross-reference that inspires us to seek traces of goodness and truth in other religions. We can only follow one path at a time — trusting that all humanity is ultimately saved in Christ.

The Truth of the Incarnation Is the Incarnation of Truth

We noted above that the "incarnation" might signify more than the idea that theological truth is revealed in the particular or in other words that the particular is the vessel of the universal. The truth of the incarnation indicates, rather, that the particular is constitutive of the truth, essential and indispensable. Truth is real, concrete, incarnate, and can only be grasped as such. This means that when we speak of Jesus Christ, God's Son made flesh, we cannot simply make a distinction between the divinity and humanity of Jesus, even although they do not coincide. God's revelation is unthinkable without the human Jesus; the human Jesus is constitutive of what we know of Jesus as Christ, of Christian faith in him. It is in Jesus, in his concrete humanity, that God is revealed among human beings, the Jew from Nazareth who proclaimed the Kingdom of God in the language and narratives of his own day and put it into practice until he died on the Cross outside Jerusalem. It is of this same Jesus that his disciples confessed after his death that he had risen, that he was the Christ, God's Son, *in* his humanity and not *in spite of* it. The one who desires to know God must look at Jesus. The first disciples expressed the results of their faith-inspired recognition of Jesus in the New Testament, in the language and stories of their day — in the same way as the faith communities that followed them have been doing, inspired time after time by these words.

Moreover, Jesus Christ reveals God and God's desire for human beings *thanks to* his humanity. Classical theology tends to explain this point in "soteriological" terms, from the perspective of "he descended from heaven for our salvation." Only if God has really become human, it is proposed, can the human person really become God; it is only because God shared humanity to the full with us that we human beings are saved. At this juncture, we rather emphasize the epistemological perspective, so the question runs: what does it say about the truth unfolded in Christ? As we have already stated, the person who desires to know God must look to Jesus Christ who, as a human person, definitively revealed God in history. At the same time, divine truth for Christians is also to be located in concrete events and narratives. It is only in the all-too-historical, the concrete, the accidental, that God can become manifest, that God becomes manifest. This does not mean that God coincides with the concrete and the accidental, but that the concrete and the accidental make the manifestation of God possible, not in spite of but rather thanks to the concrete and the accidental. Every concrete encounter, no matter how accidental, every particular and contingent event, is the potential locus of God's manifestation. For Christians, God's revelation in Jesus Christ forms the hermeneutical key in this regard.

This is what the Christological dogma of the Council of Chalcedon[12] — Jesus Christ is at the same time both God and human — can mean for us today: God is revealed in Jesus Christ, not without Jesus' humanity but in and through it; as a human person, Jesus reveals God without thereby giving up his humanity. Historically situated in a very specific context, Jesus' concrete words and deeds reveal God. Also today, every current statement about this God and this revelation must comply with the same rules. Even today, it is only possible to give expression to God's involvement in history and the world in all-too-human terms. Jesus' particular humanity, concrete history and events, Christian narratives and interpretative frameworks, do not represent a stumbling block on our journey to God, they represent the very possibility of the journey.

What we have just said is in fact true of every human engagement with the Christian faith. It is only in the particular word, narrative, ritual and practice that the profound significance of the Christian faith can be revealed. Incarnation thus demands — formulated once again in technical terms — an ongoing "radical hermeneutics" in which the particular as the possibility of divine revelation is taken seriously and at the same time relativized, since the particular never coincides with God, just as God and humanity are united in a single person, undivided and undiluted. This is the core around which the Christian tradition turns: the latter cannot be substituted nor can it be absolutized. It speaks of God — and without it there can be no talk about God — but it is not God. Where tradition is absolutized, it is precisely Godself who interrupts such self-enclosing rigidity and fosters recontextualization. It follows, therefore, that there is no such thing as a core of truths that can be distinguished as such from every form of mediation, which is given expression in ever changing historical frameworks, as many classical hermeneutic (and less hermeneutic) theologians have argued. On the contrary, theological truth is co-constituted by the all-too-human, by concrete history and context. This does not do an injustice to such truth, since it is only thus, through time and history, that we can speak about God. Likewise, it is through this tradition that God speaks to Christians today, embedded in the current historical context, whereby this tradition both perpetuates and renews itself.

---

12. For this paragraph see also my "Christus *Postmodernus: An Attempt at Apophatic Christology," in *The Myriad Christ: Plurality and the Quest for Unity in Contemporary Christology*, ed. T. Merrigan and J. Haers, BETL 152 (Leuven: Peeters Press, 2000), 577–93.

In conclusion, Christology, the theological understanding of Jesus Christ, is the cornerstone of all Christian theology and necessary for a clear understanding of what in theological terms is the truth. The all-too-human does not obstruct genuine Christian discourse about God (and to God); it is its very precondition.

4. Conclusion

As we have already stated, Christians today are being challenged by religious plurality. In the context of interreligious dialogue, they are being called upon to respect their own truth claims together with the truth claims of others at one and the same time. Rooted in their own Christian narrative background, they engage themselves as participants in a dialogue that need not necessarily lead to greater unity; the recognition of points of difference is already a major step in the right direction. As conscious participants, moreover, Christians are well advised not to misjudge the particularity of their own position as something over which the truth claims of Christianity must echo and resound, or as something that discredits the truth claims of Christianity in advance, but rather as irreducibly co-constitutive of the truth of the Christian faith. Neither the inclination to universalize the truth claim (exclusivism and inclusivism) nor the relativizing negation thereof (pluralism) are of much use. It is precisely in the combination of maintaining both their particularity and their truth claim that Christians are able to enter into interreligious communication, looking forward to the moment at which Jesus Christ reveals himself in such dialogues, as he continues to do "in the least of these. . . . "

Neither dialogue with the Enlightenment nor the contemporary confrontation with religious plurality can provide us with incontrovertible evidence in support of the Christian faith. Indeed, there is nothing to be distilled from such dialogue that makes Jesus God. It is only in faith that Jesus leads to God. The reconsideration of this faith in the contemporary context of religious plurality, however, can lead men and women to the boundaries of the faith, to the point where faith begins. The same process of reconsideration, moreover, locates Christians in the midst of the public debate on the kind of society we desire for today and tomorrow. At a time in which the master narratives of modernity have lost their plausibility, and economization and mediatization have come to dominate the public forum hand over fist, it might appear that the Christian appeal to see the truth in the concrete and the particular has little to offer — unless it is understood as a point of departure whereby Christians together with others are able to critique the said processes of globalization and streamlining, and draw attention to the "unimportant" other. Considered in this fashion, it would appear that Christianity still has something on offer for contemporary society. In the following chapter we will take these political-theological consequences a step further.

Chapter Nine

God Interrupts Time

Apocalypticism as an Indispensable Theological Conceptual Strategy

The Christian apocalyptic imagination is the result of a combination of two Jewish expectations: the coming of an earthly Messiah who was to establish a kingdom of peace and justice and the execution of God's final judgement at the end of history.[1] This stock of ideas has been broadly received in the course of the preceding two millennia in both religious and secularized senses. The apocalyptic era was to be looked forward to and promised to be characterized by salvation for the chosen, the purification of iniquity, and the destruction of the forces of evil, all of which formed part of the expectation of the definitive completion (and thus dissolution) of history. This apocalyptic fervor frequently found its way into sectarian and often millenaristic movements. Even a number of Church Fathers, such as Irenaeus of Lyon, envisaged the dawn of a thousand-year dominion as an interruption in the course of history. A serious upsurge of apocalyptic fever gave rise to figures such as Joachim di Fiori in the twelfth century as well as the *Schwärmer* movement, the "leftist" reformation, in the sixteenth century (Thomas Münzer, Hans Hut). In this instance, apocalypticism went hand in hand with significant dissatisfaction concerning the existing situation and an appeal for radical change. Chiliasm — an alternative term for millenarianism — can be discerned even today among the Adventists and the Jehovah's Witnesses. The apocalyptic imagination has also left significant traces in

1. The expectation of a messianic kingdom is to be found in the first book of Enoch, the fourth book of Ezra and in the New Testament book of Revelation (or *Apocalypse*). The devil is to be imprisoned for a period of one thousand years, a time in which Christ will reign together with the righteous martyrs. The devil is thereafter set free for a short time before his definitive defeat. It is at this point that the final judgement will take place, to be followed by the establishment of a new heaven and a new earth and the descent of the new Jerusalem from heaven (Rev 21). For further information and additional literature on this topic cf. "Apocalypses and apocalypticism," in *The Anchor Bible Dictionary*, I (New York: Doubleday, 1992), 279–87.

modern political philosophy (see, for example, the hope expressed by Lessing and Kant for an era of completion and eternal peace) and political history (see, among other things, North American political-religious rhetoric, the Marxist utopia of a classless society, or the establishment of the Third *Reich*).[2]

We are confronted today with a remarkable paradox, remarkable enough to inspire the writing of the present chapter. On the one hand, we live at a time in which apocalyptic ideas have virtually vanished from the Christian tradition, often on account of the dialogue between Christian faith and modernity: apocalypticism is considered too mythological, too dangerous, too literal, too speculative, too escapist. On the other hand, however, we are now surprisingly faced with a "post-Christian" cultural environment in which the apocalyptic is raising its head once again. It manifests itself in the form of an apocalyptic sentiment that expresses itself, among other things, in a fear of the physical end of the world, of the moral collapse of the human race, of the ultimate meaninglessness of human existence and every human aspiration or thought. Ancient biblical images seem to have become metaphors for contemporary cultural sensitivities.

1. Apocalypse Now: Symptom of a Culture Adrift?

In everyday linguistic usage, the term "apocalypse" tends in the first instance to refer to a disastrous event, one that presents a threat to the continued existence of humanity and the world, a world-wide catastrophe, the end of the world. We survived the "millennium bug," for example, which not only threatened to incapacitate our information-based society but also to hand us over to all sorts of wild scenarios of anarchy and chaos. While the entire millennium discussion fell silent a long time ago, it remains a question whether the crisis was only a well-designed, commercial peak moment for the information technology sector or whether the same sector ultimately succeeded in avoiding disaster.

Apocalypse between Cultural Pessimism and Reaffirmation of Trust

The roots of present-day apocalyptic sentiment are basically the same as they always have been: earthquakes, environmental disasters, chaos,

2. See in this regard, e.g., "Chiliasmus," in *Religion in Geschichte und Gegenwart: Handwörterbuch für Theologie und Religionswissenschaft,* II, 4th ed. (Tübingen: Mohr Siebeck, 1999), 136–44.

and war. Present-day anxiety about global warming, the safety of the food we eat and its effect on our health (bird-flu, etc.) might constitute appropriate new additions to the list. In every case, we are confronted with developments that go unchecked and remain uncheckable, developments that suddenly constitute a threat to humanity and social existence. In addition, the simultaneity of new information media technology has changed our perception of time. The flood of ominous messages of doom seems to be unstoppable and would appear to be expanding exponentially. The result is a growing sense of unease that expresses itself in insecurity and a lack of future perspective. Both conservative and progressive critics of culture tend to proclaim the same message albeit in different terminology: we live in a culture of death, drugs, and sex. We are undergoing a sort of spiritual apocalypse of which the AIDS pandemic, among other things, constitutes a significant material incarnation. Our culture has become a meaning-devouring monster that has sown the seeds of its own downfall.

Apocalypticism is also a popular theme in the world of the film.[3] Movies that exploit biblical images of impending destruction and of the ultimate struggle between good and evil are reaping in box-office dollars. The same is true of disaster movies of every sort: sinking ships (*Titanic*), erupting volcanoes, crashing airplanes, etc. We are presented with a hungry fascination for human limits and their transgression, for threats of every kind, for anything that upsets our confidence and safe lifestyle. Besides such threats, however, we often encounter an albeit Hollywood-inspired re-affirmation of our faith in the good, in life itself, and in ourselves. The good always wins out in the end (*Judge Dredd*), and our omnipotence is confirmed once again (*Independence Day*). What appeared to be leading to an end full of death and destruction is transformed into a history of victory. Nevertheless, such documents continue to represent the other side of the picture: our hidden fear of being dominated by something we ourselves have created, of machines and robots which take command over our lives, sometimes without us even being aware of it (*cyborgs* and the *replicants* from *The Terminator* which

3. Cf. *Apocalypse Now, Independence Day, End of Days, Armageddon, Judge Dredd.* See, for example, S. De Bleeckere, "De apocalyptische verbeelding: Over enkele filmische apocalypsen," *Kultuurleven* 63 (1996): 80–87; C. Martig, "Filmische Apokalypsen: Wie das Kino dem Ende der Zeit entgegenfiebert," *Herder Korrespondenz* 54 (2000): 32–38; "Populäre Apokalyptik: Weltuntergang und Neuschöpfung im Kino," *Internationale Katholische Zeitschrift Communio* 28 (1999): 545–53; R. Zwick, "Jüngste Tage: Variationen der Apokalypse im Film," in *Jüngste Tage: Die Gegenwart der Apokalyptik*, ed. M. N. Ebertz and R. Zwick (Freiburg: Herder, 1999), 184–226.

cannot be distinguished from real human beings), of apparent progress that ends in ecological catastrophe.... At the same time, however, they also remind us of our fear of those things that have always been beyond our control: fate, strangeness, etc. Such films often achieve commercial success, not only because they offer spectacular cinema with lots of special effects, but also because they seem to touch us at a deeper level. As with the reading of ancient apocalyptic texts, cultural scientists and philosophers should be on their guard against an all too literal approach to such films. Compelled by the plot, by the *genius* of the narrative and the special effects, we are probably hearing echoes of something deeper than the spectacle that flashes before our eyes on the silver screen.[4]

The "ultimate struggle between good and evil" is not only the subject of movies and fictional literature; it also raises its head from time to time in real life. Examples include the incident in Waco, Texas, in 1993 in which the FBI besieged the Branch Davidian complex headed by David Koresh for 51 days. The siege left 81 sect members dead. The latter incident is reminiscent of the mass suicide (murder?) of the members of Jim Jones' People's Temple in Guyana in 1978 in which 912 people were left dead and the ritual suicides of the Temple of the Sun and Heaven's Gate sects, to say nothing of the Oklahoma bomb attack in 1995 — supposedly the work of Christian fundamentalists — and the so-called "Serin Gas" sect and their attack on the Tokyo underground in 1999.[5] To cap it all, of course, reference can be made to Islamist terrorism that has been responsible for widespread death and destruction in New York (2001), Madrid (2003), and London (2005). The fact that the West is incapable of extinguishing (self-established) hotbeds of terrorism in the Middle East has given rise to a creeping and permanent sense of insecurity — especially when Muslim youth in the underprivileged suburbs of our major cities turn against society out of frustration (Brussels 2004, France 2005). It is equally disturbing to observe that some of us would even appear to be prepared to set aside the principles of our constitutional state in order to defend it.

Three Characteristics of Contemporary Apocalyptic Sensitivity

A closer examination of this cultural and social phenomenon allows us to discern three specific characteristics that typify contemporary apocalyptic sensitivity.

---

4. Cf. M. E. Williams, *Apocalypse Now,* in *Concilium* 33, no. 4 (1998): 3–10, p. 6.

5. See, for example, R. Hill, "Glaube und Furcht vor dem Millennium," *Internationale Katholische Zeitschrift Communio* 28 (1999): 531–44.

A. Fear of the Self-Provoked Judgement

In the first instance, it would appear that contemporary apocalyptic sensitivity involves the judgement of humanity's delusions of grandeur. In their desire to dominate and control nature, human beings have initiated a process that can no longer be stopped. Paradigmatic representations of this process include a number of human apocalypses such as the Holocaust, the Gulags, the Killing Fields,[6] and the fear of a nuclear apocalypse that has certainly not disappeared since the end of the Cold War, and has even acquired a new face in the context of recent threats from Iran and North Korea. Ecological apocalypses also have their place in the scenario: chemical disasters, residential areas built on chemical dumps, heavy metal pollution, stranded oil tankers, food safety scandals, and in particular the increase in climate temperature brought about, among other things, by CO_2 emissions and the exploitation of carbon-based fuels. The so-called "greenhouse" effect has led to a temperature increase of 0.2 degrees Celsius in the last ten years.[7] The increasing gap between rich and poor (the economic apocalypse) also continues to be a factor, with its resultant demographic evolution that is placing unheard-of pressures on the national borders of the rich North. As we noted above, Islamist terrorism combined with the apparently inextinguishable hotbeds of terror in the Middle East have seriously undermined the West's confidence in global governance. In most instances, the apocalyptic imagination expresses the awareness that we are no longer in command of things, that we have created monsters we can no longer control. Humanity has seriously overestimated itself, both at the level of planning the perfect society (with the large-scale abuse of human rights as a misplaced consequence) and in the implementation of a functionalistic and technological view of the world: the reduction of nature and the environment to that which fulfils our needs and sustains our designs. Paradoxically enough, the desire to control and dominate has led us into a confrontation with the uncontrollable and the indomitable. Apocalypse

---

6. Cf. also the 1979 film *Apocalypse Now,* which deals with the Vietnam War.

7. As a consequence thereof scientists have observed that the polar ice cap has been melting (6 percent since 1978) and that this has led to a rise in sea levels, the disruption of the gulf stream, widespread climatic disturbance (desert forming, seasonal disruption, increased hurricane activity), and the disruption of natural biotopes (relocation of breeding and nesting grounds, displacement of flowering periods). Scientists are also concerned with what is going on underground. The permafrost (upon which, e.g., the Alps rest) has already undergone a temperature increase of 1.2 degrees Celsius. Some maintain that within twenty years this will lead to instability in the Alpine valleys, the collapse of buildings, the breakdown of cable lifts, etc. (*De Standaard,* March 13, 2000).

has become a metaphor for what postmodern thinkers have referred to as the end of the master narratives because of their loss of plausibility.

B. Catastrophe Mania as the Reverse Side of the Culture of the Kick

With the demise of the meaning-giving master narratives and detraditionalization, the collective and individual search for meaning has become a highly demanding activity, a question of choices, of identity construction, situated within a complex plurality of mutually questioning, challenging, and enriching fragments and narratives. When one feels it impossible to "write oneself into" a meaning-giving narrative, or one refuses to attach oneself to something meaningful (something that gives one a reason to get up in the morning), the search for meaning and identity construction often turns into an endless search for kicks, for momentary intensifications of one's self-consciousness. While there is indeed nothing wrong with enjoying a harmless kick, when the kick itself becomes one's only source of meaning one risks being swallowed by an endless spiral of progressively heavier kicks from which there is no escape.[8]

Kicks have to do with the transgression of boundaries. Given the momentary character of kicks, however, kick and disappointment tend to go hand in hand; boundaries that one frequently transgresses start shifting. The consolation of the kick turns around an intensification of the "I-experience" sought in response to a desire for meaning that ultimately and immediately escapes our grasp. As a result, the kick's failure to hold onto meaning installs an infinite regression of progressively heavier boundary transgressions. The kick is an endless search to survive in a context of indifference, to be distinct within a milieu of indistinctness. It is the search for that which makes one different from the others, for a way to escape from a colorless existence: "I" don't belong among the impersonal masses; "I" must escape the terror of "sameness," of "lack of distinction," of "meaninglessness"; "I am alive!" Since boundaries tend to shift, however, this search for new and better kicks pushes one further and further, even as far as flirting with death (driving against the traffic, jumping from the rails just as the train passes) and suicide. The extraordinary and the unusual become the only source of meaning. A telling illustration is the case of those who live from weekend to weekend, who thrive on the nightlife from Friday to Sunday, or those who live from vacation to vacation, meaning for such people involves a

8. For a more extensive analysis of the "culture of the kick," see the fifth chapter of *Interrupting Tradition*, pp. 85–87.

transgression of the settings of everyday life because the latter no longer generates sufficient meaning for them.

The apocalyptic mentality is thus a quest for anything that interrupts the run-of-the-mill: the disruption of sameness, the transgression of the ordinary. This ultimately results in a kind of escapism, a flight from the meaninglessness of the endless series of moments, an escape from the experience of being locked up in an insignificant "here and now." Apocalypticism provides emotive language, images and experiences that break with the instrumentalist, technical, rational, bureaucratic, economic discourse, which throws people back on themselves. It has become a metaphor for the ultimate kick, the final transgression of the boundaries.

It is on this very point that the process of economization strikes back once again. Kicks are offered for sale on the market and identity thus becomes a question of purchasing power, marketing, supply and demand. This is also the point to which many forms of new religiosity are linked and a para-religious market flourishes. People are in search of harmony, consolation, fulfillment, and reconciliation in a world that has little to do with the monotony of their everyday existence.

C. Symptom of and Response to an Expanding Insecurity

In more general terms, the apocalyptic revival points to an increasing sense of powerlessness and a waning sense of trust. It bears witness to a vague sense of uncertainty and insecurity — precisely since the collapse of the master narratives that offered incontrovertible certainty and stability. The fact that we now have the freedom to construct our own identity has its negative counterpart in the instability that accompanies every identity we construct or discover. Questions such as "will we share the fate of the dinosaurs?" "will life on earth as we know it be obliterated by a meteor strike?" betray more than just speculation, they are evidence of the growing sense of insecurity that can follow after a period of exaggerated certainty: most dreams are indeed a delusion!

The rise of right-wing (political) groups is also a symptom of this growing sense of vulnerability. They are in search of security in the midst of insecurity. Strangeness, otherness is a threat to my certainty, my narrative, my stability. At the same time, their hostile conceptualization of the other helps them — via the scapegoat mechanism — to mould, stabilize, and strengthen their identity. Apocalypticism in this perspective constitutes a radical form of cultural criticism and cultural pessimism to which fundamentalist variants of religions and sects offer their support in the form of quasi-mythological solutions for the problems of meaninglessness, evil, suffering, and pain. In their view, these problems are a consequence of a culture that they evaluate in terms of superficial aestheticism, amorality and immorality, value relativism, shallowness, arbitrariness, and individualism. The only thing that can offer any certainty is a firm and stable perception of reality that contrasts sharply with such a lamentable state of affairs. It is in this regard that forms of millenarianism are often used to legitimate political and even religious power.

Theological Questions Arising from the Paradox

The paradox, namely, the fact that while apocalypticism has been removed from the theological agenda, at the present time it has become a prominent cultural reality, raises questions for present-day theologians: is the apocalyptic conceptual world passed on by the tradition still valuable for the Christian faith today? Does it still reveal something about the faith and the place of Christians in a world in which what we have called a cultural apocalyptic sensitivity is on the increase?

For the sake of clarity, it should be noted that theology, as we elaborated above, is involved in ongoing processes of "faith in search of understanding." Because of the irreducibly contextual nature of Christian faith, Christians engage in continuous processes of recontextualization due to shifts in historical and cultural contexts in order to re-establish its plausibility and relevance — both with respect to themselves and to non-Christians. Given that Christians today live in a world characterized by plurality at the level of personal and fundamental life options, and given that they now constitute a specific, albeit internally differentiated (minority) group in our pluralist European societies, they are more conscious than in the past of the fact that they are embedded within their own particular narratives and that they belong to their own particular narrative communities.

To assist our theological reflection on apocalypticism and Christian faith, we will employ two distinct yet related points of departure. The first advances the hypothesis that we will elaborate further below, while the second presents the method we intend to employ in doing so.

1. In the first instance, and in line with the argumentation of Johann-Baptist Metz[9], the father of political theology, we propose that the

9. J.-B. Metz, "Der Kampf um die verlorene Zeit — Unzeitgemäße Thesen zur Apokalyptik," in J.-B. Metz, *Unterbrechungen: Theologisch-politische Prespektiven und Profile*

purging of apocalyptic awareness from the Christian tradition stands in the way of an adequate perception of the salience of the Christian tradition. As a matter of fact, this purification process has introduced a perception of time that makes it impossible in principle to authentically conceptualize the radicality of the Christian faith. Apocalypticism is thus an indispensable theological conceptual strategy, no more and no less, to be employed in stressing the distinctive features of the Christian faith in terms of its identity and relevance today.

2. In the second instance, as to our method: contemporary global anxiety — cultural apocalypticism — provides us with the key to come to an adequate theological understanding of biblical apocalypticism. Apocalypticism can be understood in both negative and positive terms, in the same way as "anxiety" can be understood as deadly and destructive while simultaneously sowing the seeds of survival, renewal, and change. From the negative perspective, apocalypticism speaks of global anxiety. From the positive perspective, however, it tends to transform our fear of catastrophe into an awareness of crisis. Fear of the definitive end of the world then is not to be identified with the crack of doom but with paving the way for recognizing, enduring, and surviving the crisis.[10]

Before we examine this topic further, we offer a brief sketch of the apocalyptic tradition and the stages of its disappearance from theological reflection.

2. Christian Theology and Apocalypticism: A Stirring Tradition

The Apocalyptic Genre

In the strict sense of the term, "apocalypse" refers to the literary genre with which we are familiar from the Revelation (Gr. *"apokalypsis"*) of John. The genre as such, however, also occurs in other books of the bible and in particular in the so-called "inter-testamental Jewish literature" (from the third century BCE to the second century CE). Generally

---

(Gütersloh: Gütersloher Taschenbücher Siebenstern, 1981), 85–94, esp. p. 91, thesis 24 — originally published in his *Glaube in Geschichte und Gesellschaft: Studien zu einer Praktischen Fundamentaltheologie* (Mainz: Matthias-Grünewald, 1977), 149–58.

10. This thesis was developed from an existentialist perspective in U. Körtner, *Weltangst und Weltende: Eine theologische Interpretation der Apokalyptik* (Göttingen: Vandenhoeck und Ruprecht, 1988). A shorter version of his argument can be found in U. Körtner, "Weltzeit, Weltangst und Weltende: Zum Daseins- und Zeitverständnis der Apokalyptik," *Theologische Zeitschrift* 45 (1989): 32–52.

speaking, one might define "apocalypse" as a "genre of revelatory literature with a narrative structure within which a revelation is transmitted from a supernatural being to a human receptor. A transcendent reality is hereby disclosed which enjoys both a temporal aspect, insofar as it relates to eschatological salvation, and a spatial aspect, insofar as it relates to a supernatural world distinct from our own. Apocalypse is intended to warn and/or comfort a group of people who are experiencing problems by interpreting the present earthly situation in light of a supernatural existence and of the future, to influence the understanding and behavior of its audience by divine authority."[11] Apocalypse refers thus to a sort of revelation from God, Christ, or an angel, often taking the form of a vision, dream, epiphany, voices (both dialogue and oration), a journey through the heavens, or the acquisition of a heavenly document. The human recipient is often identified pseudonymously with prominent figures from the past (Enoch, Abraham). The revelation itself frequently presents world history as a pattern of calamity, crisis, destruction, and salvation: a recurring sequence of downfall, judgement, damnation, and completion. Revelation also insists on the crucial character of the actual moment, the "now": at this present moment a definitive division is being made between that which leads to salvation and to a new future and that which leads to damnation and destruction.

This definitive new future is frequently represented in a manner that emphasizes discontinuity with the existing world. God's intervention always enjoys priority because the faithful no longer trust their fellow human beings. The *Sitz-im-Leben* of these documents ought to be situated in an atmosphere of crisis: e.g., occupation (the book of *Daniel,* Maccabean resistance to Hellenism during the reign of Antiochus IV Epiphanes, 167–164 BCE), persecution (*Revelation of John,* probably under the Domitian persecution, 81–96 CE), and destruction (*4 Ezra, 2 Baruch,* and *3 Baruch* on the occasion of the destruction of the temple in Jerusalem in 70 CE). The aim of such texts is clearly to offer comfort and to warn simultaneously. They promise hope in a better future while proclaiming judgement and devastation: only those who convert will be saved.

---

11. Definition based on the standard description provided by J. J. Collins, "Introduction: Toward the Morphology of a Genre," in *Apocalypse: The Morphology of a Genre,* ed. J. J. Collins, Semeia, 14 (Missoula, MT: Scholars Press, 1979), p. 9 and expanded upon by J. Hellholm, "The Problem of Apocalyptic Genre and the Apocalypse of John," in *Early Christian Apocalyptic: Genre and Social Setting,* ed. A. Y. Collins, Semeia, 36 (Atlanta: Scholar's Press, 1986), p. 27 (with thanks to Ward Daenen).

The First Christian Apocalyptic Expectations Frustrated

The New Testament contains a significant number of apocalyptic traces and fragments. Besides the book of *Apocalypse* itself, other important examples include the preaching of John the Baptist (Luke 3), the eschatological discourse in Mark 13 (fall of the temple and of Jerusalem, end of the world) and the portrayal of Jesus as the final judge who divides the sheep from the goats in Matthew 25:31ff. A large number of apocalyptic metaphors and images add color to the pages of the New Testament witness to Jesus' words and deeds, death and resurrection. Examples include the title "Son of Man," the theme of judgement, the everlasting fire prepared for the devil and his cohorts, eternal life, the dawning of the kingdom of God, the categories of resurrection and second coming, the angels by the tomb, the appearance narratives, and so forth.

The fact that the first generation of Christians was convinced that the return of the Lord was at hand[12] is evident from several pericopes from the letters of Paul. Paul was of the opinion, for example, that it was better not to marry in light of the impending *parousia* (1 Cor. 7:1–9). As a matter of fact, the first disciples did not only believe that Jesus Christ "rose on the third day to sit at the right hand of God the Father," they also believed that he would quickly "return in glory to judge the living and the dead." The return of the risen Lord would constitute a radical interruption in human history and would definitively establish the kingdom of God. The liturgical "Maranatha" formula ("Our Lord has come" or "Come, Lord") offers a striking evocation of this fact (1 Cor. 16:22; Rev. 22:20; *Didachè* 10:6), in similar fashion to the prayer "Your kingdom come, Your will be done on earth is in heaven" taken from the Our Father.

The tense "apocalyptic" expectations of the first disciples, however, were never relieved; the end of time was postponed. The expectation of the Lord's immanent return had to be reappraised. This process is already evident in later writings of the New Testament such as the so-called pastoral letters in which the organization of the community had already become a point of discussion. As long as the *parousia* remained forthcoming, a process of institutionalization and ecclesialization set in (both of which would increase in intensity after Constantine's edict of toleration in 313). In addition, the sacraments were also afforded a more

12. For this and the following paragraphs see, for example, P. Mueller-Goldkühle, "The Post-Biblical Developments in Eschatological Thought," *Concilium* 5, no. 1 (1969): 24–41.

significant place as signs that anticipate the coming kingdom of God in the here and now.

The emergence of "an apologetics of delay" constitutes a third element in which the emphasis which was once placed on the imminent return of the Lord is now focused on the suddenness of his return. This procedure was frequently accompanied by a strong moralizing tendency; by delaying his return, the merciful God opens up new possibilities for conversion, even although the final judgement and the day of reckoning can arrive at any moment. In the last analysis, the apocalyptic tension was dissolved into a present that already considered itself to be participating in eschatological salvation (via the sacraments and the church) and a future that remained far off. "The events which had once been expected in the near future — parousia, resurrection, judgement, and the new creation — were now expected in the distant future. In this way the eschatological tension of the apostolic era was neutralized. Considerable speculation about the world to come persisted, but the note of passionate longing for it was muted."[13] The first *"de-apocalypticization'* was hereby put into practice.

Ongoing De-Apocalyptization via Hellenization and Modernization

Partly under the influence of Greek thought, the reinterpretation of the eschatological expectation led to an ever-increasing interest in the fate of the individual soul. The notion thus emerged that a special judgement would take place directly after one's death and people began to reflect on the situation of the soul detached from the body and on personal immortality. Such individualization and spiritualization (with the accent on the soul) raised questions as to what was supposed to happen in the meantime, prior to the final judgement of the world, which was to occur at the end of time. "Interim thinking" occasioned the elaboration of an "individual eschatology" (death, individual judgement, purification in purgatory) that could be distinguished from general eschatology, a distinction that functioned up to and including the twentieth century. Apocalyptic images were set aside for this final, general eschatology at the end of time: the return of the Lord, a definitive settlement of accounts with evil, collective judgement and completion ("a new heaven and a new earth"), and the resurrection of the body. The eschatological tractate thus became a "chronology of eternal life" and "a geography of the

13. Mueller-Goldkühle, "The Post-Biblical Developments," p. 26.

hereafter."[14] Metaphors and images were no longer seen as constitutive elements of a narrative whole; instead, they had become the building blocks of an eschatological system, devoid of every trace of apocalyptic tension. All this resulted in a more subtle form of de-apocalypticization.

Also important in this regard were the tensions between a Greek and a Jewish concept of time. The Jewish concept maintained a linear understanding of time with a beginning and an end — a history in which God is actively engaged and in which God intervenes. Greek thought, on the other hand, held an asymmetric duality between time and eternity. Herein time could only be conceptualized in relation to eternity — thus rather as a continuum. The church then already participated in eternity via the sacraments.

Up to the present day, therefore, history has not been interrupted in any radical fashion; it simply follows its course. Time murmurs on, even although apocalyptic fever has tended to raise its ugly head at one juncture or another in its course. Time has become a synonym for continuity and participation in eternity.

In the modern period, time was still considered in terms of continuity, albeit as continuous development or progress: history was perceived as a forward moving process on its way to completion. It was argued that the discovery of reason (which took concrete form in science and technology) and freedom (which likewise gave rise to a variety of liberation movements) would enable men and women to gradually increase their understanding of the world and their ability to manipulate it according to their intentions. Reality for the modern man or woman was caught up in a dynamic movement striving for more and better, a dynamic that one could steer in order to expedite one's own personal and social completion. The apocalyptic temporal awareness that was once so important was completely forgotten. The current cultural apocalyptic sensitivity, however, appears to react against such a modern perception of time.

Dialogue between theology and modern science and philosophy likewise led to a further discrediting of the apocalyptic expectation. Indeed, modern criticism of religion and tradition found apocalypticism to be an easy target, one that could be rejected effortlessly as superstition and myth by those who subscribed to scientific rationality. It is for this reason that modern theologians endeavored to demythologize apocalyptic elements in the same way as they removed the miraculous from the miracle

14. K. Koch, "Auch ein Problem der Zei: Christliche Eschatologie im Kreuzfeuer der Apokalyptik," *Internationale Katholische Zeitschrift Communio* 28 (1999): 492–513, p. 499.

narratives. Apocalypticism — and certainly the cosmological and temporal systematization of apocalyptic images in traditional eschatological tractates — with its discourse on demonic powers, angels, and the final struggle between good and evil, was repudiated as part of an outdated world-view. It endangered the renewed theological attempts to demonstrate the plausibility of the Christian faith in modern society. Certain theologians argued, therefore, that the message of the gospel did not coincide with the mythological terminology with which it was written. Images of Jesus from the first modern quest for the "historical Jesus," dating from the nineteenth century, were thus radically purified of apocalyptic elements and tended to represent Jesus as a great religious sage or ethical example.

The existential interpretation of Rudolf Bultmann, however, constituted the primary and most significant trigger behind the process of de-apocalypticization, *casu quo* de-mythologization. "The mythology of the New Testament should not be questioned at the level of the objective content of its presentations but rather at the level of the human existential understanding expressed in such presentations."[15] The eschaton is not some kind of dramatic moment associated with the future, it is happening here and now. Jesus is already here — in the fundamental options people make with respect to their existential orientation: believing, and thereby evading one's own shortcomings and sinful weakness, or not. Karl Rahner considered the term "apocalypticism" a catchword to designate poorly understood eschatology[16], masquerading as a report-like prediction of events to take place at the end of history. Genuine eschatology however, does not predict; rather it invites human persons to look forward in such a way that they accept their present existence "as his [sic] definitive future hidden in the present and already offering him salvation now if it is accepted as the deed of God the only ruler, the time and manner of which remain incalculable."[17] In more recent German eschatologies, such as those of Gerhard Lohfink, Gisbert Greshake, and Medard Kehl, the process of de-apocalypticization is more explicitly

---

15. R. Bultmann, *Neues Testament und Mythologie: Das Problem der Entmythologisierung der neutestamentlichen Verkündigung*, Beiträge zur evangelischen Theologie 96 (Munich: Kaiser, 1985; original edition: 1941), p. 23 (our translation). "Mythical eschatology has been fundamentally falsified by the simple fact that the parousia of Christ did not take place as the New Testament had expected, that history has continued on its course and — according to the conviction of all reasonable men and women — will continue on its course" (p. 16).

16. Cf. *Eschatology*, in K. Rahner and H. Vorgrimler, *Theological Dictionary* (New York: Herder and Herder, 1965), pp. 149–50.

17. Ibid., p. 149.

associated with the de-temporalization of eschatological expectation. It is in the very death of the human individual that the salvation expressed in our eschatological hope becomes reality.[18]

There would thus appear to be sufficient reason to disregard the apocalyptic tradition or at least ignore it as irrelevant to contemporary systematic theology. From the historical perspective, the frustration of the *Naherwartung* clearly constitutes a first major experience in this regard. From the perspective of the history of religions, heresies and sects have tended to deal specifically with apocalypticism, the latter providing the foundations of a sort of revolutionary awareness that turned itself against the reigning world or ecclesial order. Philosophically speaking, the apocalyptic understanding of time does not interface well with the Hellenistic-Platonic perception thereof, which remains virtually unquestioned in Christian theology. It is also incompatible with modern evolutionary theories of history that prevail up to the present day. Ideological exploitation of the phenomenon is far from alien to the political world, not only with respect to Nazism, for example, but also with respect to modern day right-wing conservative cultural criticism, the formation of sects, terrorism, the legitimization of violence, etc. Finally, the dogmatic systematization of apocalypticism in the neo-Scholastic eschatological tractates on the "last things" has completely lost its plausibility, especially when theologians complied with the modern critique of religion, and accordingly demythologized the Christian eschatological message.

3. Apocalypticism Today: God as the Boundary of Time

The Paradox Reconsidered

We have already referred to the evident paradox that a secularized yet often quasi-religious form of apocalyptic awareness has emerged in our culture in spite of the fact that apocalypticism has been abandoned by contemporary Christian faith and theology as irrelevant and outdated. While this awareness clearly includes elements of cultural criticism, it also has the potential, as we noted, to develop into a sort of "culture of the kick." As such, therefore, it constitutes a symptom of, and a response

18. Cf. K. Koch, *Auch ein Problem mit der Zeit,* pp. 500–501; G. Greshake and G. Lohfink, *Naherwartung — Auferstehung — Unsterblichkeit* (Freiburg: Herder, 1978); M. Kehl, *Eschatologie* (Würzburg: Echter, 1986).

to, the current context of uncertainty. The latter intrinsically accompanies the construction of identity in a postmodern context of radical plurality and has its roots in the increasing awareness brought on by the demise of the master narratives that we are apparently no longer in charge of our own lives, history, and cosmos. The major difference when compared with classical apocalypticism lies in the negative and exclusively immanent character of the contemporary apocalyptic awareness. Beyond the "all's well that ends well" character of the popular commercial film, there is no suggestion of ultimate completion or reconciliation, only (the threat of) total breakdown, devastation, and judgement.

What is most intriguing about contemporary cultural apocalyptic awareness is the fact that it expresses serious reservations with respect to the (late) modern concepts of time characteristic of our culture: (a) the modern world view proposed by scientific, technical, and social ideologies and the evolutionary perception of time implied therein, and (b) the so-called postmodern absence of clear perspectives and meaning which gives rise to a kind of circular concept of time in which nothing actually happens (beyond the occasional kick).

It seems appropriate to ask oneself the question whether it is possible at this juncture to re-establish the relationship between cultural apocalypticism and theology. Indeed, it would be something of an exaggeration to suggest that theology has paid no attention at all to apocalypticism in recent years. The political theologian Johann-Baptist Metz, for example, deserves credit for having reintroduced apocalypticism as a conceptual strategy in his fundamental-theological reflections on Christian faith. In his account, this theological conceptual strategy, moreover, has become an indispensable characteristic of a correct and legitimate way of doing theology. For Metz, apocalypticism establishes a firm claim to the intrinsic relationship between God and time: God interrupts time. It is for this reason that the Christian apocalyptic perception of time runs counter to modern evolutionary and postmodern cyclical perspectives thereon. The rediscovery of this theological conceptual strategy has the capacity to remind Christian believers that apocalypticism is not merely a matter of naive predictive speculation in need of de-mythologization but simultaneously, and perhaps more appropriately, a cry of distress and a hope-filled expression of trust in God. Against cultural apocalypticism, Christian apocalypticism calls for a shift from catastrophe thinking to crisis thinking. It is not simply a matter of devastation, catastrophe and chaos, it is also one of perspective, revelation and disclosure (which immediately reminds us of the original significance of the Greek *apokalypsis*).

In short, the apocalyptic conceptual strategy perceives the boundaries of time as determined and restricted by God. Within this limited time crisis (persecution, destruction, loss, suffering, and pain) is the precise location in which God reveals Godself as the boundary, as the one who interrupts time, the one who judges it. At the same time, revelation as interruption implies its own demands and calls for engagement. A neutral attitude at this juncture is no longer appropriate. Interruption, as the revelation of God, provokes us to assume a position; we can no longer maintain an indifferent stance to what is going on. What is called for is a critical praxis of hope. Etymologically speaking, the word "crisis" also implies "judgement." A Christian perspective on time thus requires submission to God's judgement and God's promise for the world and for humanity as revealed in Jesus Christ.

Critique of the Modern Evolutionary Perception of Time

Modern philosophies of history and ideologies have often been lax in the way they integrate the historically particular into the development of history as a systematic process. The concrete unfolding of events (and the pain, suffering, and destruction related thereto) in time and space is all too frequently passed over or too easily integrated and reconciled with the intended goal. Time and again, such perspectives on history are written from the point of view of the winners. The victims, often made up of those who suffer under the remorseless implementation of such ideologies, are forgotten from the outset or reduced to a function of the evolutionary process. As a theological conceptual strategy, however, apocalypticism finds its very point of connection here with the victims and with those who suffer.[19]

This means that the modern projects of history, of whatever ideology, must be confronted with a twofold fundamental correction. In the first instance, the meaning-creating subject of history should not be seen as an abstract principle or as an undetermined and universal potential "world-spirit" or "nature." It should not be reduced to an abstract subject such as the proletariat (or a particular nationality, race . . .), or to an abstract model such as "the human person." For Christians, the subject of history

19. These paragraphs constitute a further elaboration of elements developed in J.-B. Metz, *Glaube in Geschichte und Gesellschaft: Zeit der Orden? Zur Mystik und Politik der Nachfolge* (Freiburg: Herder, 1977). Metz provides a schematic survey of his thought in *Zum Begriff der neuen Politischen Theologie (1967–1997)* (Mainz: Matthias-Grünewald, 1997).

is God in God's eschatological dominion, a God who has made Godself known in Jesus Christ as the defender of the poor, the weak, the rejected, the marginalized, and the victims. In the second instance, therefore, the unfolding of history and the notions of reconciliation and completion should not be seen as a matter of theory but rather as one of practice. This implies that Christians, in their historical particularity and concrete history and rooted in their remembrance of Jesus' preaching of the kingdom of God, should be attentive to the places where the victims stumble and fall, and ultimately be able to identify (with) them.

From the theological perspective, therefore, apocalypticism has nothing to do with a withdrawal from the world or escapism or the abolishment of temporality. In fact, the opposite is the case! Apocalypticism calls for the *radical temporalization* of the world, with a radical awareness of the irreducible seriousness of what occurs in the here and now. The fact that apocalypticism tends to emphasize the catastrophic character of time sheds light on two closely interwoven accents. In the first place, time is seen as discontinuity, interruption, finality, the end. History becomes real history, not undone through systematization and the settling of modern processes. In the same vein, the future becomes a real future, not to be identified with seamless continuation and endless infinity. Apocalyptic awareness runs counter to evolutionary awareness in which the here and now lacks uniqueness, individuality, and particularity, and is remorselessly integrated into a dynamic movement toward a projected goal. The dramatic character of crises, catastrophes, injustice, and inhumanity becomes undermined by the false idea of evolutionary progress. At this point the second accent implied in the catastrophic view of time becomes manifest. A Christian apocalyptic awareness urges us to become conscious of the irreconcilability of history, to pay attention to the victims of suffering and injustice, to recognize the fear of God and the appeal for reconciliation and justice. It is at this point that catastrophe thinking becomes *crisis thinking:* submission to the interruptive judgement of God over history.

A revaluation of the apocalyptic tension ultimately demands the rediscovery of the *Naherwartung* which historical and systematic theology have too easily and too frequently de-temporalized into "ongoing expectation" (*Stetserwartung*) with the postponement of "judgement" to the end of the world. A restoration of the expectation of an imminent "second coming" rids history of its quietude and increases the tension; instead of paralyzing, it will provide foundation to the seriousness of a liberating praxis and emphasize the urgent and critical character of human responsibility. Discipleship of Jesus Christ must presuppose the expectation of an imminent "second coming"; otherwise it will remain beyond our capacity to endure. God can enter history at any second.

For Christians, the apocalyptic awareness of time underlines the fact that God is not only other than time, the other of time, but that God is also and simultaneously the boundary of time, the end of time and thus the guarantee of its possibility. Where God is eliminated as the one who interrupts, there can be nothing more than timeless infinity. An apocalyptic awareness of God as the one who establishes the boundaries of time cannot be harmonized at the theological level with a purely metaphorical use of the term, in order to summon up visions of ecological or nuclear disasters, for example, as scenarios of human self-destruction. A Christian apocalyptic awareness only shares an awareness of danger with such a use of the term. Just as danger constitutes a basic category in a correct understanding of the life and message of Jesus, it likewise forms a basic category in the formation of our contemporary Christian identity. The de-mythologization of apocalyptic images has all too often led to the abandonment of this element of danger in an effort to make the Christian faith easier to bear.

As Metz has noted, it is not naiveté that is a threat to the future of religion but banality.[20] Religion becomes banal when it is nothing more than a reduplication of what is going on already, what is being said and done in spite of religion. In its naiveté, on the other hand — especially its maintenance of the apocalyptic images and texts — religion is a source of irritation for the modern image of humanity, time and history, for the culture of self-realization, for apathy. In so doing, however, it comes close, at least in part, to the secret fear of the (post)modern subject: being caught up in an endless evolutionary continuum.

Critique of the Postmodern Detemporalization

Postmodernity, the category we have employed to designate the context of a modernity in crisis, is likewise fraught with ambiguities. For many contemporary men and women, postmodernity, or better still postmodernism (as the way in which one interacts with the postmodern context) has become a synonym for cultural shallowness, relativism, subjectivism, eclecticism, and aestheticism. Metz repeatedly refers to this shadow side

---

20. J.-B. Metz, *Unterwegs zu einer nachidealistischen Theologie*, in *Entwürfe der Theologie*, ed. J.-B. Bauer (Graz: Styria, 1985), 209–33, pp. 227ff.

of our culture, which he describes as a persistent all-embracing amnesia.[21] He speaks of a culture of forgetfulness in which suffering and the remembrance thereof, time and thus history, God and thus humanity, have completely disappeared. Time has become an empty and uneventful infinity in which nothing ever happens. Our contemporaries cultivate escapism as a sort of religion-friendly godlessness in which religion has been transformed into a compensatory myth of personal leisure, without God and with Nietzsche as its most prominent prophet. Metz's critique is no doubt over-exclusive in its condemnation of our current postmodern context, since it pays insufficient attention to the contemporary critical awareness to which cultural apocalypticism also in part refers. We have made it clear elsewhere that, because of his all-embracing rejection of postmodernity, Metz is ultimately no longer capable of bringing his theological intuitions into reflexive dialogue with the contemporary context.[22] This need not imply, however, that his theological intuitions — especially those dealing with God and time — do not offer elements of inspiration in support of a revaluation of the apocalyptic dimension of the Christian faith.

In support of his position, Metz appeals to Jewish theological thought, which is temporal to its very core and shaped by suffering. The Old Testament portrays Israel as a people that refused to seek comfort in myths, or better still, a nation that refused to withdraw itself from reality, however threatening it may have been. Israel's approach to reality is characterized by a *tiefe Diesseitigkeit,* which is at once the price it paid for the concept of God it ultimately acquired. Faith in God did not keep suffering at a comforting distance; rather it gave rise to lament with its characteristic lack of solace. Israel experienced God within history, not outside of it. God constituted history's boundary as (the) "one who comes." This constitutes the uniqueness of biblical theological thought and implies an equally unique perspective on reality: the imaginative observation of the

---

21. For more information on Metz's position with respect to the actual theological context see L. Boeve, "Postmoderne politieke theologie? Johann-Baptist Metz in gesprek met het actuele kritische bewustzijn," *Tijdschrift voor theologie* 39 (1999): 244–64. For references to publications on God and time after 1985 see ibid., p. 250, n. 21; cf. also, for example, "Gott: Wider den Mythos von der Ewigkeit der Zeit," in *Ende der Zeit? Die Provokation der Rede von Gott,* ed. T. R. Peters and C. Urban (Mainz: Matthias-Grünewald, 1999), 32–49.

22. Cf. Boeve, "Postmoderne politieke theologie?" pp. 245ff. For further background information based on the thought of Jean-François Lyotard, see L. Boeve, "J.-F. Lyotard's Critique of Master Narratives: Towards a Postmodern Political Theology?" in *Liberation Theologies on Shifting Grounds: A Clash of Socio-Economic and Cultural Paradigms,* ed. G. De Schrijver, BETL, 135 (Leuven: Peeters Press, 1998), 296–314.

world is framed within a temporal perception of reality, a horizon of limited (*befristeter*) time that is ultimately determined, restricted, and thus not limitless. The New Testament perception of God and time follows along similar lines. The *Naherwartung* illustrates that God's "having come" can only be grasped as a "still coming." The Johannine expression "God is love" must be understood against the background of this dynamic expectation: God will ultimately reveal Godself to us as love.[23] Such a perception of the divine also explains why biblically inspired mysticism, in contrast to myth, tends to give rise to disturbing questions rather than comforting answers. The biblical mysticism found, for example, in the book of Job, the Psalms, and the Prophets, is in essence a mysticism of suffering at God's hands. The language of prayer is "a language of suffering, a language of crisis, a language of resistance and radical danger, a language of lament and clamor, literally of the murmuring of the children of Israel. The language of this divine mysticism is not, in the first instance, a comforting response to the experience of suffering, rather it is a vexed questioning rooted in suffering, a questioning of the divinity replete with tense expectation: 'where are you, God, how long must I wait?' "[24] It is in this sense also that Metz interprets Jesus' cry from the cross: "My God, why have you forsaken me?" Negative theology thus becomes practical theology; language is transformed into despair, crushed by the unanswered yet unavoidable question of theodicy. Metz is thus inclined to suspect every contemporary theological endeavor to locate suffering in Godself as a facile attempt to reconcile ourselves with the reality of suffering by duplicating it in God and thereby universalizing, emasculating, and even aestheticizing it. Prayer in this perspective is thus, in the first instance, prayer "to God for God" (Luke 11:13). Sorrow, which has been banished from our modern world of (mythical) self-appeasement — such that every real consolation has been reduced to scant self-comfort — must likewise be understood as a longing for God. The opposite side of sorrow as "longing for God" is hope. "*Trauer ist Hoffnung im Widerstand.*"[25]

The task of the church as the narrative community of the "dangerous memory" is to remind (post)modern society that human history is also

---

23. To be compared with the self-revelation of YHWH in *Exodus* as "I will be, who I will be for you."

24. J.-B. Metz, "Theologie als Theodizee?" in *Theodizee – Gott vor Gericht?* ed. W. Oelmüller (Munich: Fink, 1990), 103–18, p. 114.

25. J.-B. Metz, "Religion, ja – Gott, nein," in *Gottespassion: Zur Ordensexistenz heute*, ed. J.-B. Metz and T. R. Peters (Freiburg: Herder, 1991), 11–62, p. 32.

a history of suffering, injustice and the absence of reconciliation. As such, it is likewise a history of anxiety and the cry for justice. It is this very awareness that dominates the apocalyptic understanding of God's imminent judgement in which history is interrupted.

4. Conclusion: God Interrupts Time

Körtner is only partly correct when he argues that cultural apocalyptic awareness has opened the door toward the re-introduction of Jewish-Christian apocalypticism.[26] It is certainly the case that the contextual critical awareness expressed in cultural apocalypticism — in which Christians also participate — exhibits some affinity with the Jewish-Christian apocalyptic concept of time. A theological rediscovery of the latter, however, implies much more than a metaphorical-narrative reduplication of this cultural awareness, if only because theology is rooted within the particular narrative tradition of Christian faith communities. Nevertheless, such an affinity clearly creates a significant opportunity for a critically productive interaction between the Christian tradition and the sensitivities of our time, whereby theological reflection can be recontextualized. Present day lack of certainty, loss of control, confrontation with uncontrollability and complexity on the one hand, and smooth economization and awkward fundamentalist attempts to ignore it or ward it off on the other, brings us face to face with the precariousness of our time, with history and our own radical historicity. The apocalyptic theological conceptual strategy reminds Christians that the time of catastrophe is the time of crisis, that history is subject to God's judgement, and that the latter sheds light on the irreconcilability of history and challenges it to a praxis of the coming of God. God does not stand outside history, nor is God a factor therein. As the other side of history, God interrupts the expectation of his "having come" in our narratives, including those of cultural apocalypticism as well as our own narratives about God.

The parable of the last judgement, "when the Son of Man comes to judge" (Matt. 25:31–46), is thus also a narrative for today and not a prediction of some future event. The parable points to the earnestness of our experience of time, of our participation in a concrete attentiveness toward and praxis on behalf of those who fall victim to the multitude of

26. Cf. U. Körtner, *Weltangst und Weltende*.

master narratives and their endeavors to forget or functionalize concrete histories of suffering. It is in our very interaction with the other, with the rejected, the victim, the poor, that we as Christians encounter the one we confess as loving Mystery. Instead of leading us away from history, apocalypticism has a place at its heart, a place in the dramatic interplay between human anxiety and human hope.

Conclusion

"The Shortest Definition of Religion: Interruption"

As was the case in our previous study, *Interrupting Tradition,* interruption has also turned out in the present volume to constitute a powerful category for conceptualizing the relationship between Christian faith and its present-day context in a dynamic and productive way. The "contextual interruption" of the Christian faith in a detraditionalized and pluralized context invites Christians — as every other context shift in the past — to reconsider and reformulate the identity, plausibility, and relevance of the Christian faith. It becomes clear in dialogue with this context, moreover, that in theological terms, the category of interruption is located at the heart of the Christian faith.

"The shortest definition of religion is interruption," is an intuition taken from Johan Baptist Metz.[1] He wanted to make clear by this statement that Christian faith can never slip unpunished into a sort of bourgeois religion, seamlessly woven into the prevailing culture and society, nor withdraw itself from or against its context. Such religion seeks a too-facile reconciliation, forgetting in the process the tragic suffering that confronts human existence. For Metz, there can be no Christian faith without tension or turmoil, without danger or menace. After all, Christians are bearers of the subversive, dangerous memory of the suffering, death, and resurrection of Jesus Christ. That is why they actively seek out the boundaries of life and coexistence, moved as they are by the human histories of suffering, that compel them toward a preferential option for the poor, the suffering, and the oppressed. By its very nature, the Christian faith disrupts the histories of conqueror and vanquished,

1. Taken from: J.-B. Metz, *Glaube in Geschichte und Gesellschaft: Studien zu einer praktischen Fundamentaltheologie* (Mainz: Matthias-Grünewald, 1977), p. 150, thesis vi; also mentioned in *Unterbrechungen: Theologisch-politische Perspektiven und Profile* (Gütersloh: Gütersloher Taschenbücher Siebenstern, 1981), p. 86. Johann Baptist Metz is one of the most renowned and influential theologians of the second half of the twentieth century. For Metz's theology, see further the collection of excerpts and articles by Metz that traces the evolution of his ideas, *Zum Begriff der neuen Politischen Theologie* (Mainz: Matthias-Grünewald, 1997).

interrupting the ideologies of the powerful and the powerlessness of the victims.[2]

In the present volume, I have tried to demonstrate how Metz's intuition can also be inspirational for current theological reflection. I have used the category of "interruption" in several senses to conceptualize the relationship between Christian faith and contemporary culture and society. Detraditionalization calls the givenness of being Christian into question and pluralization locates Christianity in the midst of a dynamic manifold world of religions and other fundamental life options. The continuity of the tradition and the overlap between the Christian horizon of meaning and the present-day context have been interrupted on account of contextual shifts. Postmodern suspicion, moreover, raises questions concerning the generalized conceptual patterns that often too quickly hark back to presupposed harmony, continuity, and consensus. In as far as modern theological methods honor these presuppositions, and function *de facto* on the basis of the aforesaid overlap between the Christian horizon and the context, they too are confronted with their own boundaries and are ultimately rendered counterproductive.

Contextual interruption, however, requires Christian faith and theology to recontextualize. Indeed, the rupture that accompanies interruption is not intended to lead to conceptual patterns that present the relationship between Christian faith and the contemporary context in oppositional terms or in terms of discontinuity. Christians may not be of the world, but they are nonetheless in the world. The crisis of modern theology does not lead to the end of dialogue with the context, but rather to a revision of the nature of this dialogue, on account of the altered relationship with the context. In contrast to the secularization paradigm, detraditionalization and pluralization sharpen our awareness that to be Christian implies an identity construction rooted in particular narratives and practices, with its own specific truth claim in a context of a dynamic plurality of often-conflicting truth claims. The postmodern critical consciousness, moreover, warns us not to be too quick to include or exclude the truth of the other, but rather to reflect on our own truth claim in relationship to the truth claims of others. The contextual interruption of theology is not possible without the context; it happens where continuity and discontinuity between theology and context encounter one another.

---

2. For a detailed sketch and constructive critique of this theological position, see, for example, my "Postmoderne politieke theologie?"

In the midst of the dialogue with the present-day context, however, "interruption" can be made productive not only as a contextual category but also, and in line with Metz, as a theological category. As a matter of fact, interruption is also capable of pointing to the way in which God reveals Godself in history and the way in which Christians bear witness to this reality in narratives and practices. God's interruption constitutes the theological foundation for a continuous and radical hermeneutic of the context and the tradition. Just as (and because) every concrete encounter with the other/Other is a potential location for God to reveal Godself today, it is only in concrete narratives and practices that the interrupting God can be testified to in today's context. Ultimately, it is the event of Jesus Christ narrated in this tradition that constitutes both the foundation and the hermeneutical key thereto. Just as (and because) the Christian narrative is interrupted, the same narrative succeeds in bearing witness to the interruption without domesticating it. Furthermore, just as (and because) the Christian narrative is interrupted by God, Christians are called to interrupt themselves and others when their own narratives and those of others close themselves off. In this sense, "interruption" is not only a formal, methodological notion, but also a substantial theological category, narratively signified by the same tradition it interrupts. In the last analysis, it is because interruption is such a thick theological a category that it legitimates and motivates its formal and methodological use.

The context in which we live thus opens a variety of paths toward the dangerous turbulence of interruption. For Metz, it is particularly the confrontation with suffering that forms the impetus behind his search for a "dangerous" theology of interruption. This confrontation compels him — in keeping with his late modern (neo-Marxist) dialogue partners (such as Adorno, Benjamin and Horkheimer) — toward developing a hermeneutics of suspicion that turns itself against those narratives that reconcile and too easily forget. Today, however, a second opportunity presents itself. Along with the cultural interruption of the Christian tradition, Christians also find themselves confronted with (religious) diversity and otherness.[3] In this instance, a theology of interruption tends rather to develop a hermeneutics of contingency, which aims to maintain

3. Metz also alludes to this intuition in his later articles, after 1985, but does not really develop it further. See, for example, his "Unterwegs zu einer nachidealistischen Theologie," in *Entwürfe der Theologie*, ed. J. Bauer (Graz: Styria, 1985), 203–33; "In Aufbruch zu einer kulturell polyzentrischen Weltkirche," in *Zukunftsfähigkeit: Suchbewegungen im Christentum* ed. F.-X. Kaufmann and J.-B. Metz (Freiburg: Herder, 1987), 93–123; "Die eine Welt als Herausforderung an das westliche Christentum," *Una Sancta* 44 (1989): 314–22; and his contributions

the radical historical and specific, particular, character of the Christian tradition without, however, closing in on itself. Such a hermeneutics of contingency, when correctly understood, includes a hermeneutics of suspicion. Whoever chooses to engage in the current dialogue with the postmodern context cannot ignore this theological lesson from the recent past. Otherwise, the rediscovery of one's own identity and its boundaries in confrontation with the other will be likely to slip once again into the facile closure of one's own narrative. The other then quickly becomes the forgotten one, the one who hastily becomes enclosed by or excluded from our narratives.

When Jesus journeyed to the district of Tyre and Sidon and encountered the Canaanite, or Syro-Phoenician, woman, he came to see God in a new and different way. He encounters the woman in question, a non-Jew, on the road and she asks him to heal her daughter (Matt. 15:21–28; Mark 7:24–30) who she claims is possessed by a demon. Jesus' initial reaction is to refuse her, arguing that he has been sent to the Jewish people ("the lost sheep of the house of Israel") and even that it would be wrong for him to bother himself with others ("it is not fair to take the children's food and throw it to the dogs"). The woman then responds, "yet even the dogs eat the crumbs that fall from their masters." At that moment Jesus' narrative about God is interrupted and he learns how to open it further in such a way that others, including non-Jews, have a place therein. God is made manifest outside the boundaries of Israel in the faith of the Canaanite woman.

---

to *Concilium* collected in J.-B. Metz and J. Moltmann, *Faith and the Future: Essays on Theology, Solidarity, and Modernity,* Concilium Series (Maryknoll, NY: Orbis, 1995), pp. 30–37 ("Theology in the Modern Age, and before Its End"), 57–65 ("Unity and Diversity: Problems and Prospects for Inculturation"), and 66–71 ("1492 – Through the Eyes of a European Theologian"); and two contributions in *Zum Begriff der neuen Politischen Theologie,* pp. 135–41 and 197–206.

Acknowledgments

A number of essays and articles published in various journals and collections constitute the preparatory work behind the present study. Full bibliographical references are provided below. References are also to be found in the footnotes to additional contributions (often of a more philosophical-theological character) in which one or more of the ideas presented here are further elaborated. The Dutch version of the present volume was published as *God onderbreekt de geschiedenis: Theologie in tijden van ommekeer* (Kapellen: Pelckmans, 2006).

The basic ideas contained in the first part were initially presented, in part, in "When Secularization Turns into Detraditionalization and Pluralization: Faith in Search of Understanding" *Bulletin ET* 12 (2001): 258–70, and "Religion after Detraditionalization: Christian Faith in a Post-Secular Europe," *Irish Theological Quarterly* 70 (2005): 99–122, especially as regards the first chapter, and "Zeg nooit meer correlatie: Over christelijke traditie, hedendaagse context en onderbreking," *Collationes* 33 (2004): 193–219, for chapters 2 and 3. For chapter 2, see also my programmatic essay "Beyond the Modern and Anti-modern Dilemma: *Gaudium et Spes* and Theological Method in a Postmodern European Context," *Horizons* 33 (2007) no. 2. For the third chapter, see also "La pertinence de la foi chrétienne dans la société contemporaine: Entre sécularité et pluralité," *Ephemerides Theologicae Lovanienses* 77 (2001): 441–55.

With respect to part 2, reference can be made for the fourth chapter to "Theology and the Interruption of Experience," in *Religious Experience and Contemporary Theological Epistemology,* ed. L. Boeve, Y. De Maeseneer, and S. Van den Bossche, BETL, 188 (Leuven: Peeters Press, 2005), 11–40. The text that formed the basis of the fifth chapter is "The Sacramental Interruption of Rituals of Life," *Heythrop Journal* 44 (2003): 401–17. We also made use of "Schatbewaarder én spoorzoeker: het één niet zonder het ander," in *Jezus, een eigentijds verhaal,* ed. M. Bouwens, J. Geel, and F. Maas (Zoetermeer: Meinema, 2001), 87–91 for the conclusion of this chapter. Chapter 6 is a slightly reworked version of a lecture delivered on November 3, 2006, at a conference on science, faith, and ethics in Celje (Slovenia) (to be published in the proceedings).

Chapters 7 and 8 of part 3 were initially prepared in the following contributions. Chapter 7: "Cultural Apophaticism: A Challenge for Contemporary Theology," in *Rethinking Ecumenism: Strategies for the 21st Century* (FS Houtepen), ed. F. Bakker (Zoetermeer: Meinema, 2004), 79–92, and "Negative Theology and Theological Hermeneutics: The Particularity of Naming God," in *Der Name Gottes,* ed. I. Dalferth, K. Schmid, and P. Stoellger (Tübingen: Mohr Siebeck, in press); chapter 8: A. J. Godzieba, L. Boeve, and M. Saracino, "Resurrection – Interruption – Transformation: Incarnation as a Hermeneutical Strategy: A Symposium," *Theological Studies* 67 (2006): 777–815, 795–808, and "Religious Truth, Particularity and Incarnation: A Theological Proposal for a Philosophical Hermeneutics of Religion," in *Religion and Contingence,* ed. D.-M. Grube and P. Jonkers, STAR (Assen: Van Gorcum, 2007, in press). Chapter 9 is an updated version of "God Interrupts History: Apocalyptism as an Indispensable Theological Conceptual Strategy," *Louvain Studies* 26 (2001): 195–216.

The conclusion was partly prepared in "The Shortest Definition of Religion: Interruption," *Communio viatorum* 46 (2004): 299–32.

Index